blue
rider
press

THE LOST DAUGHTER

ALSO BY MARY WILLIAMS

Brothers in Hope:
The Story of the Lost Boys of Sudan

The Lost Daughter

MARY WILLIAMS

BLUE RIDER PRESS

A MEMBER OF PENGUIN GROUP (USA) INC.

NEW YORK

blue
rider
press

Published by the Penguin Group
Penguin Group (USA) Inc., 375 Hudson Street,
New York, New York 10014, USA

USA · Canada · UK · Ireland · Australia
New Zealand · India · South Africa · China

Penguin Books Ltd, Registered Offices:
80 Strand, London WC2R 0RL, England
For more information about the Penguin Group visit penguin.com

Library of Congress Cataloging-in-Publication Data

Williams, Mary, date.
The lost daughter / Mary Williams.
p.   cm.
ISBN 978-0-399-16086-8
1. Williams, Mary, 1967—Childwood and youth.   2. African Americans—California—
Oakland—Biography.   3. African Americans—California—Oakland—Social conditions—
20th century.   4. Adoptees—California—Biography.   5. Black Panther Party—History.
6. Mothers and daughters—California—Biography.   7. Fonda, Jane, 1937–   8. Oakland
(Calif.)—Social conditions—20th century.   9. Oakland (Calif.)—Biography.   I. Title.
F869.O2W55   2013   2013001245
979.4'053092—dc23
[B]

Printed in the United States of America
1   3   5   7   9   10   8   6   4   2

Book design by Gretchen Achilles

ALWAYS LEARNING   PEARSON

FOR MY MOM

AND

FOR MY MAMA

All of us have moments in our childhood where we come alive for the first time. And we go back to those moments and think, This is when I became myself.

—RITA DOVE

THE LOST DAUGHTER

I AM ABOUT TO ATTEMPT time travel. Once I pass through airport security and board US Airways flight 2748 to Oakland, California, I will be transported to a place I fled nearly thirty years ago. Although I have taken on physical challenges, like a cross-country bicycle ride and a five-month stint on a research base in Antarctica, I have generally shied away from emotional ones.

Six years ago I quit my well-paid job, left my fiancé and sold my three-bedroom home in Atlanta, abandoning a life of materialism and attachment to pursue one that included solitude, travel and adventure.

Now in my mid-forties, I spend half the year working all over the country for federal parks and nonprofits, doing odd jobs like manning a visitor center, clearing trails or assisting researchers. So I often live in constrained quarters with an assorted lot of scientists, dreamers and vagabonds. The rest of the time I enjoy self-imposed exile in my tiny Arizona condo, happiest when left alone to hike, read or watch YouTube. I'm especially drawn to makeup application and hairstyling videos, even though I seldom wear cosmetics and my hair is two inches long; I like the girl talk without the hassle of actual girlfriends. I was hesitant to try Facebook, but after a colleague at an Alaskan wildlife refuge introduced me to the site, insisting that with my reclusive lifestyle it would be the ideal way to stay in touch, I decided to give it a shot.

That's how I found Neome Banks, someone I haven't seen since childhood. And that's why I'm headed back to Oakland. I want to see the place that formed me, find the people I left behind. Rediscover family.

I once heard that families are like fudge: mostly sweet with a few nuts. But a family can also be like a country. It can thrive in times of prosperity in one moment and in the next be embroiled in senseless conflict. Its once well-loved leaders corrupted and its citizens numbed, beaten, violated, murdered. Some left displaced and in search of refuge. I know because I once had a family like this. It has taken me decades to weave together the moments of peace, despair and resurrection into a makeshift treaty that will finally allow me to lick my wounds and go home to see what I can salvage.

The word "home" feels strange on my tongue, like a bitter aftertaste that lingers long after a meal. Though I have lived in many places, home has always been Oakland. As I prepare for the journey, I stare at my face in the mirror a lot because soon I'll be with people whose faces and voices are slight variations of my own. But mostly I think about what life was like before everything disintegrated as if in the wake of an atomic bomb.

CHAPTER 1

I WAS BORN at Kaiser Hospital in Oakland, California. It was 1967 and there was much more going on than my painful, bloody struggle to free myself from the womb. The world was caught up in a swirling storm of violence, revolutionary zeal, sexual freedom and creative expression. The Vietnam War was in high gear, with the number of American troops serving reaching nearly half a million. Stateside, anti-war protesters were out in full force too. One of them was Muhammad Ali, who in this year was stripped of his boxing world championship for refusing to serve. Israel was feeling especially scrappy and was at war with Syria, Egypt *and* Jordan. Cities throughout America exploded in race riots and looting. Pot was groovy. Sex was free. The Beatles were the number one band in the world. Microminiskirts and go-go boots were in vogue, as was (for a brief time) paper clothing.

Despite the violence, sex, drugs, rock and roll and bad fashion, my mother managed to carry me safely through the long, hot Summer of Love and deliver me on a Friday the 13th in October. No baby pictures exist to mark my birth. I don't think this was out of indifference. I just happened to be number five in a growing brood of girls. I imagine my arrival was like seeing your favorite movie for the fifth time. Enjoyable but lacking the excitement and anticipation of the first couple of viewings. I was named Mary Lawanna, though because my mother's name is Mary, I was called by my middle name. I would be followed a year later by a little brother who would garner a great deal of excitement because he was the long-awaited boy. I'd come to view him as the wee-wee-packing changeling who displaced my coveted role as the baby of the family.

My mother was a cook. In my earliest memories she is bent over a steaming pot of gumbo, waiting to feed whatever group of Panthers had gathered at the local community center to discuss the latest news regarding conflicts with the police or strategies on how to improve education at the Panther-run elementary school. She would also hit the streets to sell the Party newspaper, *The Black Panther*, for twenty-five cents a copy.

My father quit his job as an apprentice welder to join the Panthers. He was a captain in the Panthers' militaristic hierarchy. He participated in one of the most controversial programs, the armed citizens' patrol. Working in rotating twelve-hour shifts, he and other Panthers would spend long days and nights tailing police cars and doing foot patrols, ready to defend any blacks they saw being threatened by police.

Oakland, California, was at the heart of the social upheaval that gave rise to the Black Power movement. My parents were members of the Black Panther Party—an organization founded in Oakland during the mid-1960s to stop police brutality toward African Americans and to help those who lacked employment, education and healthcare. Some of the many accomplishments of the Party would include the Free Breakfast for Children Program that would be replicated by public school systems across the country. Other free Panther services to underserved communities included clothing distribution, classes on politics, economics, self-defense and first aid. They also opened free medical clinics and offered transportation to upstate prisons for family members of Panther inmates.

Revolution was a day-to-day reality of my early childhood, resulting in bloody shoot-outs and confrontations between the police and, well, us. From shortly after I was born in 1967 through 1969 nationwide, police–Panther clashes would result in nine police officers killed and fifty-six wounded. Ten Panthers would be killed and there were no statistics for the wounded; hundreds more would be arrested.

These hostilities ignited soon after J. Edgar Hoover, then the director of the FBI, issued his notorious statement against the Panthers as "the greatest threat to the internal security of the country." This proclamation was followed by U.S. Attorney General John Mitchell creating his "Panther Squad," which would begin carrying out a series of pre-dawn, shoot-first-ask-questions-later police raids, like the one in Chicago that killed Panthers Fred Hampton and Mark Clark.

When I was about three years old, I remember hiding out in the basement of a house during a Panther confrontation with the police. From above, I heard glass breaking, heavy footfalls and shouting muffled by distance and floorboards. I was held tightly by some woman (not my mother), and all around me were other little kids whimpering and whining. The woman holding me was rocking me and stroking my hair and whispering "Shush, child" over and over. But the strange thing was that I have no memory of feeling scared. I actually liked the uncertainty, the presence of bodies in the damp darkness, the feeling of tenseness in the air. It's a good memory.

As the FBI began to crack down more and more on Party members via intimidations, arrests and assassinations, some Panthers went into exile in other countries or went underground. When I overheard adults saying things like, "Well, you know Sister So-and-So went underground last week?" all kinds of crazy images would form in my head. I'd daydream of Panther members living in candlelit dirt tunnels, shivering in the dark, feeding on dangling root vegetables like a frightened Bugs Bunny hiding out from Elmer Fudd.

I wondered if my father, who seemed to be around the house less and less, was actually underground. So it came as a relief when I learned that my increasingly absentee father wasn't underground at all. He was serving time at a place called Soledad State Prison.

In 1970, my father, Louis Randolph Williams, had risen to the rank of captain within the Panthers. He was twenty-nine, and for years he had been working odd jobs by day and participating in the armed citizens' patrols at night. In April of that year, he and two fellow Panthers had been on patrol when they saw a paddy wagon and several police officers arresting four black marijuana suspects. They ambushed the officers, wounding three. Backup police units were called and the Panthers fled the scene, leading thirty patrol cars on a high-speed chase into downtown Oakland and discouraging their pursuit with Molotov cocktails. My father was captured, charged with assault with intent to murder and sentenced to seven years in prison.

At first, my mother took my five siblings and me on long bus rides to Soledad prison to visit him. Prison seemed like a fine place to me. Unlike for the first few years of my life, I knew exactly where my daddy was at all times. On our visits he was always smiling and we got to play in a large room filled with tables and benches, vending machines and lots of other families. Daddy would buy us candy bars and soda, and we'd all stand in front of a large, faded mural of a forest and take pictures. We took turns sitting in his lap while he and Mama talked. When I asked if I could stay the night with him, he'd laugh. I loved to make him laugh. He was so handsome. Caramel skin, shiny teeth, tall and lean-limbed. Perfection.

But after a few months, Mama stopped taking us to see Daddy; the long bus rides with six rambunctious kids were starting to take their toll, and it turned out their marriage was a lot shakier than I had imagined. Mama would get mad at me whenever I asked when we were going to see him again. When I told my oldest sister, Deborah, how great it would be if Daddy would come home, she said, "You don't know nothing! I'm glad he ain't living with us no more." When I asked why, she told me I was too young to remember when Daddy lived with us—true enough. She told me how Daddy and Mama fought all the time because he was always seeing other women. They fought so badly one night, Daddy ripped Mama's clothes off and beat her until she ran into the street naked to get away from him. "It's better he stay where he is."

Though my father was heavily involved in Panther activities, my mother limited her support to attending the many Free Huey rallies. But at this time any involvement in the Panthers attracted the attention of the FBI. It didn't take long for them to home in on her. One afternoon, the FBI paid us a visit, surrounding our apartment building and threatening to subpoena my mama to appear in front of a federal grand jury investigating the Party. Sufficiently frightened by this encounter with the FBI, my mother called the Party leadership, which promptly got her a lawyer. Luckily the FBI's secret grand jury investigation turned up nothing, and my mother emerged from the experience unscathed. Her involvement in the Party deepened, however. She quit her job at the post office and moved us into Party housing with several other Party members. People slept in shared rooms and in the basement and living room on pallets and mattresses. People were always coming and going.

As a fully fledged Panther, she took various jobs within the organization, including cooking at headquarters and in the free breakfast program. Though my mother would leave the Party in 1973, my father would remain and we children continued to attend the Party school. My mother went back on welfare for a time before taking a 28-week welding course at the East Bay Skills Center and soon after became the first woman welder at Ameron Pipe. She'd rise to the position of journeyman welder and win a spot on the grievance committee of Teamsters Local 70.

My mother's position as a welder meant more money and a move away from government cheese. In its stead, we ate out at all-you-can-eat buffets once a week and got actual store-bought toys we wanted on Christmas: skateboards, pogo sticks and Big Wheels. She even got a steady boyfriend named Tracy. He was tall, dark, gentle-natured and doted on our mother. These were good times until they weren't.

In my father's absence, his younger brother stepped in as a father figure for us. He was also a Panther. Uncle Landon, who was a former U.S. Army Vietnam War paratrooper, was invaluable to the Party as its security chief and weapons expert. His job included training Party members in militaristic maneuvers. He had recently been released from prison for the suspected torture and murder of a police informant (the government would eventually drop the case against him) just as my father began his seven-year sentence. He did his best to provide us with a strong male presence in our father's absence.

While my father was handsome and charismatic, his younger brother was the more stable and intellectual of the two despite his fearsome reputation as a Party enforcer. He was a young father supporting two children from a previous marriage and a child younger than one in his current marriage. Unlike other Party rank-and-file who lived in Panther housing, which meant bunklike quarters and often sleeping on pallets, my uncle chose to live in his own tidy little apartment in a good neighborhood with his new wife, Jan, and their baby, Ayaan. At the time, they were both pursuing bachelor's degrees.

Jan was very fair-skinned, short and compact, with the waist-length, thick black tresses of an Indian princess. They never argued or raised their voices. At least twice a month they invited us (usually two at a time) to spend the weekend in their light-filled apartment that smelled of patchouli incense and was decorated with African textiles, art and potted plants. They also had bookshelves overflowing with books covering topics like political economy, radical theory, philosophy, social theory and history. I helped my aunt feed my baby cousin, whom my uncle called Apples because her cheeks were so full it looked as if she were holding one in each cheek. There was an atmosphere of unflappable calm in their home that sedated my usually rambunctious nature. In their home I was content to work on a puzzle or catch up on homework. I didn't miss not being able to watch TV. Occasionally they'd take us on outings to the Exploratorium and Knott's Berry Farm.

Very rarely did we misbehave with Uncle Landon. A stern glance from him was usually enough to get us to abort any acts of tomfoolery we were contemplating. Those glances gave us a rare glimpse into a side of his personality that he saved strictly for his enemies and that we wanted no part of. But there was a time when I did something so bad that my uncle had no choice but to discipline me. It happened one afternoon before dinner when my aunt was changing the baby and my uncle was studying for an exam. I left my sister Louise in the living room and went to read a book in my uncle's big bed. As I propped up the pillows, I discovered a gun hidden underneath. I'd never seen or held a real gun before. I sat on the bed and took aim at a vase and then the doorknob, with my finger resting on the trigger. I blew air between my pursed lips emulating rapid fire. Then I turned the gun around and looked down the barrel just as my uncle walked in the room.

When he saw me with his gun, he froze in the doorway then grabbed onto the doorjamb as if he suddenly could not hold himself up. All the color left his face. I knew I was in trouble, and as if to erase it, I shoved the gun back under the pillow and jumped off the bed. My uncle, with the color slowly returning to his face, barked at me to go to the living room and stay there. That's when the tears came. When I got to the living room, my sister Louise must have heard my uncle yell, and when she saw me crying she said, "Oooo! Whatchu do?" "Shut up!" I snapped, and flopped onto the couch and buried my face in the cushions. "What happened?"

she asked with worry in her voice. I told her I found Uncle Landon's gun. She stared at me with eyes so wide I thought they'd fall
out of her head and roll across the floor. Then with the solemnity
of a doctor informing her patient that the cancer has metastasized,
she patted me on the back and said, "You gonna get it, but good."

I already knew I was going to get a beating for what I'd done. I
got whipped at home for things far less dire than playing with a
loaded gun. Something as simple as giving my mother a dirty look
could get you lashed with an extension cord, a wire hanger, a shoe,
a pot. Anything close to hand when the offense occurred was fair
game.

I'd never been disciplined by my uncle but I had no reason to
suspect it wouldn't be like what I'd get at home. Usually, punishment at home was swiftly meted out. But it seemed like a long time
since Uncle Landon ordered me to the living room. When he came
out of the bedroom, I instinctively wrapped my arms tightly around
my sister's waist as she frantically tried to extricate herself from
my grasp. But instead of reaching for me, my uncle did not even
glance our way. He calmly walked into my cousin's room where my
aunt was and closed the door. Louise and I crept over and put our
ears to the door to hear what they were talking about but could not
make sense of their whispered conversation. When we went back
to the sofa, my sister punched me in the shoulder. "Because of you
they probably talkin' 'bout us not coming here no more!" I rubbed
my bruised shoulder and let flow a whole new round of tears. A few
minutes later my aunt and uncle emerged from the bedroom as if
nothing had happened. They told us to get washed up for dinner.
My sister and I washed up, all the while giving each other disbe-
lieving looks. Had I really dodged a bullet—so to speak?

Dinner was as enjoyable as always. We all cooed over the baby and talked about school. My uncle was his usual smiley, affable self. When we finished dinner we got dessert, fresh fruit salad. And that was that. So I thought. We played dominoes and then took our nightly shower in preparation for bed. Louise helped Aunt Jan pull out the sofa bed. Then Uncle Landon told me to go into his room. My guts dropped. I looked over at Aunt Jan, whose face always reflected her every thought and emotion. The look I read there was not unlike what a loved one would give a prisoner just handed the death penalty. My eyes pleaded with her to intervene but I got no succor there. I walked slowly into the room, followed by my uncle, who shut the door behind us.

My eyes welled up when he took his belt off. But I wasn't the only one. I could see the tears welling up in his eyes too. "You can't play with guns. You could have hurt yourself. If you had, your father would never forgive me." His voice cracked and I could see he didn't want to beat me any more than I wanted to be beaten. Then he bent me over his knee and gave me about ten half-hearted lashes. I screamed like I was being flayed alive because I didn't want to hurt his feelings. He obviously was not very good at giving whippings.

My family moved often. Sometimes we were evicted. Sometimes my mother just wanted to be somewhere new. But each move took us only a dozen or so blocks from the previous apartment. We never left the confines of Oakland.

I adored my mother. I loved the way she looked, the way she smelled (she wore Jean Naté perfume). Nothing made me happier than to be near her. Every Saturday, after we stopped going to the prison, we made our weekly family trip to the drive-in movie theater. I helped my mother prepare bologna and cheese sandwiches, and pack them in the cooler with grape and orange soda. We piled into our old wood-paneled station wagon, all seven of us. My mother made the three oldest kids sit cross-legged in the backseat and draped a blanket over their laps. The three smaller kids (including me) curled up in the foot well, hidden under the blanket so we didn't have to pay for the extra tickets. I was a happy little girl, sitting in that car that smelled of bologna sandwiches and family.

When the movie started, I'd sit on my mother's lap, or my oldest sister Deborah's; she always sat up front with Mama. We saw *Star Wars, Eyes of Laura Mars, Jaws.* The films were always horror and sci-fi, which we all loved despite our tender ages. To this day watching horror films brings on a sense of comfort rather than fear. If it was a double feature, we younger kids would leave the car during intermission to play in the drive-in's playground. I enjoyed the velvety feel of the warm summer night stroking my face and bare legs as I tried to swing myself high enough to kick the moon.

There were several ways our big family coped with the stress of living in small apartments. Mostly it was by being outside as much as possible. But we also had coping strategies while inside. My mother coped by staking a clear claim on her private space: her bedroom. Though she allowed us to watch TV in her room (which we did every night) and even occasionally sleep with her, we all knew it was her space. We six kids slept from three to six to a room, depending on the size of the place we lived in. There was a lot of fighting and arguing over who owned what and what part of the room we could claim as ours. Then one day, one of my sisters came up with the idea of pitching a sheet tent in the corner of the room, held up by thumbtacking the corners to the walls and using books to anchor the hanging section to the floor.

My sister was proud enough to give us a brief tour inside. It was cozy and I loved the way the light inside took on the orange-sherbet glow of the sheet. She had a pillow and her comforter set up on the floor, along with her personal possessions safely out of reach. Brilliant! We all went in search of spare flat sheets and thumbtacks. Soon the tents got really elaborate. Some were broadened with two sheets and took up half a wall, with a broom stuck in a bucket in the center for support and string attached to a section and tacked to the ceiling to allow the occupant to walk upright. Inside were sleeping and seating areas. We created flap windows by cutting holes in the sheet, and closed the flap for privacy with safety pins. Everything was fine until someone decided they wanted to add a new addition that infringed on the "property line" of another. Fights would break out. Secretly, tents would be vandalized. Mama had to arbitrate disputes between neighbors until she got fed up and razed our little shantytown.

My poor mother. She couldn't keep anything in her home nice. We kids tore up everything. It's a wonder she continued to clothe and feed us. While roughhousing, we knocked out the picture window, scuffed up the walls, ripped curtains from the rod, flooded the bathroom and stained the carpet. My mother loved tropical fish. She bought a 20-gallon aquarium full of fighting fish, angel fish, oscars and tetras. It sat against the wall in the living room on a wrought-iron stand. She was very proud of her aquarium and decorated it elaborately with brightly colored gravel and lost treasure chests, spinning windmills and porous volcanic rocks for the fish to hide in. For night, she installed neon lights that gave the tank a serene glow. Whenever I learned she was going to the pet shop for supplies, I was the first one in the car.

She had to go to the pet shop often for new fish because we kids loved to feed them. Even when my mother told me not to, I'd get the fish food when no one was around and sprinkle so much in that it would cover the surface like fall leaves on a pond. I liked to see the fish dart to the surface for the treats. It didn't quite click in my head that overfeeding them could kill them. *Food makes you strong not weak. The more food the better,* I thought.

At least twice we knocked over our mother's beloved tank while playing or fighting too near it, sending twenty gallons of water and a dozen terrified fish across the living room carpet. My siblings and I scooped up the flopping fish and placed them in bowls and cups filled with tap water until we could get the tank righted and scoop up the gravel.

When Mama came home, she knew something was up because someone offered to help her with her coat and my older sisters had dinner prepared. We younger kids were sitting peaceably on the couch reading. But despite our best efforts, we could not distract our mother from noticing how her feet squelched as she walked across the carpet or draw her gaze from the cracked tank half-filled with cloudy water and two-thirds of her prized fish floating on the surface. She beat us all and sent us to our room. We could hear her crying on the phone to a friend, "I can't have nothin'! They keep tearing everything up!" The next morning the tank was gone. It would be the last we'd ever see one in our home.

CHAPTER 2

WE GREW UP QUICK. It was not uncommon for the other single mothers in my neighborhood to send small children outside alone. To gain this privilege, the child only had to demonstrate that she or he could walk upright most of the time, have sense enough to avoid getting hit by a car, and possess an aversion to dog poo. If you could wrap your mind around these few things, then you could pass through one of the first and most significant ghetto rites of passage: running the streets without adult supervision. I was six years old the first time I was allowed on the streets alone. The magnitude of this event, in my eyes, was no less significant than a young Maasai killing his first lion, or a Native American brave on a spirit quest.

The week before school started, Mama would take us all down to the local Goodwill to shop for school clothes. For years I didn't know where clothes could be purchased new. I awaited the yearly trip to Goodwill with more anticipation than Christmas. I loved the worn, spotted linoleum floor, the fluttering fluorescent lights and the racks and racks of clothing. Most of all I loved the smell, a combination of floor wax, mold and cheap perfume that seemed to permeate the building and clothing—the ghetto version of the new car smell. What I loved about shopping at the Goodwill was not that I'd be getting something "new." What I loved was what it signified. It meant the end of one year and the beginning of something new. A whole new year of adventures and learning and moving closer to being a grown-up.

Before our mother let us run loose in the store, she gave us the four rules of Goodwill shopping:

1. Stay away from the toy and book section because we ain't here for that.

2. Get two pairs of pants, two shirts, a pair of shoes and a warm coat.

3. TRY THEM ON! If we get home and they don't fit, you will be wearing it anyway.

4. Be back at the cash register in an hour or you can walk home with nothing.

And with that we were off. Two pairs of pants, two shirts, shoes and a coat may not seem like a lot for an entire school year, but it was more than many kids got in my neighborhood. Plus, if we got everything in polyester fabric, it could not only survive the school year but World War III as well. The fact that my mother could do this for all six of her children (she spent about two dollars per child) was nothing short of astonishing. Though she worked full-time as a welder, she struggled to support us and was not above supplementing the family larder with government cheese.

Government cheese was processed cheese packaged in unsliced blocks and distributed to welfare and food stamp recipients starting in the 1960s. It was originally used in military kitchens to feed soldiers during World War II. Once a month, government cheese and butter was distributed from the local elementary school. Lines of needy families stretched down the block. Usually the folks standing in line were children, as many parents were ashamed to stand in line for government handouts. It was a time when welfare was a dirty word. If you wanted to disparage someone whose family was on welfare, you could say, "At least we don't live on government cheese!" That statement alone could send the toughest bully running home in tears.

But times were hard and Mama would send all of us down to the school the minute word reached her that government cheese was to be had. We came home with huge blocks of butter and cheese that Mama kept in a chest freezer. The entire neighborhood feasted on grilled cheese sandwiches fried in butter, mac and cheese, cheeseburgers, cheese omelets and cheesy fries for weeks.

Intercommunal Youth Institute was a huge, utilitarian two-story building equipped with eight classrooms, an art room, a curriculum center, a full kitchen (serving breakfast, lunch and dinner daily), a cafeteria and an auditorium with a seating capacity of 350 used for drama presentations and other school programs. All of this was surrounded by a sea of concrete and a chain-link fence, and located a few blocks from our apartment.

Our school had two mottos: "Educate to Liberate" and "The World Is Our Classroom." It was fully accredited by the state and tuition-free, serving children between the ages of two and eleven years old. There were over a hundred students enrolled and placed in eight ungraded groups based on skills and abilities, not age. The Party's Socialist leanings ran deep and could be seen in the flattening of hierarchy that existed in the relationship we students had with the teachers. We did not address our teachers as Ms. or Mr. So-and-So. We addressed our teachers as Sister Erica or Brother Ed. Also, students were empowered to take a strong interest in how the school was run. This egalitarian perspective was manifest in a youth committee comprising three representatives from Groups 2 through 8 that had input into academic and activity-related decisions at the school. Our school was a direct response to the substandard and often demoralizing atmosphere that prevailed in the public school system of the time.

My classmates and I started each day with a hot breakfast followed by calisthenics, classes and afterschool activities like art and music lessons (I played clarinet), sports, and readings from Chairman Mao Zedong's manifesto, *The Little Red Book*. Although not formally members of the Communist Party, Panthers were Socialists, and we were taught to sympathize with revolutionaries like Mao and Che Guevara. We spent all day at school from eight A.M. until well into the night, when we would be dropped off by bus to our respective homes.

My father being in prison brought me a certain amount of cachet at school. He was considered a real revolutionary willing to sacrifice his freedom for the people. I'd smile with pride when adult Panthers would spot me and say, "Hey, there goes Randy's little girl. She gonna grow up and be a soldier like her daddy!" I worked hard to be the best at school, to live up to my father's image. I excelled in the classroom and on the playground. I was a tough kid, fearless on the monkey bars and just one of a few willing to swing full revolutions then hurl myself into space and, just when it seemed I'd crack my head open on the concrete, stick a perfect landing.

I was often mistaken for a boy. My mother never straightened my hair or pierced my ears. I wore my hair in a short afro. Because I played hard, my mother stopped dressing me in frilly girl clothes when I turned four. Before that, I remember she would dress my sister Louise and me—we were separated by one year—in short gingham baby-doll dresses with matching bloomers, because Louise and I looked so much alike. Louise wore the blue version and I red. We Williams kids strongly resembled one another, but there were some stark differences. Half of us had the darker skin and stocky frame of my mother's side of the family, the other half had the golden skin tone and lean frame of my father's side. What united us were our faces—baby faces with expressive, almond-shaped eyes, full lips and rounded cheeks we did not outgrow—faces that compelled many to say, "If you seen one, you've seen 'em all." So my mother was able to convince folks for a time that her youngest daughters were twins.

It was a struggle for my mother to get me dressed up in anything feminine. The only time I would acquiesce was during the holidays, especially if we were going to visit my paternal grandmother. (My mother's mother died before I was born.) She lived with my step-grandfather in a neat little house with fine furniture and a big picture-glass window. She made us homemade vanilla ice cream and sumptuous Thanksgiving meals. One Thanksgiving at Grandma's, my mother noticed that I'd ripped a hole in the bodice of my holiday dress (a long granny dress with white ruffle down the front) while roughhousing with my cousins. She promised to "Light my butt up" when we got home. I ran crying to Grandma and begged her to let me stay the night with her, and she convinced my mother to let me stay.

After everyone had gone and everything was cleaned and put away, I sat on my grandma's lap in her big chair and stroked her veiny, caramel-colored hand, the same color as my father's. "Your skin is so soft, Grandma. Why is your skin so soft?" I asked. "Oh, it's probably because I'm old and it's rotting," she replied nonchalantly. My grandma was like that. She didn't dumb things down and she told it like it was. That same evening as we prepared for bed, I told my grandma I didn't like my mama and I wanted to live with her. My grandma told me I shouldn't say that about my mama. I should be happy to have my mama. Then she told me an extraordinary story. She said she'd never known her birth mother. Soon after she was born, someone wrapped her in newspaper and put her in a trashcan in an alley. She cried and cried because she was cold and hungry. A lady taking out her trash thought the cries were from a cat, so when she lifted the trash lid and saw a baby, she was very shocked. My grandma said that lady became her mother—my great-grandmother was still alive and well at that time—and took very good care of her. I stared up at my grandma with my eyes and mouth wide open. How could someone throw away my beautiful, dainty, soft-spoken, gentle grandma? When my mother came for me the next morning, no longer angry about my dress, I left thinking I had the coolest grandma in the world. I'd find out decades later from my uncle Landon that Grandma's tale of being an abandoned baby in the trash was completely false. I don't fault her for it. She simply wanted to teach me to appreciate our family.

I had a love-hate relationship with being a girl. Growing up, I found that sex roles were so clearly defined that it was difficult for me to indulge in the full spectrum of things I liked to do without suffering the taunt of "tomboy." While I liked dolls and play-cooking, I also liked climbing trees and rock fights. Nothing stressed my nerves more than being in a situation where I was forced to identify solely with being female. As we students shuffled from one class to the next, we had to get in two lines side by side, one for boys and one for girls. To separate the class in this way seemed wrong because most of my friends were boys. Boys shared my interests in bugs, dirt and scary movies. They liked me because of my antics, like the time I unwittingly ran straight through the plate-glass window in the dining hall without so much as a scratch. I also had a special gift that my classmates envied. I put on a little exhibition of this talent every day at lunch when teachers weren't around. I'd take a swallow of milk, put my head down between my legs, allowing the milk to fill my sinuses, straighten up and let the milk run from my nose. *"Ewwwww!"* screamed the girls. "Cool!" yelled the boys. I was famous!

Kids in my neighborhood could create a toy or game out of anything. Rocks and a piece of chalk meant hopscotch. A piece of string became a game called Cat's Cradle. A blank sheet of paper was folded into a Chinese fortune-teller. An old clothesline was a jump rope. A bag full of rubber bands became Chinese jump rope.

I was not one to limit myself, so when I tired of playing with girls, I'd join the boys.

Though there was no shortage of raw materials ripe for the taking throughout the neighborhood, we sometimes kept our play simple. Hours were spent playing hide and seek, rock-paper-scissors, freeze tag, patty-cake and exploring. Of course the best places to explore were off-limits: abandoned buildings, rooftops and drainage ditches.

One of my favorite escapes was a place we kids called "the creek," which was really just a small pond fed by an old metal culvert. At a time when there were still vestiges of nature in the city, the creek was hidden from the street in a depression surrounded by overgrown weeds and scraggly scrub brush. I spent a lot of time there with a ragtag gang of siblings and other stray kids from the neighborhood. We caught tadpoles and sold them for bait to the men in our neighborhood who liked to fish. The tadpoles were a penny each.

The creek was also the setting of one of the most epic dirt-rock battles in our neighborhood's history. My siblings and I took up positions on the upper slopes of the dirt embankment leading down to the creek. Our less fortunate opponents had the far inferior position of defending the low ground. They were tasked with using scrub brush for shelter and throwing their dirt rocks up-hill, despite the fact that they lacked the upper body strength to lob their missiles any farther than halfway up the slope. We, on the other hand, pummeled our opponents with a hailstorm of dirt clods reminiscent of a summer's-night meteor shower. There was something very satisfying about the way the dirt clods exploded into dust when they made contact with a target. The battle raged on for twenty minutes before our opponents gave up and ran home, with us hot on their trail pelting them with dirt rocks the whole way.

But the real adventure at the creek was the culvert itself, which all the adults in the neighborhood warned us not to go into, which only made us want to go more. The bravest among us would usually only get in about fifteen feet. After that, what little light remained faded to total blackness. Inevitably, one of us would yell "Rat!" and that would send us all screaming back toward the entrance. One day we got serious and vowed to break the fifteen-foot barrier. We made a pact that we would follow the culvert wherever it led, no matter how long it took. We met at the creek with packs full of rope, our favorite toys, soda, Doritos and other essential survival gear.

The six of us—one of my sisters, my little brother and three friends from the neighborhood—arranged ourselves in a conga-line formation. Our cheery mood quickly deteriorated as we passed into complete darkness. Except for our rapid breathing and the occasional gasp at some imagined attack from a creepy-crawly, all was concentrated quiet. It felt like an eternity before we noticed a disk of brightness at the end of the tunnel. Someone yelled "Rat!" and we all surged forward, laughing and yelling triumphantly as we scrambled back into the light.

There were very few things that could tear us kids away from our play. Not beckoning mothers. Not grumbling tummies. Not the threat of a whipping for being out past the time the streetlights came on. The most spirited rock fight, baseball game or jump rope competition, however, stopped on a dime when two vehicles rolled into the neighborhood: the Ice Cream Truck and the Bookmobile.

The tinny, out-of-tune serenade emanating from the ice cream truck sent every kid in the neighborhood scurrying home from the treetops, under bushes, abandoned lots, behind cars and street corners like cockroaches exposed to the light of day. "The ice cream man! The ice cream man!" could be heard up and down the street. Piggy banks were raided, parents were nagged, coins liberated from change purses. The collective blood pressure and stress level of the children in the neighborhood were dangerously elevated until a quarter found its way into a grubby little fist. Then there was a reverse mass migration out of houses as the now coin-bearing children raced to queue up outside of the ice cream truck, garishly decorated with a cornucopia of mouth-watering images of ice cream that included Drum Sticks, orange cream bars, sundae cones, Fudgsicles, Bomb Pops, rainbow snow cones and Neapolitan ice cream sandwiches (my favorite). After buying ice cream, we stood in a group slowly savoring our treats while regarding, with barely concealed contempt, the sad faces of the kids unable to get money for ice cream, who eyed us like hyenas on the fringe of a lion kill.

Another cause for excitement was the bimonthly visit from the bookmobile. Bookmobiles are mobile libraries designed to service communities without access to libraries. My love of reading can be directly attributed to my access to a bookmobile. I scoured the shelves for children's books about the Greek and Roman gods, animals and dinosaurs. My fiction preferences leaned toward *The Berenstain Bears, The Cat in the Hat, Where the Sidewalk Ends, Cu-*

rious George and any of the Aesop fables. It was in the bookmobile that I discovered Ezra Jack Keats's *The Snowy Day*. This book was a revelation because it was the first children's book I ever read that featured a black child. His name was Peter, a pudgy, dark-skinned kid about my age dressed in a red jumpsuit, out in the hood exploring after the first snowfall of the season. Peter was a dude I could relate to. I checked the book out so often the librarian suggested I leave it for others to read. I'd eventually move on to other books but *The Snowy Day* would always be the first book that reflected who I was and what I felt as a small child growing up in the city.

My mother and father divorced eventually. My mother told me my father had been physically abusive and emotionally abusive even before they married, but she was too terrified to divorce him. She saw his imprisonment as the perfect opportunity to get out. After their divorce, my mother would go out partying with her friends a couple of weekends a month. I was never happy to see her getting dressed up in her tight, polyester, bell-bottom slacks and loose-flowing shirts with colors and patterns bold enough to be seen from space. I'd stand by pouting as she retrieved her wig, which was a glossy black helmet of hair indicative of the early Supremes. She'd preen in front of the mirror and spray the wig down with a thick coating of Aqua Net hairspray, which wreaked havoc on our lungs but got the wig as shiny as wet tar. Then she'd apply her makeup: a bit of red lipstick and black Maybelline eyeliner that she'd sharpen with a pocket knife and heat up with a match to the tip before tracing her upper and lower lids. Lastly she'd douse herself in the cloying sweet citrus aroma of Jean Naté perfume. While

I enjoyed taking in the spectacle of her out-on-the-town routine, I didn't like that it meant once Mama left, my eldest sister, Deborah, would be in charge.

Weekend nights normally meant we could stay up late and watch TV and play board games. These plans changed on the few occasions Mama was out and Deborah was in charge. Deborah was my mother's favorite. She knew it and we knew it. This was made clear by the fact that they often giggled together in secret conversations; and when my mother went on errands, she always took Deborah. Deborah was even privy to the one thing nearly every child was denied access to: Grown Folks' Business. Whenever my mother and her adult friends began to shift benign conversation about children, clothes and recipes into the realm of Grown Folks' Business, which usually meant topics like sex, drugs, gossip or violence, we younger kids were banished to the outdoors while Deborah was allowed to stay. Her special privileges also included her word being taken above ours, riding shotgun, not having to do chores and taking charge whenever Mama wasn't around.

Deborah had a leonine presence, with her golden skin and huge, perfectly spherical afro that seemed as pristine and impenetrable as a primeval forest. Her prison guard approach to babysitting was hated by all. As soon as the door clicked shut and the *thock, thock, thock* of Mama's heels faded as she strolled across the concrete yard to her car, Deborah had a belt in hand, which she used to back us into our room like a lion tamer. With backup from my sister Donna, her rule was absolute over us younger kids. She was quick to squash even the hint of rebellion with threats and violence. She'd demand we go to sleep as soon as our mother left at eight P.M. We balked. "But *Night of the Living Dead* is on tonight!" "Too bad!" We'd try to shame her into letting us stay up by screaming, "We ain't your slaves!" to which she'd reply "Tonight you are!" She'd shut us in and threaten us with a beating if we so much as peeked through the keyhole.

But she wasn't fooling us. We knew as soon as Mama was gone and we were banished to our room, fourteen-year-old Deborah and thirteen-year-old Donna would invite their friends over, which included boys. We'd hear them laughing and playing records all night. They'd always manage to get their friends out and the house back in order before Mama came home. No amount of tattling from us would convince my mother that Deborah was anything short of an angel. The special intimacy she shared with our mother could not be breached.

Deborah could make our mama laugh, real gut-busting laughs that brought tears to my mother's eyes. They held whispered conversations on the couch with their heads nearly touching like girlfriends. In fact that's how I viewed Deborah. Not as my mother's daughter but as her friend. My mother's relationship with the rest of us was cordial, friendly at times, but nothing that I ever felt was affectionate. There was a sense of duty to keep us clothed and fed but never kisses and hugs and *I love you*'s. Deborah never got that either, but when they were together I felt their emotional bond and it fed my own need for love just to witness it between them, even though I somehow knew I would never be on the receiving end of it. Despite her many children, I didn't get the sense that my mother particularly enjoyed children. There was tolerance, and every once in a while surrender to her predicament, but never joy.

Only once did I ever see my mother look on me with pride. A neighbor, distressed by my tomboy appearance, decided to dress me up and press my hair straight. I sat in a metal folding chair in her kitchen and let her swipe a hot comb through my hair saturated in Crisco cooking oil. The stench of burning hair and smoke made my eyes water. She followed up the press with a curling iron. Then she had me put on one of her daughter's dresses that she'd outgrown, a short white frilly thing that reminded me of something Shirley Temple would wear. When I stepped outside, it seemed the whole block was abuzz with my transformation. So much so that someone was sent to get my mother from her friend's house up the street. She came with a group of her friends and they surrounded me. "She's gorgeous, Mary!" "Mmm-hmm! A doll!" My mother never said a word. She just looked at me, her eyes wide and a big smile on her face. A smile that told me she was proud and I was beautiful. A look usually reserved for Deborah.

Despite our rivalry, Deborah was my idol. She was fearless, sassy, beautiful and widely admired at school. At the age of eleven, she was the Panther school's first graduate and was the mistress of ceremonies at the 1974 graduation. In a white dress, she stepped up to the podium surrounded by the school director, her teachers and my uncle, and gave a speech in which she praised Wednesday field trips, her favorite classes (math and reading) and the instructors. She remarked that she was sad to be leaving the school but happy that her experiences would prepare her to overcome the evils of the racist public school system where she would complete her education. She was especially sad to leave her teachers who "are not just teachers as they are in some schools—they are also our comrades." Later she brought the house down with a trombone solo of the song "Sunny" by Bobby Hebb. She was quoted in *The Black Panther* paper: "One of the most important things I have learned at the Institute is what freedom means . . ." When complimented on the confidence displayed by the graduating students, Ericka Huggins, the school director, would comment, "Our children are not afraid." Between 1974 and 1977, three more of my sisters would graduate but none with the fanfare and promise of the first.

Soon after graduating and entering puberty, however, all traces of my confident, talented and intelligent sister began to fade. It seemed she'd peaked as an eleven-year-old graduate, and from that moment on, slowly wandered away from us. The first clear sign I saw that the fearless, free girl was in decline emerged when she came to pick me up at school three years after she graduated. An older boy from Deborah's graduating class was picking on me. I had climbed a tree on the playground and when I tried to come down, he would whip my legs with a switch to prevent me.

I was relieved when I saw my sister approaching. "You gonna get it now. My big sister gonna beat yo' ass!" The boy looked over his shoulder to watch Deborah's approach. "Who? Her?" he said with a sneer. It had never occurred to me that everyone wasn't afraid of Deborah. She was such a force in my family and at school, I'd assumed the mere mention of her name would send tsunamis of fear washing over anyone fool enough to mess with her or us.

He threw down the switch and turned his back on me, crouching in the bare branches of the oak, and turned his tormentor's eye on my sister. "So you gonna beat my ass, hunh?" he said as he stood half a foot above my sister with his chest puffed up. For the first time I saw fear on my sister's face. When she looked up at me in the tree, I could also make out shame. Shame that this boy was belittling her in front of me. "I asked you a question, bitch!" he shouted in her ear and then shoved her in the face, sending her pinwheeling backward and landing solidly on her backside. She sat there on the concrete as passive as a puppy, with her chin in her chest. "I didn't think so!" he chuckled as he strutted off with a stiff-armed swagger.

That's when I jumped from the tree and ran to help my sister up. She swiped me away and stood up. After she brushed her clothes off, she said, "Let's go," as if the hero of my life had not just been felled. Seeing my big sister vulnerable and afraid was as devastating as some other kid being told Santa Claus isn't real. She saw my disappointment, so she tried to play it off by telling me the boy was lucky she didn't feel well or she would have cracked his head. But her bravado did little to repair what had been shattered. We walked the last few blocks home in silence. I didn't know it then, but Deborah wouldn't be the first girl I'd see lose her power after entering young womanhood. I made a promise to myself as I walked home with my big sister that I'd never let anyone make me feel small. The years would teach me it was easier said than done.

CHAPTER 3

THE YEAR 1977 was one of big change. My father was released from prison, though I wouldn't lay eyes on him for several weeks until one day he showed up unexpectedly at my school. I was playing dodgeball when I noticed the school principal, Ericka Huggins, leading a man across the yard then tapping the man on the shoulder and pointing in my direction. I knew him immediately even though the last time I had seen him, seven years earlier, I was three years old. He was wearing a black leather jacket and tan slacks with creases sharp enough to slice bread. His hair was trimmed short and he was smiling. Smiling at me! My classmates gathered around me to see what I was staring at. "Who's that?" someone asked. "That's *my* daddy!" I said, puffed up with pride. Then I ran to him and he scooped me up in his strong arms. "How's my baby?" he asked over and over again, with his face in my neck, squeezing me so hard I could hardly breathe but I hoped he'd never stop. I couldn't believe he was back and he was mine.

He spent the rest of recess watching me play. To have him there so handsome and well respected felt like being the daughter of a rock star. I without a doubt had the coolest daddy in the city and I wanted everyone to know it. After recess he kissed me good-bye and promised to come see me at home the next night.

Mama had us all take a shower and put on clean clothes in preparation for Daddy's visit. She'd spent the day cleaning the house and rearranging the furniture in the living room. After five different configurations of our humble furniture, she seemed satisfied. She then changed into one of her muumuus, a floor-length floral dress that she told us was worn by women in Hawaii. Next she hit the kitchen and within a few hours had a big pot of gumbo with sausage, chicken, crab legs and shrimp simmering on the stove next to a large pot of white rice.

When Daddy knocked on the door, we four youngest kids all surged forward wanting desperately to be the first to let Daddy in. I got elbowed and shoved and gave as well as I got. Before a full-on riot erupted, Mama shooed us out of the way and opened the door herself. Daddy kissed Mama briefly on the cheek before turning his light on us. He bent to kiss us all even though he was burdened with two large heavy-looking bags, which he gave to us. It took two of us to carry one bag, which we carted off to the kitchen. The bags contained milk, eggs, flour and sacks of sugar. We squealed like we'd never seen groceries before and thanked our daddy over and over.

He laughed and let us take turns sitting next to him. My two oldest sisters, Deborah and Donna, seemed cautiously happy as they sat to themselves on the other side of the room answering our father's inquiries about school and life with one-word declarations. Now that he was back, he told Mama, he was gonna take us to spend time with him. He'd gotten an apartment near Lake Merritt so we could even spend the night on weekends. This announcement sent us into near paroxysms of joy. Then Mama asked Daddy to help her move the coffee table against the wall, freeing up the center of the room—which could only mean dancing! Mama put some music on the record player, blasting "Car Wash" by Rose Royce, "Boogie On, Reggae Woman" by Stevie Wonder, and our favorite,"Kung Fu Fighting" by Carl Douglas, as we kids formed a Soul Train line and shuffled across the living room in front of Daddy. We got down with the Funky Chicken and the Robot, anything that would garner praise from our father, who'd cheer us on from the sidelines with "Aw, sooky sooky!" "Look out now!" "You outta sight!" "Get down wit da boogie!"

Afterward we ate dinner, which Daddy declared the best gumbo he'd ever had after each bite. Mama followed up the gumbo with a homemade peach cobbler with vanilla ice cream. Then she had us clear the table and wash up and told us to go watch TV in her room so she and Daddy could talk in peace. I couldn't concentrate on TV with my daddy so near, so I sneaked back to the living room and poked my head in. Mama and Daddy were sitting on the couch and Mama was trying to kiss him, but he was pushing her away. He brushed her hands away when she tried to touch him. When he saw me, he stood up and said, "Baby girl! Go get your brother and sisters. I want to kiss them good-bye."

I ran back with his request. As he held each of us, he promised he'd be back and pick us up to go stay with him. "Would you like that?" he asked. "Yeah!" we trumpeted. Mama stood to the side and watched, smiling in a way that didn't touch her eyes. Then before Daddy left, I kissed and hugged him one last time for Mama.

A few weeks later, Daddy came back as promised and took my sister Louise and me to spend the whole weekend with him. After picking us up in his sporty new car that smelled like the little pine tree that swung from the rearview mirror, he drove to a nearby neighborhood. "I thought your place was near Lake Merritt, Daddy," I said, peering at the shabby houses and apartment buildings that were as lackluster as the ones on my block. Surely Daddy didn't live here. When he pulled up to the curb next to a large gray and white bungalow with an oil-stained and cracked driveway and an anemic lawn, he got out of the car and stuck his head back inside to tell us, "I have to see someone. Wait here for me." Then he slammed the door and walked up to the house, straightening his shirt sleeves and adjusting his shirt collar. He knocked on the door, it opened, and he disappeared into the shadows of the house, which promptly sealed itself in his wake.

We sat waiting in the car for him for what could not have been more than twenty minutes but in the world of restless children equated to hours and hours of senseless confinement. That's when my sister dared me to go knock on the door to see what was going on. "We didn't come to sit cooped up in no hot car! Go tell Daddy we hungry and ready to go." Anxious to free myself from the car, I slipped out the backseat and approached the house. I could see that there were worn-out Hot Wheels cars and the chewed-on twisted bodies of plastic toy soldiers strewn across the cracked concrete porch. I could hear conversation coming from the house as I stood on the porch but couldn't make out the words. I tried to take a peek in the front window but the curtains were drawn tight.

After a few minutes of hesitation, I banged on the door and

the conversation stopped. I could see there was a peephole in the door and I stood with my hands on my hips looking up at it. Then I heard my daddy say, "Is there a little girl out there?" and then a lady's voice said, "I don't see a little girl. Looks like a little boy though."

Normally I never took offense to people mistaking me for a boy, but this time my face got all hot and my chest tightened. When the door opened and a pretty, slim lady with long braids, wearing bell-bottom jeans and a tight T-shirt answered, I was so angry I told her with my fists planted firmly on my hips, "I ain't no boy, I'm a girl!" Then I brushed past her and stomped over to my daddy, who was sitting on the couch in the living room. "I came to tell you we tired of waiting out in the car and we hungry."

The lady and my daddy started laughing, which only made me angrier. "Whew! She feisty, hunh?" the lady said, staring down at me. My daddy grabbed me around the waist and pulled me onto his lap. I struggled to keep my feet and my temper, but then Daddy reached for my tickle spot, my neck, and I dissolved in giggles.

"I want you to meet Ann," Daddy said. "Ann is a friend of mine and I want you to be nice to her." I gave Ann a look that said, *Don't count on it.* "I also want you to meet your brother." *My brother? I already know my brother!* I was about to say when Ann left the room and came back with a little boy about the same age as my little brother. "Lawanna, meet your other brother, Randolph." Not only was a new brother being sprung on me, he also had the same name and was a damn near carbon copy of the brother I already had. We stood in the middle of the room facing each other. He blinked at me. I blinked at him. "Give her a hug, Randy," the lady said, as if being confronted with my father's other family was the most normal thing in the world. When the boy reached out his skinny arms to hug me, I instinctively drew my fist back to punch him in the face, which got him to back off real quick. "Whoa, baby girl! What you doing?" my daddy asked, grabbing me by my cocked arm. "I'm going to wait in the car!" I announced, ripping my arm from his grip and heading out the door.

I never saw the boy or the woman again, although later as a young teen I would learn that I had many more half-siblings. Most were boys and, á la George Foreman, my father would name all of his boys after himself.

There were a few more trips with Daddy in which we spent the evening with him at his glass-and-steel high-rise apartment overlooking Lake Merritt. We knew he shared it with a woman, but this time he had sense enough to ask her not to be around when we were there. When we went out with Daddy in public, women were drawn to him. They laughed and giggled at things he said that were not funny. Stared into his eyes too long, extended conversations well beyond necessary, and their hands somehow found themselves squeezing a bicep or landing on his chest like wayward butterflies. I was proud that women found my daddy attractive, but I did not want to share him with them.

Our love affair with Daddy's return began to wear for all of us. The rumors of secret families scattered across the city and his increasingly infrequent visits took a toll. Daddy avoided our mother and chose to pop up at our apartment to leave food and clothes for us at very inopportune times. Like on days we were playing hooky from school. Right in the middle of my sisters and I watching daytime soap operas, we'd hear a tapping on the front window and see Daddy peering in at us through a crack in the drapes. We'd scatter like rats on a sinking ship. "I saw you in there! Open the door!" But we knew if we ignored him long enough, he'd go away and then we'd retrieve the items he'd leave by the door.

We began to associate him with being in trouble because eventually his visits became limited to disciplinary encounters. My mother would call him whenever we kids got into trouble beyond the pale. Which didn't occur often. But when it did, the prospect of being on the receiving end of Daddy's wrath was nothing to joke about.

I noticed an increase in the amount of whispered conversations between Party members in the fall leading into 1977. The topics of these conversations were obviously Grown Folks' Business so I had to employ a host of tactics ranging from listening under open windows or, if I was in the room, pretending to be engrossed in a game or book in order to discern what had the adults in my life so agitated. Sometimes I'd blow my cover by openly listening to the adults, at which point they'd stop talking and my mother or another adult would say, "Get out of my mouth!"—a way of telling me to mind my own business. From what I gathered from stolen bits of conversation I hoarded like a pack rat, the Party was under a lot of external and internal stress.

The FBI's Counter Intelligence Program (COINTELPRO), founded in 1967 and designed to identify what it characterized as "Black Nationalist Hate Groups," was in full effect. It initially targeted groups including the Southern Christian Leadership Conference (SCLC) and the Student Nonviolent Coordinating Committee (SNCC). Agents were expressly directed to focus on black leaders they labeled "messiahs" to prevent them and their organizations from "gaining respectability," leaders like Martin Luther King Jr., Elijah Muhammad and Stokely Carmichael.

The Black Panther Party did not make the COINTELPRO list until 1969, when J. Edgar Hoover would make it the program's main target, with an aim to "disrupt and neutralize." By July 1969, the Party would become the target of 233 of the total authorized "Black Nationalist" COINTELPRO actions, which would include numerous infiltrations of FBI agents. Many of the actions taken against the BPP were unlawful and strove not to prevent crime but to foment violence and unrest through infiltration and by "intensifying the degree of animosity" between the BPP and other nationalist groups as well as between its members. Some of these tactics included letter forging, unlawful wiretapping and telephone voice impersonations.

These tactics, in conjunction with a growing tolerance within the Party for misuse of funds, extortion, random violence and drug abuse, would lead to its eventual downfall by creating a climate of fear from within and without. The marriage of external attacks and internal power trips also led to a cancerous culture of extreme misogyny, which I witnessed firsthand when the bully who'd chased me up a tree at school turned on my sister Deborah and assaulted her on the playground. This didn't just happen among students. It was not unheard of for Party women to be coerced into sex and sometimes outright raped by fellow Panthers, and beaten when they lodged complaints. Teenaged girls were a common target as well. With five female children to care for, my mother turned her back on an organization that was created to protect and empower but in the end would leave many of its members traumatized, disillusioned and beholden to a new master that was slowly taking over the bodies and minds of the community: cheap cocaine.

Despite the unrest that was brewing, I never believed we would leave the Party. It was all I knew and had become a strong part of my identity. I took great pride in telling people where I went to school, that my father was a revolutionary prisoner and my comrade was Huey P. Newton. I fully expected to be the fifth person in my family to graduate from the Intercommunal Youth Institute, despite the fact that like my mama, my daddy, upon his release from prison, became less involved in the Party. I believed this right up until the day I was in the middle of math class and the school's director, Ericka Huggins, stuck her head in the room and beckoned me to join her in the hall.

Like any kid called out of class by the principal, I racked my brain to uncover what trouble I had been up to that would warrant this visit. When I got out in the hall, she informed me I was to go straight home. "Why?" "You can't come to school here anymore." Then she handed me a sack lunch and sent me on my way.

Stunned and confused, I walked through the gate to the sidewalk. Then I turned back toward my school, opened the brown paper sack and threw the peanut butter and jelly sandwich over the gate, followed by a boiled egg, an apple and carrot sticks. Then I ran home.

Within a week my mother enrolled me in the closest elementary school near our home. I was bored by the activities that involved writing the alphabet in cursive over and over again until it perfectly resembled the chart on the wall above the blackboard. Science class was devoid of animals or field trips or outdoor exploration. The course was strictly book-based and involved reading and discussion only. The kids in public school were different too. As the new kid, I got picked on for being a Panther. Many people in the community viewed the Panthers as little more than power-hungry thugs. The girls, who all wore their hair relaxed, made fun of my afro and my secondhand clothes. The boys wouldn't play with me.

I made connections with my teachers, who seemed more interested in my background as a Panther than the kids did. I was known as a teacher's pet, preferring to spend my recess time cleaning blackboards, doing extra credit assignments and reading. I was constantly inadvertently offending some kid at school and had to sneak out early or stay late in order to avoid being jumped on the way home.

I went from being extremely independent and outgoing to a virtual recluse. When I could not avoid the bullies, I'd cut school until things calmed down. Despite my absences, I still managed to do well in school. It was around this time that I became obsessed with small spaces. I'd see a cabinet or a box and wonder if I was small enough to fit into it. I'd crawl in and out of cabinets at school and home. I found it peaceful folding myself into these tight dark spaces that released me from having to think about the things that were falling apart around me. My favorite place to hide was an attic crawl space in our house. The darkness, the cobwebs and the stifling heat did little to deter me from seeking this place out when I needed comfort. I began to bring up my favorite things. A diary, polished stones, my favorite books. Things I wanted protected should something catastrophic happen.

I wasn't just imagining the worst. There was very bad tension building in the house from the most unlikely of sources. Deborah, my mother's golden child, was in full rebellion. Now fifteen, she and Mama were fighting more and more, verbal confrontations that would end with Deborah leaving the house and not returning for days. Mama began to drink more and more. Eventually, my mother heard a rumor that Deborah was working as a prostitute. My mother told my father. The last time I'd see my parents in the same room was when Deborah returned home after more than a week on the street. She plopped down on a chair and I climbed into her lap. My mother secretly telephoned my father.

Deborah tried to leave when she saw him standing in the doorway. My parents argued with her, and the argument became a beating. My father chased her outside and continued beating her in the street. My mother did not interfere. Deborah eventually slipped free and ran into the night. Mama told us not to let her in the house if she were to return. But it would be nearly a year before I'd see her again.

Deborah's absence from our family was like suddenly realizing that our once sturdy home was really little more than a lean-to in a storm. There was nothing and no one who could hold us up or keep us together. Things got even worse when a knee injury caused Mama to lose her welding job, making her dependent on disability checks and welfare. She also cozied up to more alcohol and drugs. She grew distant from us. Family activities ended. She was sad all the time and started drinking heavily. She'd sit on the couch for hours with her chin on her chest, listening to blues records and weeping. All she would say is, "I'm tired. I'm tired."

Nothing would cheer her. Daddy stopped coming around. My

older sisters seemed to close up as much as our mother. Although I did not want to admit it, I was on my own.

My adjustment to public school was long and difficult. Though my new school was just a few blocks from the Panther school, it might as well have been another continent. I simply didn't know how to interact in the community outside of the Panthers. The disequilibrium I experienced upon entering public school was not unlike culture shock.

I was proud of my family's involvement in the Party and took any opportunity to inform my new teachers and classmates that my father spent time in Soledad as a revolutionary prisoner. Instead of being impressed, the teachers looked at me with pity in their eyes and my classmates teased me for being the daughter of a jailbird. What was once a badge of honor became a liability. I'd lived a sheltered life in the Party. I did not know the Black Panther Party had deteriorated as an organization and, in the process, lost respect in the eyes of the community it originally sought to serve.

By the time I entered public school, many people in the community viewed the Panthers as a violent and corrupt group. The accomplishments of the Party began to be overshadowed by what many thought was its corruption of young black males, manifested in an alarming increase in black-on-black violence in Oakland and across the nation. Some blamed the Party for creating a "gang mentality" and a "romance with the gun" in young black males.

It was in this climate that I entered public school. I went from being loved by my teachers and respected by my classmates to being bullied. I was bullied for being a Panther and also bullied by a group of "well-off" kids because I didn't have nice clothes. While my Goodwill ensembles served me well at the Panther school, they drew negative attention from the kids in public school. I quickly became the target of a group of popular girls. Their leader coolly informed me that if I came to school the next day wearing my blue jeans or tan pants or my white or striped shirt, she and her friends were going to beat me up after school. They'd basically described every article of clothing I owned.

I was scared because I knew it would be tough to get my siblings to lend me anything of their clothing, as we were all very protective of the few things we owned. So it wasn't surprising when both Teresa and Louise refused to let me borrow their clothes. In order to avoid getting beat up, I had to resort to plan B. I got up in the middle of the night and stole a pair of one sister's pants and another's shirt. I got up extra early the next day and went to school before they saw me. The plan worked and I avoided getting beat up by the cool kids that day. But my sister caught me at school in one of her shirts and got so angry she demanded I take it off on the spot. So though I pilfered clothes to avoid getting in a fight with the cool kids, I ended up in a fight with my sister.

The kids also made fun of my mother whenever she came to the school. If there were papers she needed to sign or a teacher to see, she came dressed in her old welding clothes—a beanie, heavy boots, a man's jacket and baggy pants. The kids made fun, saying my mother was a bull dyke. They refused to believe me when I told them she dressed like that because she had been a welder. It was the first time I was ever ashamed of her.

They also accused me of being lesbian because I didn't wear

dresses and I wore my hair in an afro when most of the girls wore their hair pressed straight. There was one instance when a substitute teacher mistook me for a boy, which sent the entire class into hysterics and me to the restroom in order to keep the kids from seeing me cry.

Another big adjustment was the indifference of the teachers toward the well-being of students. I was used to being coddled by my teachers at the Panther school. In public school I felt like I was tolerated. The teachers ignored the bullying that was an everyday occurrence and even turned a blind eye to fights that took place in the parking lot after school almost every day. After leaving the relative security of the Panther school, I found myself the target of male sexual predatory behavior that seemed rampant in the wider community.

Despite my difficulty fitting in socially, I enjoyed learning. I was especially fond of science and English. In junior high I joined the school newspaper and helped work on the school yearbook. I avoided group sports and other social clubs like death itself. It was difficult for me to make friends and so I spent my free time with my siblings and Panther friends after school, especially Neome. But more than anything I began to enjoy my solitude. I spent most of my free time between the pages of a book, usually Stephen King.

Every neighborhood has at least one weird family. On one of the many streets on which we lived it was the Taylors. They were a mother and father with a teenaged son and two daughters about the same age as the youngest girls in my family. They lived in a house whose backyard abutted the back of our apartment building. A tall wooden fence obscured by high, thick brush separated the two properties.

The Taylors initially came to my attention when their house burned down in an electrical fire. When we saw the flames leaping high into the air over the back fence, my sister Louise and I high-tailed it around the block to see what was burning. We arrived in front of the burning house just as the fire engines arrived. It was a large, pretty house with two stories and large windows. I thought it a pity that such a house was engulfed in flames, with smoke pouring out of its windows and up the branches of an old oak in the front yard.

We, along with a street full of neighbors, watched as the firemen put the fire out but not before part of the roof caved in and a section of siding burned away. What was left looked like a torched dollhouse, in that part of the exterior wall was gone and one could easily see a cross section of the house. With most of the excitement extinguished with the fire and it growing dark out, we rushed home to tell our family everything we saw.

We went back a few weeks later to see if the house had fallen down. To our dismay it was still standing. A man with a pot belly and a wreath of kinky hair circling his otherwise bald pate was out front with a boy of about fourteen. The boy was light-skinned, lanky, with a big afro. We knew him as a boy our older sister had a crush on. With hammer and nails they were sealing up the busted-out windows with plywood. We could see that they'd already covered the holes in the roof with large tarps. We stood across the street and watched them work.

When they took a break, we walked across the street and up to the curb, where the man and his son sat drinking colas, and started talking to the boy. We wanted to know why they were boarding up a burnt-up house. The boy had nice white teeth. He was shirtless and skinny, but you could see he had a few muscles. The father sat a short distance away but was staring at us with obvious interest. We knew the father to be one of many neighborhood perverts who cruised around in their cars looking to pick up fast girls. He was well known because when he cruised around, he did it in an old van that we saw parked in the driveway.

We were ignoring the old man, so he left us with his son and went back to work on the house. After a few minutes of our annoying inquiries, the boy called out some names and two girls about our age came around from the back of the house. They were his sisters. They asked us if we wanted to come play in their backyard.

We left the boy and father to their work and followed the girls back down the driveway past the van, which was a funky throwback to the heyday of the hippie era. Their father was known to host prostitutes inside that van.

The girls told us since the fire the family had been living in various makeshift shelters in the backyard. The Taylors had a big backyard that was blanketed in weeds and years' worth of dead leaves that had fallen from several large trees. In the back there also stood a large garage with peeling sky-blue paint and dirty beige trim that was probably white in another life. It looked more like a barn than a garage, with its two large swinging doors and pitched roof. We asked if we could look inside.

When the girls brought us into the garage, Mrs. Taylor asked who we were, but her daughters told her to mind her business. They ignored her follow-up questions, too, and told us to do likewise, so we did. I was a bit shocked. I'd never seen anyone get away with talking to their mother like that.

The garage was crammed full of the items they'd managed to salvage from the fire: a couple of chairs, garbage bags spilling over with clothing, photo albums, stacks of papers, board games, an old trunk. There were also lots of pots and pans and dishes, two sets of bunk beds, a card table with four metal folding chairs near another trunk that held a hot plate and acted as a makeshift kitchen. The electric hot plate was connected to a series of extension cords that ran along the floor and out the door and eventually connected to an outlet in a helpful neighbor's house.

There were also several large plastic coolers and a large wooden bookshelf holding lots of canned food and several cases of generic soda pop. One of the sisters peeled off a couple of colas and offered them to us. They were warm but we drank them anyway. I asked about several kerosene-burning lanterns I saw lying about. They, along with flashlights, were used by the family to get around at night.

There was a corner of the garage that was separated from the rest by an old army blanket folded over a piece of cord nailed to the wall. Behind it was a single mattress on a folding metal frame dressed neatly with decorative pillows and a pretty handmade crocheted blanket with red roses. The night table was two stacked milk crates covered with a piece of white lace. That's where the mother slept. It was behind the curtain that Mrs. Taylor fled when her daughters ignored her.

The garage was poorly ventilated because there were only two small windows. There was a horrible stench of unwashed bodies and rotting food. I saw a plate of what looked like half-eaten ravioli crawling with maggots. Roaches were everywhere. They used a corner of the yard where Mr. Taylor had dug a trench as a toilet, and they washed their clothes and bathed in a big metal tub behind plastic sheeting hung from a line. Far from being repulsed, I was fascinated by the Taylors. They were like an inner-city Swiss Family Robinson.

I became quite close with one of the sisters and played with her in the backyard nearly every day after school. The only hazard was Mr. Taylor. His hands had a way of creeping over me if I was caught unawares. One afternoon I was climbing up to join my friend on the top bunk when Mr. Taylor came over and grabbed me from behind, putting one hand between my legs and the other one on one of my breasts. When I slapped his hands away and gave him a dirty look, he looked back at me sheepishly, ensuring me he was just trying to help me up.

"You're nasty!" I screamed.

"What's going on?" Mrs. Taylor asked, pulling the hanging blanket aside to see out. She was a pudgy, soft-bodied woman who was bullied just as badly by her husband as her children.

"Nothin's happening," Mr. Taylor said, still staring up at me feigning innocence.

"Nnh-uhn!" I said. "He was putting his nasty hands on my coochie!"

"No! I was just helping her up," he said as he walked out.

I wanted Mrs. Taylor to hit him with her shoe, or cuss him out at the very least. Instead she just let the blanket fall back into place, sealing herself away from her family.

My friend then whispered to me, "Just watch where he is at all times. That way you have time to get away."

My fascination with the Taylors quickly waned after that incident. The novelty of their unconventional living situation had worn off. I would have remained friends with the girls but the neighborhood kids bullied them because of their father and how they lived, so they never wanted to play anywhere but in their backyard, which for me was too close to their father for comfort.

It was at this point that fear crept into my life like a goblin that lived in the pit of my stomach promising ruin. I knew my childhood was coming to an end. The end of childhood for girls in my community meant being vulnerable to the predatory advances of men who saw young girls, especially girls without the benefit of stable homes, as fair game. I'd seen it many times. Girls in my school and in my own family who were strong and vital and curious became suddenly cowed, abused and abandoned soon after puberty. Many were saddled with children and adult responsibility before finishing junior high school.

It happened to Deborah and my sister Donna. At just ten, it had begun to happen to me. For most of my childhood I looked like a boy, dressed like a boy, played like a boy. This gender bending allowed me the freedom to explore my community with ease. But my body began to betray me, tiny, swollen boobs began to grow and blow my cover. Teachers and shopkeepers and neighborhood men took notice. Men old enough to be my grandfather started offering me sweets in exchange for sexual favors. I became adept at fending off their groping hands and unwanted attention. I didn't know to tell anyone. Snitching was not allowed, even if you were the victim. I knew it was up to me to stay out of harm's way.

I went from a child who loved being outside to one who spent as little time outside as possible. The most risky part of the day was the two-block trip to the bus stop to go to school. There were always a few perverts who liked to hang around there waiting for girls traveling on their own. We learned there was safety in numbers and made arrangements beforehand to arrive at the stop at roughly the same time. In the chill of early morning on any given weekday it was common to see girls huddled together at bus stops emboldened by their numbers, hurling insults at the perverts as they slowly glided by in their cars looking to give a girl "a ride" to school. The trip home was equally harrowing.

It was during this time that I developed a slight stutter and began seeking out hiding places that only I knew about. The attic space at home. The crawl space under the stage at school. Places where I could stash food and my favorite things. Places where I could ride out the coming apocalypse that was puberty. I also turned heavily to books to escape. I was particularly attracted to horror fiction and sci-fi: *The Hobbit, The Lion, the Witch and the Wardrobe* and lots and lots of Stephen King novels. They read like survival manuals, teaching me how not to fall victim to monsters. I also learned from some members of my family and people in the community how abuse of drugs and alcohol, partying and running the streets could ruin a person. I vowed from a very young age that I would never drink, smoke, do drugs or have sex.

My mother had no problem letting us watch films that had graphic sex scenes and she certainly had no problem talking about sex with her friends within hearing distance of us, but when it came to educating her kids about sex and the changes our bodies would go through, she never broached the subject. It left me thinking that sex and the female body were shameful and only good for crass jokes and secret conversations. Open educational sex talk didn't happen in our home despite the fact that my mother was raising five girls. Most of what I knew came from afterschool specials, books, gossip and a sex education class at school.

The sex ed class was a bit more helpful. It was taught by an old white woman who seemed overly excited about the subject. She had long white hair with scraggly ends that hung down past her butt. She was too old to be a hippie but she dressed like one, in her peasant blouse and bell-bottom jeans that even then were a bit out of style. Her skin was as sun-ravaged as the dashboard of an old car. Her face was tan and cracked and would not have looked out of place on a shar-pei puppy, but her eyes were young. They were clear, blue, jovial and landed on each of us with the intensity of a searchlight.

As she began to unpack her teaching aids from a big duffel bag, all I could think about was her being somebody's granny. Somebody's granny who was handling a cross section of an erect penis. There were nervous snickers as she unpacked a bag that also contained a cross section of a female pelvis.

She began her lecture with a slide show. The first slide was of the male reproductive system with the various parts labeled. We were instructed to repeat back to her each part: "Head." "Head!" "Shaft." "Shaft!" "Testes." "Testes!" "Anus." "Anus!" She encouraged us to say each word loud and clear. It was exhilarating. It felt like Teacher was giving us permission to say dirty words in class. She repeated the exercise for the female reproductive system.

Then she showed us a short movie of sperm swimming toward the egg. She described the fertilization of the egg as the world's tiniest footrace, with millions of sperm racing to reach the finish line. This part of the lecture was like listening to a synopsis of a movie. Each sperm released was full of ambition and hope. They raced along like spawning salmon to fulfill their destiny. Many would lose their way and Teacher pointed out deformed sperm with crooked tails that swam in circles, sperm that had two heads or two tails that couldn't swim at all. Then there were the star sperm. They were the Sidney Poitiers and John Waynes in the story of reproduction, who raced along like little minnows, each as hale and hardy as the next; but only one was destined to win the grand prize and have its genetic material incorporated into a fertilized egg.

This whole sex thing was exciting and as interesting as an episode of *Wild Kingdom*. So later when Teacher asked for volunteers, I threw my hand up and was selected along with another girl and a boy. We shuffled to the front of the class. Then Teacher reached into her bag and presented each of us with a condom and a cucumber. When she told us to put the condoms on the cucumber, the class erupted into a chorus of raucous laughter, elbow jabbing and crude jokes. I was mortified. Even more so when I tore the condom trying to get it on. Teacher just laughed and said, "It happens." As awkward as sex ed turned out to be, it filled in many of the gaps in my knowledge of the subject.

My mother would not discuss sex but she was not averse to having lots of it. From a young age I knew what the banging headboard and grunting noises that were still audible over the music blaring in her bedroom meant. It meant Mama and her boyfriend were doing the nasty.

Growing up in a sexually ignorant home had its consequences. One day, at age fifteen, Donna began asking us younger siblings to walk on her stomach.

"What for?" I asked, eyeing her suspiciously.

She told me her stomach hurt and walking on it would help.

"Why don't you tell Mama you don't feel good?" Louise asked.

"It don't feel bad enough for the doctor. I just need you to walk on it. And don't tell Mama."

When I was convinced there would be no repercussions, I was more than happy to walk on my big sister, which she asked me to do several times a day for weeks. Then one evening she woke up the whole house screaming as if she were about to die. Mama rushed her to the hospital, leaving the rest of us alone at home to speculate about what was happening. We all knew she'd been complaining of bellyaches for months and I thought maybe I'd hurt her by walking on her belly. Mama returned a few hours later to inform us that Donna had had a baby. She'd managed to hide her pregnancy from all of us for seven months, then gave birth to a baby girl two months premature. How she managed to hide her pregnancy in a house in which true privacy was only achieved in REM sleep was beyond us all.

When we went to the hospital to see Donna, she lay in her bed crying, refusing to look at us as she was so ashamed. Mama told us that all the way to the hospital Donna denied she was pregnant right up until she delivered her baby. I felt sick when I realized that the reason she'd asked us to walk on her stomach was because she was trying to miscarry.

We left Donna and went to the NICU to see the baby that Donna named Latasha. She was just two pounds, incredibly small, lying there in an incubator too premature to regulate her own body temperature or breathe on her own. She was hooked up to an impossible number of tubes and doodads. I'd never seen a baby so small. She looked like an ugly old man but I loved her on sight. The nurses called her a miracle baby because she thrived despite the lack of prenatal care and being born way too early. If only they knew that Latasha also had to contend with her mother actively trying to end the pregnancy too. She was indeed a miracle. She came home to us a few months later healthy and hearty and became the center of my world. It was like having the baby sister I'd always wanted. I helped with her feeding, as Donna did not breast-feed, as well as with diaper changes and cuddling. I loved to stick my nose in the space at the base of her neck where the sweet smell of baby was most concentrated.

She grew into an active and inquisitive toddler. She loved to scribble on paper with markers. One afternoon when she was left alone, we discovered that she'd gone around the apartment marking walls, doors and furniture with a little slash of purple. While I believed most kids would have found a spot and scribbled the pen dry, I thought it evidence of Tasha's brilliance that she chose to mark many spots as if to convey "Tasha was here!" For weeks we'd run across undiscovered slashes of purple in odd locations, like on the underside of tables and one even inside the refrigerator.

The stress of helping to raise Tasha put a strain on my mother and sister's relationship. They began to argue frequently. Mama threatened to kick her out. In order to get away, Donna got a new boyfriend and moved to Texas, taking Tasha with her. I missed my niece but just like with Deborah, we simply had to cope with the loss on our own. After they left I had to go on as if my heart wasn't missing. Instead of feeling sad it was much easier for me to feel angry. My anger began to replace the love I once had for my mother, who I viewed as responsible for my sister's leaving. Along with anger there was also fear. Fear that getting on my mother's bad side would get me put out too. Instead of whippings, her new form of punishment became threats of putting us out on the street— threats that I knew weren't idle.

It was around this time that Mama really checked out. She was drunk nearly every day. I did my best to stay out of her way. We all did. My sister Teresa used academics as a way out. She managed to get a scholarship that included early college admission with student housing. Sometimes she'd invite Louise and me to the UC Berkeley campus to visit her. We'd play video games like Pac-Man and Donkey Kong in the student lounge. But eventually we had to return home.

CHAPTER 4

IT'D BEEN ABOUT A YEAR since I'd last seen Deborah the night she fought with Daddy. After she ran away, Mama told us not to let her in the house if she came by. Deborah was deep into her crack addiction and Mama feared she'd steal things if she got into the house when she wasn't there. I could tell my mother missed her because after she left, that's when she started drinking more than ever. But once Deborah left, it was like she was erased from our family. Aside from the caution not to let her in the house, her name was rarely mentioned. Overnight my big sister was out of my life, but it would be because of her that I would learn sooner than later that being female was a scary, helpless thing to be.

The first lesson came one weekend afternoon while I was home sitting on the porch. A man pulled into our driveway in a slick blue car thumping loud music. He rolled down his window and waved me over with a hand laden with thick gold rings. Even as he sat in his car I could see he was a big man, broad-shouldered and light-skinned. He was handsome and flashed a smile at me before he turned his music down and asked if Deborah was home.

"She ain't here," I told him.

"What's your name, sweetheart?" he asked, looking me up and down. I knew the look. Every girl over ten knew that look. Although he hadn't laid a hand on me, that look made me want to run and hide. But I knew the worst thing I could do was show fear. Instinctively I crossed my arms over my tiny bosom and gave him my dirtiest look. The man pouted, tilted his head to the side, and looked up at me with puppy eyes. He knew he'd spooked me, but that Mr. Innocent look he gave me only made him look even creepier.

"If she ain't here, can you tell me where she at?" he asked, giving me a full smile with big horsey teeth. His goofy smile reminded me of Mr. Ed, a talking horse in one of my favorite TV shows, and I smiled despite my unease. He took my smile as an invitation and reached his hand out to me. I backed away and could not have been more startled if his hand were a dead rat.

"She ain't here!" I said, trying to sound unafraid while edging my way back up onto the porch and near the front door should I need to run inside. He changed tactics.

"If you tell me where she is, I'll give you a dollar."

A dollar was a lot of money to me and the prospect of getting it was tempting. I didn't know where Deborah was but I wasn't averse to telling him a fib to get that dollar.

"Give me the dollar first!" I said with my hand on my hip, trying to look tough.

He laughed.

"Come get in the car. Ride with me to the store so I can get change. I only got twenties," he said, pulling out his wallet and tilting it slightly toward me so that I could see it was stuffed with bills. When I saw all that money, I felt my eyes bug out far enough to pop loose and roll down the street.

He reached a hand out toward me again, wriggling his fingers in a way that made me think of serpent tongues. When I hesitated, he opened the car door and began to get out. That did it. Something deep within me said *Run!* It was an instinctual fear as clear and undeniable as the fear of snakes or the fear of falling. This man was a predator and I knew as sure as I knew my own name that if I got in the car, I wouldn't get a dollar. I'd get a world of hurt I was unlikely to recover from. I dropped any pretense of being unafraid and ran into the house and locked the door.

Once inside the house behind a locked door, I peeked out at the man through a crack in the curtains. He was leaning against his car and was digging in his jacket for what I saw was a cigarette and a book of matches. I watched him light the cigarette, and by the way he smoked it—holding it tightly between his thumb and index finger and sucking on it with his face all squinched up like a fist—I knew it was dope.

"Get out of here!" I said under my breath, willing him to burst into flames or get beamed up to a hostile planet somewhere in another galaxy. Instead he lingered in the driveway and took his time smoking the joint before he got in his car and disappeared down the street. It angered me that I couldn't make that man go away when I wanted him to. He could have hurt me and been sure the police would not be called. Even for people who were not ex-Panthers, it was rare to call on the police for help. I knew my greatest defense was to show no fear. When Mama came home, I told her about the man. She said she thought he might have been Deborah's pimp and that I did the right thing by locking myself in the house.

Many months later I was home alone playing Pac-Man when I heard pounding on the front door. I was so startled I dropped the joy stick. A pounding like that could only mean the police or somebody looking to settle a score. I sat quietly, with my heart beating in my throat waiting for whoever it was to go away. After what felt like minutes it did not stop, so I crept into the living room and peeked out the window. I saw a skinny woman in a tube top and tight jeans hammering the door, all the while staring furtively over her shoulder. It took a moment for me to register that it was my sister Deborah. She was at least twenty pounds underweight. Her cheekbones were protruding and her eyes were sunken.

I cracked the door open using my foot to keep her from pushing her way in.

"Open the door, Lawanna!" she said, trying to push the door open.

"Mama ain't here. She say you can't come in if she ain't here."

I could see that my sister was scared of something but I was even more scared of what Mama would do to me if she found out I let Deborah inside.

"Let me in, baby girl! Somebody is trying to get me!"

I stepped aside and let her in, and she quickly locked the door. She turned to me and said, "If a man comes looking for me, don't tell him I'm here." Then she ran to the back bedroom and closed the door.

Within a minute there was another round of furious knocking on the door. I cracked the door again using my foot as a doorjamb and I was relieved to see a short, skinny man instead of the big pimp from before. The scrawny guy was trying to see past me into the house.

"Whatchu want?" I asked.

"Deborah! I saw her come in here," he said, now trying to push the door open.

I pushed back.

"She ain't here, now get the fuck off our porch!"

The man suddenly pushed the door with all his might, sending me across the room and onto the couch. He walked right in like he owned the place, opening the door to the downstairs bathroom and violently pulling back the shower curtain. I didn't have sense enough to be afraid. I still had a little bit of tomboy in me telling me that I was fearless and fully capable of defending myself from most dangers. So I trailed behind the man, cursing him out as he searched our house.

He ignored me and continued his search. When he reached the bedroom in the back where Deborah was hiding, he opened the door and saw her. He stepped into the room and closed the door in my face. I was about to enter behind him when I heard an awful sound that stopped me in my tracks and sent my tomboy spirit running for cover. I heard the sickening thud of a fist violently colliding with flesh over and over again. He was beating my sister and I could hear her grunts as she took the blows.

After a minute or two, he came out of the room breathing hard and rubbing his fist. I shrank away from him, suddenly realizing that I too was in danger. That I was in danger the minute he pushed his way into the house. I was only spared because he was so focused on finding my sister.

The man seemed not to notice me now that his mission was complete, and I was relieved to see him walk out the front door. I locked the door behind him and went to check on my sister. She was just getting up from the floor when I came into the room and I helped her to stand. I noticed her arms were just bones when I gripped her upper arm. Her face was just beginning to bruise up, her nose bleeding, and she was holding her stomach.

"You OK?" I asked, nearly in tears.

"Yeah. I'm OK," she said, as if nothing unusual had occurred.

Then she made her way to the living room and out the front door without so much as a good-bye. I was terrified. Hours later I was still terrified. That afternoon was the moment I realized that being female in my hood was to be vulnerable. The only power grown women had was over their small children. I wouldn't be a kid for long. I was quickly approaching puberty and the phase in my life when I would no longer feel safe in the world.

CHAPTER 5

RELIEF CAME FOR ME that summer when Uncle Landon came over one evening to ask Mama if she was interested in sending me, Louise and my brother to summer camp in Santa Barbara. Mama was quick to agree and I was excited to get a break from her and Oakland. I didn't know where Santa Barbara was, but I knew it couldn't be worse than Oakland.

Landon told Mama the camp was owned by Jane Fonda and her husband, Tom Hayden. Both Jane and Tom were supporters of the Black Panthers and friends of Uncle Landon. They'd recently returned from a working trip to Africa. The camp taught theater arts and self-esteem to children of varied races and socioeconomic backgrounds. Jane told my uncle that it would be a good idea for some Panther children to attend the camp. My uncle agreed. That summer my siblings and I were put on a Greyhound bus. It would be my first trip away from home.

Laurel Springs Children's Camp stood on a hundred and sixty acres in the hills above Santa Barbara. At 2,800 feet above sea level, it offered spectacular views of Los Padres National Forest and the Pacific Ocean.

Before I attended Laurel Springs, I had not known I was poor. I brought a light jacket, one pair of pants, two shirts and a pair of shorts that doubled as a swimsuit when worn with a T-shirt. Toiletries? A bar of Irish Spring soap, a worn-out toothbrush and an afro pick.

I couldn't believe the stuff coming out of my bunkmates' suitcases! One girl brought four swimsuits and a fresh pair of undies for every day of the week. (I knew this because the days of the week were printed on the back of each pair.) The other children received care packages from home crammed with food, magazines and books.

When we talked at night around the campfire, I found out many of them had their own rooms *and* bathrooms at home— and they thought about the future, speculating about careers. Would they understand anything about my life? I doubted it. So I put on a happy-go-lucky front, said little about my background and threw myself into theater arts, writing and performing skits with the other kids.

I signed up to try everything that was offered: arts and crafts, canoeing, swimming, hiking, baseball, gardening; but my favorite was theater. I loved getting onstage and becoming someone else. I played a nurse in my very first play. After a performance, the counselors were always very complimentary, as if no other kid in the history of the world could have played a better nurse.

I became close with the head counselor, a woman named Marin. She was a petite brunette who I saw as a maternal figure. We'd become pen pals when the summer ended. The other camp counselors were a ragtag group of hippies who made everything easy and fun. I felt I could mess up without it being seen as a character flaw.

I was devastated when my first summer at Laurel Springs came to an end. We all stood weeping, kids and counselors, in the world's biggest group hug. Then I reluctantly grabbed my bag, jumped in the van and headed back down the mountain toward my real life back in Oakland.

When I got home I wouldn't shut up about camp for weeks. My siblings were not as enamored as I was because they chose not to return the next summer. I went on my own. In fact I returned to Laurel Springs for several summers in a row, and I got to know Jane better. Smiley and chatty, she often wore snug sweatpants and a T-shirt baring her toned midriff, her hair bouncing and behaving. She invited me to her cottage for lunch one day and coached me on monologues. She focused on me, taking in everything I said as if it were the most fascinating thing she had ever heard. She hugged me whenever we crossed paths at the camp, held my hand when we walked together, scratched my back when we sat next to each other. This touch, this healthy loving touch, was a revelation.

I got to know her children, who also attended the camp. There was Vanessa, who was my age. She was a spunky girl with a pixie haircut who seemed even as a young girl to know exactly who she was. Then there was Jane's son, Troy, who was a few years younger than me. He was spider-monkey thin and full of mischief, but he was a kind boy and seemed drawn to me. I enjoyed his company. They were my ready-made summer family and I looked forward to seeing them each year.

School was the closest thing I had to a safe haven outside of Laurel Springs. But it too became dodgy when I entered puberty. I was tall for my age, and to my abject horror I was developing sooner than the other girls. When I started growing breasts, the few girls I called friends singled me out for bullying because of it. On more than one occasion my hall locker was set on fire. The arsonist would squeeze lighter fluid between the air vents in the locker door and follow it up with a lit match. I got into physical fights with the boys, too, who made fun of my developing body. One boy made the mistake of copping a feel in the hall between classes only to find himself gasping for air in a headlock after I wrestled him to the ground. A male teacher also took notice and I had to look out for his groping hands and scanning eyes. I resorted to wearing baggy clothes and a jacket even on the hottest of days to hide the hateful new body that I believed was out to destroy me.

I envied the girls whose bodies remained as curveless as a boy's. They didn't have to worry about being betrayed by boobs and hips set on drawing negative attention like a picnic drew ants. My new wiggly parts prevented me from participating in games I loved, like baseball and basketball, because that involved running and jumping. The worst part was feeling that I could not talk to anyone about my problems. Personal problems were not shared in my family, especially if they were related to sex. Having problems that one couldn't solve on one's own was a sign of weakness, and I'd learned from an early age not to show weakness. One of the worst things you could be called in my neighborhood was a punk, which was someone incapable of defending themselves.

Mama was drunk nearly every day and I did my best to stay out of her way by heading straight to my room after school or visiting Uncle Landon and Aunt Jan. My remaining sisters looked for more permanent solutions to the problems at home. Teresa was enrolled in college, Louise devised a different plan. When home became unbearable for Louise, she moved out and, in the process, dropped out of school. I didn't know where she'd gone and pined for her because she was my best friend. About a week after she'd gone, she showed up at school one day and told me she was living in the basement of an empty house. I could see she was quite proud of herself for finding her own place to live even though it was a basement. I was glad to know she was OK and eagerly accepted her invitation to visit her place after school.

I was expecting a dank, dark basement in a run-down, abandoned house but it turned out to be in a newer home that for some reason was empty. The room was dry and had windows that provided natural light. The floor was smooth concrete and she'd managed to furnish it: stacked cinder blocks and a piece of wood with a cloth over it was a table, a few beanbag chairs to sit on, a piece of carpet remnant for the floor and several layers of comforters on the floor for her bed. I was actually jealous of her setup and would have moved in with her, but I was scared of sleeping there at night because she had no electricity. She only lived in the basement for a few weeks, after which she enrolled herself in Job Corps and moved out of state, where she eventually would work for a GED and learn a trade.

I had no plan of escape. It was my summers at Laurel Springs that enabled me to get through the stresses of my life in Oakland. Even when I wasn't attending camp, just looking forward to camp each summer kept me motivated. I was also staying in contact with Jane and my camp counselors via letters. Their communiqués were always encouraging and I relied heavily on them to keep me feeling good about myself because they were always full of praise. They helped to keep me from internalizing the verbal abuse I was receiving from my mother, who was keen to call me worthless, no good and destined to be a teenaged mother.

It was around this time that my half-sister, Clara Jean, who was my mother's firstborn by a different father, came into my life. She was raised by my mother's parents so I never saw much of her when I was a young child. Mama said my father would not accept her when they got married so she left her with her parents in the same little house on Church Street where she met our father, whose family lived next door.

Clara lived in that little house throughout her childhood and the death of our grandmother. She was a young woman in her twenties and taking care of our grandfather, who was called China because when he was a baby he was fat and bald just like the Buddha. China had a lot of health problems. He had diabetes and was paralyzed on one side of his body as the result of a stroke. He was also an amputee, having lost his left leg from the knee down as a complication of his diabetes.

The house they lived in was run-down and Clara Jean was no housekeeper. The place was infested with cockroaches and mice that stayed active throughout the day and night. When Clara Jean entered college, she found it hard to study, have a social life and take care of our grandfather. While I was visiting with them one day, she offered to pay me to spend the evening with China on the weekends so she could go out with friends. I jumped on the opportunity to make a few bucks and get away from Mama.

Though being in that filthy house and taking care of a cranky old man was a challenge (I had to help him go to the toilet, dispense medication, clean and dress his stump and prepare meals), it was far better than what I had to put up with at home. Soon a few weekends a month turned into nearly every day when Clara Jean got a boyfriend and began spending more and more time with him.

A home health aide took care of China during the day and I relieved her after school. I slept on a worn-out couch in the living room that harbored a family of mice. China and I spent the evenings watching TV and bickering over his cigarette smoking, which his doctor forbid him. Though I knew it was bad for him, and for me since I had to breathe his secondhand smoke, I knew he'd keep me up all night banging a cup against the frame of his metal hospital bed if I didn't get him his smokes.

When summer rolled around, Clara rewarded me for helping her out with China by taking me to see a performance of the musical *Dream Girls*. It was the first play I'd ever seen and it inspired me to think about becoming an actress and using acting as my way out of my mother's house and even out of Oakland. I'd had a bit of experience acting in plays at Laurel Springs, but I knew I'd need more training if I was going to make it as an actress. When I told Clara that I wanted to act, she offered to enroll me in a class at the Young Conservatory, an acting program for young people between eight and nineteen at the American Conservatory Theater in San Francisco.

I was the only black person in the class and initially felt uncomfortable, but the experience I had interacting with other races at Laurel Springs made adjusting easier. Like at Laurel Springs, I was embraced by the class and treated just like everyone else by the teacher—a cheery, openly gay man who used huge sweeping motions with his arms whenever he talked. My secret nickname for him was the Human Fly Swatter.

He selected scenes from Thornton Wilder's *Our Town*, about the day-to-day happenings in a small American town in the 1930s, as our first group piece. I found the plot and the dialogue extremely boring. The most exciting things going on in the town were people going off to war and eloping, but nothing happened that I thought worthy of having a whole play written about it.

I thought it would be a much better play if it were set in my neighborhood. The play could open with a slumlord getting shot to death in a drug deal gone wrong. There could also be a scene in which a young teenager was arrested for shoplifting and, after a short scuffle with police, was able to break free and outrun the two overweight officers while being cheered on by neighborhood residents. Now that was a play I could have gotten into! Though I would have liked to share my ideas for spicing up Wilder's play with the teacher, I kept my thoughts to myself.

I was paired with a boy my age to practice a scene. He was kind of nerdy and reminded me of Danny Bonaduce's character in *The Partridge Family*, with his flaming red hair and annoying personality. He was a talkative fellow who, were he born a decade or two later, would have been a good candidate for Ritalin. After working with him a few times, I got the feeling he had a crush on me. Because he was so nerdy and I'm sure I could have kicked his ass if I had to, I didn't feel too threatened by his attentions.

Then one day during a break, he sneaked up behind me and grabbed me playfully by the waist. It startled me, and instinctively I turned around and punched him in the chest hard enough to send him pinwheeling backward a few feet. I was so angry I called him a stupid nigger. I was using "nigger" as a generic term, not to describe a black person but in place of a word like "jerk" or "asshole"; the white folks who saw me gave me the oddest looks. Looks that said to me, *"We thought she was different, but it turns out she's just like the rest."*

I immediately regretted my overreaction. I apologized to my partner and later apologized to the whole class at the behest of the teacher, but they never looked at me quite the same. I didn't blame them. I knew I was slowly becoming a product of my surroundings. The constant stress and need to protect myself was causing me to have a short fuse. I was having trouble controlling my temper, which could be set off by the slightest insult, eliciting a very violent response. It was a defense mechanism that was necessary for survival in my hood, but I was learning it would serve me ill anywhere else. If I didn't get away soon, this side of my personality would spread like cancer and take me over, leaving me unfit to live anywhere but places like East Oakland. When the course ended, Clara Jean offered to pay for another course. I declined.

When the summer came around, I decided not to go to Laurel Springs. I was focusing on getting my acting career off the ground. I was sure that if I worked hard at it, in a few months' or a year's time I could claw my way to Broadway or even motion pictures. I spent the summer auditioning for plays in Oakland and San Francisco. The first role I got was a small part in a Langston Hughes play. It was in a tiny theater in Oakland with barely enough seating for thirty people. The stage was about the size of a California king-size mattress. It might as well have been Broadway for how proud I felt.

I was only fourteen but because I looked old for my age, I was able to lie and get the part. The director was an African-American woman who was very supportive of me and often pulled me aside to give me encouragement. I was a nervous wreck the first performance but was able to get it together enough to do well in the five following shows. My role called for me to kiss a grown man, and during one performance he decided to put his tongue in my mouth. It took everything I had in me not to go into a rage right there on the stage in front of an audience. After the performance was over, I cussed the man out and went to complain to the director. She seemed shocked by how angry I was and told me I shouldn't get so riled up over a kiss. I saw it as just another instance in which I was being taken advantage of, with no one coming to my defense. I stormed out and never went back.

Though my first experience ended badly, I was still determined to make it as an actress. I read the paper daily looking for open auditions and found one for a new musical. I read they were looking for African-American females who could sing, dance and act. I had no formal training as a singer or dancer but I didn't see how that should get in the way of my getting the part. I practiced singing Whitney Houston's rendition of "The Greatest Love of All." After I felt I'd mastered the piece, I asked Teresa to come with me to the audition, which was in San Francisco. We arrived at the location, signed in and took seats in a crowded waiting room. When the first person was called in to the audition room, we could hear her performing through the thin walls. It gave us waiting an opportunity to size up the competition. There was a young girl sitting next to me. She was short, a little chubby and wore glasses. An older boy sat with her, who I presumed was her brother because they shared a similar geekiness. I quickly dismissed her as a threat.

When she was called in, I listened closely. But it turned out I didn't have to because that munchkin had a good set of pipes on her. She belted out "I Feel Pretty" from *West Side Story* in a voice that rang out so sweet and true it was as if there wasn't a wall separating us. It was magnificent. She was able to show great range and personality. When she finished, we could hear the producers and the director applaud her performance. Even some of the people in the waiting room were applauding. When she came out, I prayed I wouldn't have to follow her. Of course they called me next.

Teresa wished me luck and I entered the room. It was devoid of furniture except for a long table with three men and a woman facing me. They asked my name and asked about my experience. I told them about the Langston Hughes play, my classes at Laurel Springs and ACT. Then I sang my song. I forgot the words after the first few lines and asked to start over. When I started over, I remembered the lines but found I couldn't sing above a whisper. They told me they'd give me one more chance. I took a moment to center myself. I was letting the performance of that little troll doll who went before me get in my head. Then I let out the first few words in a clear melodic voice that quickly devolved into atonal gibberish when my nerves got the best of me and I forgot the lines again.

I left the audition room thoroughly humiliated and entered

the waiting room where there was no applause. In fact, no one even looked up at me. My sister and I slunk out together.

I went to my next audition alone. It was for a part in Shakespeare's *A Midsummer Night's Dream*. It was requested that we pick one of several preselected monologues from the play to perform. I'd heard of Shakespeare but I'd never read anything by him. I went to the library and checked out *A Midsummer Night's Dream* and selected the longest of the suggested female monologues and memorized it. I didn't know what many of the words meant or even how to pronounce them, but I did my best to memorize it and spent hours practicing until I felt comfortable. The last thing I wanted was to forget my lines again or let my nerves sink me.

I arrived at the audition, which was being held in a small university lecture hall, an hour early. The room was empty. It had high ceilings and tiered seating arranged in a semicircle like at a movie theater. The place where the professor lectured was where we would be auditioning. I took a seat front row center. The room smelled comfortingly of old books and chalk. I sat in the humming silence for a while taking account of my feelings. I wasn't nervous. I knew I had my piece memorized. I got up and went to the front of the room and looked out onto the empty seats. My adoring fans. I went through the piece twice without a hitch. I was about to do a third run when people began to trickle in.

I returned to my seat and watched as folks began to fill up the first few rows of seats. They arrived in groups of twos and threes, chatting and joking. Many were practicing their monologues with their companions. The serene silence of the room was gradually pushed back by chatter, laughter and sudden bursts of surprised yells that rang out like bird calls every now and then when one person called to another across the room.

I could see they were all older than me—early to late twenties, some even older—and seemed very sure of themselves as they joked and greeted one another. They also looked like real actors. Most were dressed in loose-fitting black clothes and looked a bit underfed, dirty and disheveled, as if they spent all their free time studying their craft. There were at least forty people auditioning.

Then the room fell silent when a man entered carrying an armful of papers and an old leather bag with a long strap slung low across his chest. He had the disheveled look too. I could hardly see his face, which was partly obscured by floppy black hair. He made his way to the front of the room, greeting people he knew along the way. He was tailed by a young woman with stringy blond hair equally laden with papers, who stood by his side when he reached the front of the room. He introduced himself as the director. He was in his early thirties (old) but had a boyish look due to the mop of hair and twinkly, curious eyes.

He told us that he'd like us to take the stage, give our names and any other information about our acting background before performing our monologues. After the performance he would thank those he did not wish to hire and they could leave. Those he wanted could return to their seats. Then he and his companion made their way to seats a few rows behind the actors.

When he sat and settled himself, he called out, "Who's up first?" There was a bit of nervous laughter and chatter from the actors. Heads swiveled back and forth looking to see who'd rise first. After a few seconds I found myself on my feet and walking toward the stage. It was like my body was on automatic pilot. One moment I was in my seat, the next I was looking out into an audience of curious white faces.

I gave my name and talked a bit about my limited experience. I told them I was really serious about acting. Then I went into the monologue. I found myself staring at the ceiling a lot but forced myself to look out into the audience from time to time like my acting teacher instructed. When I was finished, I thanked the audience, bowed and waited. When I looked into the audience, I saw that several people were talking to each other behind their hands. Some were staring at me like I was a circus freak but most were looking in their laps. I stood there in front of them with my head held high. The room was as silent as the moment before the Big Bang. Every millisecond I stood there felt like hours as I waited for the director to tell me to stay or go. Then, after what felt like a week and a half, I heard him clear his throat and say, "Lawanna?"

"Yeah!" I responded, unable to keep a defensive tone out of my voice, as I was sure he was about to send me on my way.

"I'd like you to come up here and sit by me."

The audience was suddenly humming with urgent whispered conversations.

"Uh . . . OK," I replied. I went back to my seat to gather my coat and bag and made my way toward the back of the room with every eye in the place tracking my progress. When I got to the back, the director stood and shook my hand before waving me into the seat next to his. He remained standing and, with his hand on my shoulder, he called out, "Next!"

I sat there next to him not knowing what to think. I just stared ahead stiffly, pleased that I had been asked to stay. After a while I relaxed, relieved to be released from the anxiety of performing, and watched the auditions. I sympathized with a woman whose voice warbled with nerves the whole way through her piece and a man who struggled to remember the lines. Both were thanked and sent on their way. When a woman took the stage and brilliantly performed the same monologue I had, I was mortified. I realized that I had pronounced a lot of words incorrectly and I sank into my seat. The director noticed and patted my hand encouragingly.

Over the course of the evening many people were thanked for their time and shown the door. A few, like me, were asked to stay but none were invited to sit with the director. When the auditions were over, there were less than a dozen people, including me, who were asked to stay. That's when the director turned to me and told me I didn't have the part. He'd asked me to stay as an inspiration to him. He let me know I'd done a terrible job with the monologue but he admired my guts and told me that he knew experienced actors who didn't have a tenth of the courage and confidence I had. He encouraged me to continue to practice and go after my dream. Then he gave me a pat on the back and sent me on my way.

I smiled all the way home.

CHAPTER 6

I WAS VISITING TERESA at UC Berkeley when I saw an ad tacked to a crowded bulletin board in the student union. I almost didn't see it through the overlapping layers of flyers seeking roommates and selling used furniture. I pulled the flyer down, folded it and stuffed it in my back pocket. That night back at China's house, I took it out and reread it. It was basically a call for actors to audition for a new acting company. There was a phone number and the first name of the contact: David.

I called the number. The man who answered identified himself as David and seemed pleased when I told him I was interested in auditioning. His voice was warm and had a smile in it. He asked me to share more information about myself—my age, where I was from and my acting experience. I told him everything and was happy to know he was OK with my being only fourteen.

He told me he was an actor turned director and had done a lot of theater in the Bay Area but had recently decided he wanted to start his own acting troupe that he hoped to fill with actors of different races and ages.

We talked for about thirty minutes, with him asking a lot of questions about my family. I felt comfortable and he seemed sympathetic, so I told him about my problems at home. He listened and said the best actors have had troubled lives because they can draw on those experiences to enrich their craft. He said I seemed like a good fit for his company and invited me to a group audition he was holding the following week. He told me to come prepared with a monologue of my own choosing and apologized that the audition would have to be held at his house in San Francisco because he was still in the process of looking for a theater space to rent. I told him I didn't mind and wrote down his address along with the day and time of the audition. Before we hung up he asked for my phone number and my address and I gave it to him. I let Clara Jean know I couldn't watch China that day and she wished me luck.

The next day I was at the library looking for the perfect monologue. I didn't want anything to do with Shakespeare or Wilder. Since I could choose, I wanted to do something by a black person. I asked the librarian for suggestions. She handed me a book of the collected poems of James Weldon Johnson opened to the poem "The Creation." I sat down and read it. It is long, twelve stanzas about the creation of the earth, that begins:

And God stepped out on space,
And He looked around and said,
"I'm lonely—
I'll make me a world."

And far as the eye of God could see
Darkness covered everything,

Blacker than a hundred midnights
Down in a cypress swamp.

Those powerful lines sent chills down my spine. I told the librarian I loved the poem but it wasn't a monologue. When she told me the husband-and-wife acting duo Ossie Davis and Ruby Dee performed many poems of African Americans as dramatic pieces, I was sold.

I spent the week memorizing and performing it. I practiced projecting my voice and infusing it with what I thought was a godlike resonance. My practice was interrupted repeatedly by China telling me to shut the hell up because he couldn't hear the TV over the racket I was making.

When the day of the audition came, I felt confident. The audition was set for four o'clock, so I gave myself plenty of time to get there and have a bit of time to rehearse beforehand. The address brought me to a pretty Victorian house in a nice neighborhood. I rang the bell and a big white man dressed in jeans and a T-shirt answered. He was clean-shaven, with dark curly hair, well over six feet tall and a bit chubby. He identified himself as David and smiled broadly, waving me in.

The interior of the house was not as nice as the exterior. The wood floors were scuffed and stained, a threadbare area rug did little to hide the imperfections. The only furniture in the living room was a large desk covered in paperwork, a tall bookshelf overflowing with books and file folders, and a large couch blanketed with a tie-dye flat sheet. The arms of the sofa were exposed and spewing bits of foam rubber. The nicest thing about the room was an elaborate cut-glass chandelier hanging from the ceiling.

David offered me a seat on the sofa, which I accepted. I was about twenty minutes early so I wasn't surprised not to see any other actors. I'd wanted to rehearse with the extra time but David sat down next to me and soon we were talking about acting and our favorite movies. The next time I looked at my watch I saw it was a little after four P.M.

"The others should be coming soon," I said.

David looked at his watch and shrugged and said, "Actors," with a long-suffering expression on his face. Being early made me feel as if I'd have a leg up on the others when they arrived. We talked more. I started to feel a little uneasy when 4:30 came and still no other actors. Then David moved closer to me on the sofa, close enough that his outer thigh was pressed against mine. Then he threw his arm around my shoulder, pulling my upper body into him, and tried to kiss me.

At first I thought he was trying to reach over me. Then his face was close to mine; I could smell the minty gum he was chewing. I pulled away from him and tried to stand up but he grabbed my arm. That's when I realized I was in trouble. My adrenaline was pumping and my anger surfaced. I tried to twist out of his grip, cursing and yelling at the top of my voice. He let me go and I was on my feet backing my way toward the door. He stood up showing me the palms of his hands.

"I'm sorry. Calm down. I didn't mean to scare you," he said.

I just kept backing away from him glaring pure hate. Then he lunged at me and got me by the throat, pushing me up against the wall. Anger gave way to terror. I fought him, but nothing I did could get him off of me. He was choking me, with his angry face inches from mine. Then everything softened and went black.

When I came to, I had a hard time taking in breath. I was on my back on the floor with David on top of me. I couldn't feel anything, just the weight of him. I was numb. I just lay there pinned to the floor and looked up at the chandelier, the last pretty thing in the world.

When it was over, he watched while I got dressed, which weirdly was the most shameful part of everything that happened. After I was dressed, he lifted my face and examined it closely.

"You might have a shiner tomorrow," he said clinically. "Next time don't struggle and save yourself some grief."

The words "next time" exploded in my head, but I didn't say anything. I just wanted to leave. He grabbed some keys from his coat pocket, took me by the upper arm and walked me out of the house. It was dark out. I got in the passenger seat of his car and he drove me to the train station. Before he let me out of the car, he kissed me and said he'd call me later.

I went home. Not to China's house. I went to Mama's house. She was in her bedroom watching TV. I went in and she looked up at me with alcohol-clouded eyes, then turned her attention back to the TV.

I took a hot shower. Afterward, when I wiped the condensation from the mirror, I didn't recognize the girl staring back. That's when the tears came. I saw David a couple of times a week for the next few months. Sometimes he'd pick me up. Other times I'd come to the Victorian. I always left hurt in some way. When school started up, he told me it was over. I was relieved but a part of me also felt abandoned.

It took a long time for me to understand how it was that I had switched so quickly from a self-assured girl into a passive victim.

Despite the cloak of specialness I'd pieced together for myself from the kind words and encouragement I got from Jane, camp counselors and others, I had been subtly groomed to be a victim all my life. Experience, in my family and in our community, had taught me that being a girl was to be vulnerable. I had witnessed firsthand attacks on my sisters, friends and strangers. From the moment I showed signs of sexual maturity, I was forced to be on constant vigil even from people a young person is taught to trust. When I was finally brutalized, I believe I experienced a feeling almost of relief, that this unavoidable event had finally caught up to me. I had been a hamster on a treadmill trying desperately to outpace the inevitable. So when it happened I was resigned to my fate. I gave up the fantasy that girls like me could aspire to anything more than early pregnancies, violent relationships and welfare. My attacker rendered me sullied and unredeemable. I gave up on myself and gave myself away.

The following summer I went back to Laurel Springs. On the ride up the mountain, I stuck my head out the van window and breathed in the fresh, cool air. Being in the mountains made me feel clean again. I'd forgotten how beautiful the world looked from a mountaintop. When we arrived at the lodge, my friends were there to greet and embrace me. There were some new faces, but many of the original counselors and some of the original campers were still there. I luxuriated in the feeling of being in a safe place again. But I was not the same girl. I could not bear to be touched, had nightmares, didn't like being surrounded by lots of people and wanted to sleep constantly.

Unbeknownst to me, the counselors began reporting to Jane the strange changes they saw in me. I was not as vibrant as I used to be; they told her I was a candle on the verge of flickering out. When pressed about what had caused the change, I told my counselors about the rape.

When the news got to Jane, she came to have a heart-to-heart talk with me. I told her everything, even revealing my desire to get pregnant so that I could finally have someone to love and someone to love me. Jane was appalled and told me I'd be better off getting a puppy. "Having a baby and being a single mother at your age would be a disaster. You have to think about your future." I told her I hardly ever thought about the future. I simply assumed I'd lead a life similar to my mother's, sisters' and other women's in my community. My sad confession would later inform much of the work she would go on to do with adolescents in Georgia for her nonprofit organization, the Georgia Campaign for Adolescent Pregnancy Prevention (GCAPP).

After our talk, she told me she'd help me get out of Oakland. What she needed from me was to spend the next school year getting my grades back up. If I did, she would welcome me to come live in Santa Monica with her family for as long as I needed. She also wanted me to tell my family about the rape. I agreed to it all.

When I left camp at the end of summer, Jane kept in close contact with me via letters and phone calls. She also began helping financially. I was stunned by her kindness. Stunned that someone was giving me an opportunity to get away. I had given up on myself and my grades at school suffered, but Jane's proposal renewed my interest in school. She threw me a lifeline and I grabbed it.

A few weeks after my return, I got up the nerve to talk to Uncle

Landon and Aunt Jan about the rape and Jane's proposal. They were heartbroken to hear about the abuse. Uncle Landon told me I should have told him. I told him I was sorry I hadn't. He said I should have told my father too. "He'd kill for you, you know." I could see the sadness in his eyes when I responded that I didn't have any faith in my father coming to my defense. They both said they would miss me when I left, but both agreed living with Jane was a great opportunity for me. Next I told Mama. She asked a few questions, then never brought it up again. Her response, or lack thereof, did not surprise me.

Jane paid for me to see an Oakland therapist. I visited her twice a week over the course of the school year. I never felt comfortable talking to her in detail about the rape, which is what she wanted. I simply wasn't ready. Instead I spent my time with her talking about superficial things, refusing to go any deeper than which subjects I was taking in school. But I stuck to the appointments out of respect for Jane.

By the end of the school year my grades were up and, as promised, I sent my report card to Jane. In return she sent me a plane ticket. It had been an eventful year. I had unburdened myself from a painful secret and was finally realizing my dream of leaving Oakland with the blessing of my Uncle Landon, but I was far from happy. I hadn't experienced a moment of happiness since the rape and I wasn't convinced that a therapist's couch or a change of scenery was going to change that, but I was up for an adventure. At sixteen, I packed up my few belongings and took my first plane ride to Los Angeles and into the care of Jane Fonda.

CHAPTER 7

WHEN MY PLANE LANDED at LAX, Jane and Troy were waiting for me at the gate. Tom was away on business and Vanessa was spending the week with her father. They both embraced me and looked me over, telling me how well I looked. The public display of affection was a bit overwhelming. This family was very touchy-feely. Back rubs, hugs and kisses on the mouth were normal. It took some getting used to. Troy was wearing a Dodgers cap and a goofy grin. He grabbed me by the hand and dragged me out of the airport and to the car, talking a mile a minute about how glad he was I was finally here. I loved this little boy with the dimensions of a spider monkey, who for some inexplicable reason seemed to adore me. Jane, with eighties big hair, walked beside me, holding my upper arm as if I would suddenly bolt like a caged animal.

I was a bit curious about what type of car Jane drove. I assumed a movie star would have a chauffeured car or a big shiny Cadillac. I soon saw she drove a Chrysler station wagon with wood paneling.

Inside there was a smell I was totally unfamiliar with but I would soon learn had a name: new car smell.

The seats were covered in caramel-colored leather as soft as living tissue. And sitting on the console was, wonder of wonders, a mobile phone! It was black and boxy and as big and solid looking as a construction worker's lunch box. Jane chatted happily, asking if I was hungry and what types of food I liked because she was planning on cooking something special. Troy wanted to take me to the mall where there was a new restaurant he was crazy about called Chick-fil-A. "They even give out as many free samples as you want so you don't even have to buy anything!" he said enthusiastically.

I mostly stared out the window watching L.A. slide by. My first impression was that L.A. made you want to look up. I looked up at the tall buildings, the palm trees and the billboards hawking movies and high-end office space instead of cigarettes and cheap liquor like in Oakland. Even the sky itself seemed higher and brighter despite the smog. In Oakland I never looked at the sky.

The station wagon was like a spaceship entering the orbit of an alien world. Freeways gave way to a city center of skyscrapers higher than anything I'd ever seen, then we cruised in for a landing in a residential neighborhood in Santa Monica full of large, well-made homes on wide streets lined with palm trees so tall they seemed to lean in toward their neighbors across the street like giants conferring on important business. I noticed the lack of foot traffic aside from the occasional jogger, usually a skinny, tan, blond woman in a tiny tank top and white shorts who would not have made it one hundred yards wearing that getup in my neighborhood. I noticed the absence of graffiti, gang members, drunks, drug addicts, dirty old men and bubble-gum-popping fast girls. Where were the familiar candy and cigarette wrappers that blew along the street like citified tumbleweeds? No churches, no liquor stores, no stray dogs roaming the streets like lion prides roaming the savanna. I wondered where the black folk were.

We pulled down a back alley behind the houses. Jane pushed a remote control attached to her sun visor, and a large gate slid back on rollers, revealing the back side of my new home on 4th and Alta, which we referred to as the Alta house. Taxi, the family's big black lab, bounded over to greet us with a huge avocado in his mouth like the world's most slobbery welcome home gift. As I stepped out of the car, I saw where he got it from. The back-yard was dominated by a huge avocado tree laden with fruit. A dozen avocados had fallen to the carpet of thick green grass in the shade under the tree. After a couple of belly scratches and a pat on the head, Taxi was content to return to his shady patch under the tree and resumed gnawing contentedly on his prize. Another dog, a border collie named Scottie, was a little more standoffish. He eyed me from a distance as if to let me know, unlike Taxi, I would have to earn his affection.

The smell of the sea was heavy in the air, as we were less than a block from the beach. There was also the strong aroma of fresh flowers. The backyard was partly a flower garden. There were rose bushes and other flowering plants I did not know the names of. Flowers poked out from every tree and bush, a profusion of color and fragrance. We entered the Spanish-style home through the kitchen. The flooring was handmade Mexican terracotta tiles. Jane pointed out where a little dog had left his footprints on several of the tiles, perhaps while they were left to dry in some tiny village in

Mexico. I thought it odd that she would take such pride in the tiles that were marred instead of the pristine ones.

I marveled at the large dining room table that looked like a cross section of an ancient felled tree. One could still see the scars and knotholes though the wood had been sanded and polished. Two long benches of equally old wood served for seating instead of chairs.

Troy offered to give me a tour of the house while Jane got started on dinner. Two steps led up to a two-story living room with white adobe walls in which there were no straight angles. Jane told me the workers who built the house used bottles to roll away the right angles. There was a large sofa and love seat covered in a fabric crowded with giant pink roses. It was overstuffed and looked like a big bed with sofa arms. One could get lost in all the pillows that were piled upon it. A large-screen TV looked enticing.

Also in the living room was a large antique credenza that seemed to sag under the weight of dozens of antique silver picture frames filled with family photos: black-and-white photos of Jane as a cherub-faced toddler as well as photos of Henry Fonda and Jane's mother, Frances Seymour, lying out on a blanket with a young Jane, a young Peter and their half-sister Pan. There were more recent photos of Vanessa and Troy and Jane's husband, Tom. Images of Jane at award ceremonies. There was one where she is in a beaded gown raising the Oscar triumphantly overhead. A group photo of Henry Fonda receiving his first Oscar at the age of 76, infirm in a wheelchair surrounded by his family. Photos of smiling, happy, accomplished people. *How in the hell am I supposed to fit in?* I wondered.

The most magnificent room in the entire house was a tiny room to the right of the front door. Behind a solid wood pocket door was a small library with bookshelves reaching all the way to the ceiling. Like at a real library, there was even a ladder on a runner one could use to reach the books high up. Later I would put my Stephen King collection on the highest shelf. There was a large window with a view of the front yard, which also boasted a flower garden in bloom and a large fence with tall bushes that obscured the house from passersby on the street.

Next I was led upstairs to where the bedrooms were. I'd be sharing a room with Vanessa. Her room had a loft area where I would sleep and Vanessa would sleep on a futon below. I could see that Vanessa had wallpapered an entire wall in photos: photos of her cradled in her mother's arms shortly after birth; many photos of her with her father, the famous French director Roger Vadim. Vanessa on the deck of a boat in a bikini pulling for all she is worth on a fishing pole longer than herself. Vanessa as a child sitting just offstage while Jane, sporting a pixie haircut and clothes that were fashionable in the early seventies, is in the middle of an impassioned speech with a fist raised in protest. There were dozens of photos of friends, family, vacations and her beloved dog, Taxi. This was her life on the wall and, from what I could see, she was a loved girl who had seen and done a lot.

The minute I dropped my duffel bag in Vanessa's room—Vanessa was spending the week with her father, who lived a few minutes away—Troy dragged me into his room, which was across the hall. He had a collection of Dodgers memorabilia. "I'm going to play professional baseball one day!" he told me, pulling a signed photograph of Tommy Lasorda from the wall for me to admire. He also had a small collection of books about the Mafia, which he was obsessed with. He told me about his favorite mafioso, Al Capone, and said if baseball didn't work out he'd be a mobster. Then he told me he had a secret place he wanted to show me.

In Troy's closet there was a panic room. Unbeknownst to me at the time, Jane and Tom had recently built the house with a great emphasis on security. Protestors of Jane's anti-war involvement in Vietnam and of Tom's political aspirations had thrown objects through the window of their previous home, and bomb threats were a regular occurence. The threats prompted them to install a remote ignition device that started their car's engines from afar in case a bomb was lurking beneath.

If I had known all this, I would have been even more intrigued by the little door in the back of his closet, which opened onto a tiny room barely big enough for two people. I poked my head inside and saw that Troy had used it mostly like a little cave, where he had drawn several primitive drawings on the walls in crayon. "If something bad happens, like a home invasion, this is where I'll go. You can come too. We'll be safe in here. It's even fireproof." The fact that this family that looked so secure and happy had a safe room made me feel my fascination with hiding spaces wasn't so strange.

After I unpacked and had a shower, Jane called us down to dinner, which she had prepared herself. We were having fried chicken with a salad of lettuce, green apples and walnuts with vinaigrette. I only ate the chicken and explained to Jane that I didn't eat green things, which Troy found hilarious. Jane looked at me with an expression that I would learn said, *"I'll fix that."* For dessert, there was baked Alaska. *Oh the things white people come up with!* is all I thought as I devoured the rich treat.

At the end of the evening, Jane tucked us into bed, Troy first, then me. She pulled the covers up around my neck and told me how happy she was I agreed to come. She kissed me on the cheek and wished me a good night, clicking off the light before closing the door, leaving me to sleep. I lay in the dark willing myself not to be afraid, but the panic began to build and I knew it would overtake me soon. In defeat I crept out of bed and down the ladder from the loft. I took a chair and propped it under the door handle, effectively preventing anyone from coming in while I slept, a habit I had gotten into in Oakland during the past year. Once I had secured the door and checked to see if the windows were locked and the curtains drawn, the panic abated and I was finally able to surrender myself to sleep.

Soon after getting settled in, I reverted to my couch-potato ways and began to spend most of my time on the big floral sofa in the living room watching a new station called MTV. It was summertime and from the moment I woke up until it was time to go to bed, I vegetated in front of the big screen. I knew it annoyed Jane that I was not taking advantage of the beach and the world-famous Santa Monica Pier that was just a stone's throw from the house, but I wasn't convinced yet that I'd be safe if I ventured out on my own.

Occasionally, when Troy wasn't at baseball practice or over at his friends' houses, I took him to the mall. There we would pop in and out of toy stores and pawnshops where he salivated over vintage baseball cards. Troy chattered incessantly, mostly about his desire to be rich. He believed he would achieve his goal via the lottery. Because I looked old for my age, he begged me every chance he got to buy lottery tickets for him, which I gladly did. After I bought the tickets, we'd huddle up on the sidewalk outside the store and I'd watch while he scratched the gray film away with a dime, hoping for a big win. He never won anything more than a few dollars or another ticket, but the whole exercise brought him joy and I liked to see him happy.

One day I asked him why he wanted money so much. "Your family is already rich." He looked at me as if I was daft. By Hollywood standards, his family lived quite modestly, especially in light of the fact that at the time Jane was one of the silver screen's biggest stars. In addition to being Hollywood royalty, she was also a savvy and successful businesswoman who hit it big with her Jane Fonda Workout tapes, clothing and studios. The majority of the money Jane earned, however, went to support Tom's political aspirations and charitable causes. The house they were currently living in was a recent move. And though it seemed palatial to me, I realized in hindsight that it was an upper-middle-class abode. Before that house, Troy grew up in a fixer-upper on a not-so-nice street a few blocks over. So while most Hollywood spawn lived in mansions with more staff than family members and tooled around in sports cars and boasted allowances larger than the yearly income of an average working-class family, Troy and Vanessa were not indulged to that degree.

Vanessa was just ten months younger than me, and during my camp days I'd chat with her whenever she wandered over to the lodge. She reminded me of the character Peppermint Patty from the *Peanuts* comic strip, with her tomboy ways and short haircut. She had a raspy voice reminiscent of the actress Debra Winger that only enhanced her mystique. I could tell that even as a young girl she knew exactly who she was and to hell with anybody who tried to give her grief. I envied her confidence and outgoingness, mostly because it reminded me of how I used to be.

When I came to share a bedroom with her years later, she welcomed me with open arms. She would split her time between the Alta house and her father's nearby apartment. She adored her father and did not have as close a relationship with Jane, so she spent most of her time with him, but when she was home, we'd pass the time listening to her music collection in our room: Cat Stevens, James Taylor, The Beatles, Bill Withers, Bob Dylan, Marvin Gaye. Her music was cool, her style of dress was cool, she spoke French, she was a gifted student. She was so cool she didn't have boyfriends, she had lovers. I was thrilled that this girl who was everything I wanted to be actually enjoyed my company despite the fact that I was her complete opposite. While I enjoyed being around her to live vicariously through her exploits, I had no idea what she found intriguing about me. When she was home, I didn't sleep in the loft. Instead, we chatted until all hours of the night together on her futon until we fell asleep with a snoring Taxi between us.

Vanessa had lots of friends but her best buddy was an African-American girl named Gigi. The three of us would spend a lot of time hanging out at Vanessa's favorite restaurant, a deli that made her favorite dish—bagels and lox. Afterward we'd go visit Vanessa's father, Roger Vadim, at his funky little apartment that he shared with his girlfriend, a slim, raven-haired beauty. The apartment was small but light-filled and cluttered in a way that gave the place charm: lots of photos and book piles, eclectic furniture. I felt at ease in Vadim's place and in his presence. He was a man who loved females and had a knack for making us feel admired and welcome, especially Vanessa. His face lit up whenever she was around and I understood why she spent so much time with him.

Gigi and I spent a lot of time together with Vanessa right before she went off to Brown University at the age of sixteen. We were all very proud of her. I missed her terribly when she left, but knew we'd be together again when the holidays rolled around. Little did I know we'd see her sooner than that. One afternoon Jane, some of her friends and I came home to find a large package sitting in the hall. Her friends told Jane it was a gift from them. When Jane opened the box, Vanessa popped out with a big smile and a hug for her startled mother. Jane's friends had secretly flown Vanessa out from the East Coast for a surprise visit. She knew how to make an entrance.

I'd learn years later that Vanessa resented her mother for bringing me into the family. She felt my presence took up time that she desperately wanted from her mother. But to Vanessa's credit, she never once took out her frustrations on me. On the contrary, she bent over backward to make me feel accepted and was the first to proudly introduce me to her friends as her sister.

In addition to using money earned making movies to support various causes, Jane and Tom often threw star-studded fundraisers at the house. They were fun events and I loved to stand on the sidelines and watch as a procession of my favorite movie stars strolled into the house one after another. For one event that was raising money for antiapartheid efforts in South Africa, Bishop Desmond Tutu was on hand. The party guests included Oprah Winfrey, Quincy Jones, Robert Downey Jr., Daryl Hannah, Jackson

Browne, Marisa Tomei and Rae Dawn Chong. I'd dart out of the shadows every now and then with my notepad and a pen collecting autographs. Jane would transform at these events. She'd shed her sweats and don a pretty party dress. Her speech was punctuated with "Fabulous!" and "Marvelous!" She became a true Hollywood diva, dazzling her guests into loosening their purse strings for a worthy cause.

Paparazzi would buzz around the front gate like flies, snapping pictures of the guests coming and going. Crowds of fans would gather outside too. I'd wander out to marvel at the spectacle, and often fans would beg me to take in an 8x10-inch photo of Jane from her classic film *Barbarella* or some other photo for her to sign. I was all too happy to take them to Jane, and she was always happy to sign. When she was busy, I'd sign her name myself, not to be mischievous but to avoid having to tell the fan I couldn't get a signature. They seemed to always know it wasn't her signature and threw dirty looks at me for ruining their photos.

These parties took a lot out of Jane. At the end of the evening when the last of the stars walked or stumbled out the door, Jane would kick off her shoes and collapse onto the big sofa. I'd sidle up next to her and we'd discuss the evening. She'd ask if I thought it looked like everyone was enjoying the evening. I'd give my opinion and she'd listen intently, taking in every observation.

To get me off the couch, Jane would often take me to work with her at her production company in a little two-story building not too far from the house. She and her team produced films like *9 to 5* and *On Golden Pond*. It was in her office that I first came face to face with an honest-to-God Oscar. I stood in the doorway to her office stunned to see not one but two of the statuettes sitting on a shelf. She'd won them for Best Actress in *Klute* and *Coming Home*. I reached out and grabbed each one in my hands, awed by the heft and beauty of them. Jane smiled at me as I stood there with a statue in each fist.

Then she told me a funny story about Katharine Hepburn. Ms. Hepburn starred with her and her father in *On Golden Pond* and won her fourth Oscar, to Jane's two, for her work in the film. A few days after her win, Jane discovered that Ms. Hepburn had a very competitive side when she called Jane and cackled triumphantly into the phone, "You'll never catch me now!"

I'd spend the day listening in on meetings she'd hold with her producers. I was especially excited when she told me she was thinking of remaking the old black-and-white classic *All About Eve*, about a famous aging stage actress who is backstabbed by a young actress she takes under her wing. We watched the film together one evening, which heralded the beginning of my lifelong love affair with black-and-white films and the indomitable Bette Davis. Jane was to take on the Bette Davis role and she told me she was going to hold a meeting with Madonna, whom she was considering for the role of the scheming ingénue played in the film deliciously by a young Anne Baxter. Madonna was a rising star at the time and I begged Jane to introduce me to her. Unfortunately the project fell through.

To keep me occupied, Jane also sent me to aerobics classes at her successful Jane Fonda Workout studio. She had me outfitted in tights, leotards, leg warmers and the modified off-the-shoulder sweatshirts á la *Flashdance*. I'd be the only black girl in a class of skinny white women jumping around and feeling the burn. The classes became addictive and I'd sometimes do two a day. I got so into working out I'd often wear my leotards out and about as if they were street clothes. For a while it was a status symbol for folks to see how seriously you took your workout. Strolling into a supermarket in a sweat-stained leotard showing off your fit body was all the rage, and I jumped on the bandwagon for a time.

One day Tom invited me to accompany him and Troy on a visit to his office at the capitol building in Sacramento. Tom was a state assemblyman at the time and I was excited to see the state capitol. We all flew up together and that evening we went out to dinner at a restaurant with a few of Tom's colleagues. I remember the restaurant was a steakhouse and the décor was leather and dark reds and greens, like a rich man's drawing room. I don't remember much about the conversation. The most memorable part of the evening was watching Tom interact with Troy. Troy sat close to his father, who stroked his back and bent to kiss him on the top of his head from time to time. His pet name for Troy was Sweetie. As the hour grew late and Troy began to doze off, Tom cradled him and gently rocked him as he continued his conversation. I found the whole scene heartbreakingly tender and intimate. I'd never seen a father be so openly affectionate with a child.

Troy and I spent the following afternoon playing Frisbee on the capitol lawn and watching a woman's miniature Doberman chase and be chased by the aggressive gray squirrels that patrolled the lawn raiding the blankets of unwitting picnickers. When it got too hot, we took our game of Frisbee indoors, tossing it up and down the halls. Then Troy threw me the Frisbee when I wasn't paying attention and it hit me in the nose, causing it to bleed. Troy was immediately remorseful. A staffer witnessed the incident and made a big deal of having me fill out an incident report, which he insisted must be filled out whenever an injury occurred on state property. We were scared of what Tom would think when he found out we'd been roughhousing in the halls and instigated an incident report. But when Tom was informed, he laughed and told us to be careful next time.

On the last evening of our visit, Tom took us to a social gathering. It was held in a large room in an official-looking building. Most of the attendees were older white men. After I took a bathroom break, I couldn't see Tom and Troy anywhere when I came out. I searched for them in the crowded room. All the while I could feel a panic attack coming on. I gave up my search and ran out into the street to escape the collapsing room and the men who were beginning to look more and more ominous. Even after I calmed down, I couldn't gather the nerve to go back inside. So I sat on the steps outside and waited for Tom and Troy to come out. I learned later they were both looking for me, too, and were worried that something had happened to me. They were relieved to find me unharmed on the steps. When we got home, Tom told Jane about the incident.

Jane worried about me. Though I was getting out more, I still had trouble making friends and suffered from nightmares and panic attacks. She suspected my nightmares, panic attacks and bouts of agoraphobia stemmed from a form a PTSD I got from the rape. So, soon after the incident in Sacramento she signed me up to start seeing a therapist again. She even sat in on the first few sessions with me. The therapist was a well-meaning African-American woman, but I lost patience with her when she asked me, "How did being raped make you feel?" I responded with, "How do you think it made me feel? It sucked!" I could see that Jane was

tickled by my response to the stupid question and she congratu-
lated me for speaking my mind.

Though I continued with therapy, I found the most rewarding
conversations about my inner turmoil took place on the two-hour
drives Jane, Troy and I would take from Santa Monica to Laurel
Springs nearly every weekend. True to form, within twenty minutes of hitting the Pacific Coast Highway, Troy was knocked out in
the backseat and would stay that way for the duration of the trip.

Jane and I would pass the time talking about how I was coping
with the change, my fears and my plans for the future. I told her a
lot of things still scared me—sleeping alone, crowds. Sometimes
I'd say things that made her cry. Like how I found it odd that Jane
and Tom did not beat their children. Didn't all parents beat their
children? I was also a sounding board for her and listened as she
shared her thoughts with me. At the halfway point we usually
pulled off the highway in a little town that had an ice cream shop
that made date shakes. We'd all get one and stretch our legs before continuing up the coast, sliding along the highway between
the mountains and the sea.

By the end of my first summer in L.A., I found myself at home
alone on the big sofa watching Michael Jackson moonwalk with
zombies on the TV when I decided I was sick of being scared. Sick
of people worrying about me. I wanted to reclaim a piece of the
brave young girl I used to be. I decided to face one of my greatest
fears head on.

I got off the couch, grabbed my sunglasses, a sun hat and a blanket and headed out the door. I took the five-minute walk down to
the beach and spread out my blanket and sat down on it, staring
out to sea and ignoring the voices in my head that were urging me

to return to the safety of the couch. The beach was not very crowded this day and I was able to get a patch of sand to myself. I sat cross-legged and as still as the Buddha as I waited for my heart rate to return to normal. After a while I lay back on my blanket and closed my eyes. It didn't take long for the voices to fade, pushed aside by the squawk of sea birds, the pounding surf and the children at play. Without knowing exactly when, I fell asleep. When I woke up, the sun was much lower in the sky. I was thrilled! I shook out my blanket, folded it and tucked it under my arm. Not only did I go out alone without the world crushing in on me, I actually went to sleep outside in a public place. It was a huge deal for me and I was very proud of myself.

As my first summer began to draw to a close, Jane approached me about where I'd go to finish high school. At the moment she was between films and was able to be around a lot. But she had a film coming up that would demand all of her time. Troy had Tom to look after him and Vanessa went to her father. Jane didn't want me to be left without support, so we discussed the possibility of boarding school. We visited several before deciding on a tiny school called Happy Valley halfway between Santa Monica and Santa Barbara in a town called Ojai.

It was close enough for me to come home every weekend if I liked. I was afraid I might not be able to keep up academically, since many of my schoolmates would be coming from some of California's finest private schools. I was particularly concerned about my vocabulary and I told Jane so. She went out and bought me copies of *Huckleberry Finn*, *Les Misérables*, *Catcher in the Rye*, *Pride and Prejudice* and other classic works—real literature and a big step up from my usual diet of horror fiction. Before she and Troy dropped me off at school, Jane placed the books in my arms and challenged me to make a list of all the words I didn't know, then find their meaning and come to her and use them properly in a sentence. I took her up on her suggestion. With patience and great effort, I made my way slowly through one of the books. To show Jane I was sticking to the challenge, I sent her a small card. It had black-and-white etchings of fairies on it. Inside I wrote, "These fairies are ethereal."

Happy Valley was not the stereotypical boarding school. There were no uniforms or military-style codes of conduct. It was quite the opposite. If a band of hippies got together to create a boarding school, it would be very close to Happy Valley.

The setting was rural and the buildings were open and decorated with handmade artwork. Some of the classes included basket weaving and thrift store shopping. Field trips were often to the beach to catch some rays. Many of the students were from the Los Angeles area and were attending the school because of their parents' hectic work lives. For me the school felt like an extended summer camp.

For the first time in a long while I made friends. I joined a clique of very wealthy Jewish girls from the valley. It didn't take long for my Ebonics to give way to valley girl speak: "Grody!" "Gag me with a spoon." "That's gross!" I picked up a bit of Yiddish and spoke of "schlepping" and "kvetching." I even got in the habit of sighing "Oy vey" whenever I was annoyed, with the naturalness of a little old woman from Israel.

When Jane wasn't working, she picked me up on the weekend,

which we'd spend at Laurel Springs. On several visits she was also hosting some of her friends. One weekend, Sophia Loren stopped by. She was warm and engaging and taught me how to pick and slice up ripe cactus fruit. On another trip I met Bonnie Raitt. I recall her being quite funny and that she talked incessantly, as if she had something very important to say and was fearful of being cut off.

When it was just us, we'd read lines if she was preparing for a film or we would go for a leisurely hike. We spent many afternoons at opposite ends of the little house engrossed in books. During Oscar season we would go to the Alta house. We had a tradition of what we called "movie marathons." Jane compiled a list of movies she needed to see in order to vote on them for Oscar consideration. She then compiled the theaters and showtimes. The marathon began with a matinee and could extend through to the final evening showing. We often found ourselves racing between theaters on opposite ends of town, taking breaks for lunch and dinner in between showings. Nowadays members of the academy get screening DVDs sent to their homes. The DVDs are more convenient but I miss the good ol' days of battling L.A. traffic to get to the theater before the opening credits. Especially since we had it down to a science.

When Jane was working and couldn't pick me up, I'd go home with one of my friends. They introduced me to the L.A. scene. One of my friends had a BMW and she'd drive us to Hollywood, where we'd walk around and people-watch. They especially loved to eat sushi, which I found totally gross but pretended to like in order not to seem square. We spent most of the evening riding around in the BMW with the windows down, waving to cute boys. Then we'd all crash at somebody's house and spend the day doing our nails and gossiping.

I enjoyed my time at Happy Valley, but by the end of the school year I let Jane know that I didn't feel challenged academically. She took me out of Happy Valley and enrolled me herself in a high school program run out of Santa Monica Community College not far from the Alta house.

I loved the new school because it was in a college setting and made me feel a bit grown up. I liked that the classes took place in the same rooms college courses were taught in. I felt quite mature sitting in a big lecture hall, especially after Happy Valley, where class size maxed out at about ten and sitting in a chair was optional.

It was here that I came to love writing after taking a creative writing class with a very eccentric teacher. I don't remember the teacher's name, but he was a little man who looked and dressed a lot like Albert Einstein without the wild hair. He'd stand in front of the class and read passages from the works of Dickens, Hemingway, Shakespeare. He wouldn't just read the words, he'd allow them to dance off his tongue, and his arms would spiral in an arabesque when he read a particularly beautiful piece. "Did you hear that! Lovely! Let me read it again!" Most of the students found him comical but I got what he meant about words. That it was artful how they were strung together, not randomly but with thought and craft, like the weaving of an intricate carpet or the strokes of a brush wielded by a master painter.

When the school year ended, I had enough credits to graduate. Jane and Troy attended the ceremony. Jane wore a floral dress and Troy was decked out in his finest. I was beyond proud of myself.

There was a time I didn't think I'd ever see graduation day. I presented Jane with my diploma, letting her know it was because of her that I have it.

I was almost eighteen years old. I would no longer be a minor and I was relieved that I had almost reached the age of maturity without my mama demanding I return to Oakland. In my heart of hearts, I wished she would have fought for me or at least tried to stay in touch. It was around this time that Jane sat me down for a serious chat. Up until then our relationship had been undefined. Jane told me she felt as if I had become an important part of her family and wanted to know if I'd feel comfortable being referred to as her daughter. I told her I'd like that very much.

After I got my high school diploma, I enrolled in college-level courses at Santa Monica College in preparation for transferring to a four-year institution. I moved out of the Alta house and in with roommates. I also became infatuated with bicycles. Jane bought me a beautiful Cannondale touring cycle that I rode along the boardwalk. Jane joined me on a few rides and became hooked herself. We went on several rides together before I headed off to college at Pitzer, a small, private liberal arts school just an hour outside of L.A. Jane and Troy dropped me off at school and Jane helped me unpack while she chatted up my new roommate, a Latina woman named Maria from Los Angeles. Maria was an alternative student, which meant she was an older student—twenty-five years old—who was attempting to get a degree because finances and other problems were a barrier. Maria was on several scholarships and had to work to make her tuition.

From the intense way Jane was grilling my roommate, I knew that she was planning something. Jane had been financially supporting struggling students (many of whom she met at Laurel Springs) for years. Sure enough, a few days after she dropped me off, she called to speak to Maria. I left the room to give Maria privacy. When I returned, Maria's happy expression told me what I already knew. Another worthy had been rewarded because she, like me, was fortunate enough to cross paths with Jane. Her decision to help Maria paid off. She would graduate ahead of schedule with honors.

My love affair with the bicycle intensified during my first semester of college. I'd go on long sojourns through the town of Claremont and environs. My eyes were always drawn to the snow-capped mountain that dominated the landscape: Mount Baldy. I asked the locals about it. Turns out it was 4,000 feet at its highest elevation and was home to a popular ski resort. I asked if the road up was good for cycling and a shopkeeper looked me up and down and said he wouldn't attempt it, but when he drove up to go skiing, he did pass crazy cyclists from time to time pumping their way up the mountain. He told me there was a place called Mount Baldy Village that many cyclists shot for at about mile eight.

I set my sights on Mount Baldy even though I hadn't biked anything steeper than a slight incline. The next day I biked to the base of the mountain and saw that the road was steep, but I'd been told that it was heavily switchbacked. I put my bike in the lowest gear and started climbing. Within ten minutes I was winded and I turned back. A few days later I tried again and I was still unable to make it much farther than I had before. Now when I saw Mount Baldy in the distance, I didn't see a beautiful mountain, I saw a nemesis. I began to feel that the mountain was taunting me. Nearly every day I peddled back out to the mountain, forcing myself to climb just a little bit farther than the last time. On my visits I noticed another biker, a young white guy suited up in spandex biking shorts and a bright yellow racing shirt. A real biker. He zipped by me without a second glance.

As the weeks turned to months, I was making progress. I could get well past the halfway point before turning around, and the biker dude was noticing. Now when he passed me, he gave a nod and I nodded back.

One weekend, I was in the middle of my climb. I was reaching the halfway point and feeling fatigued and contemplating turning around early when Biker Dude pulled up beside me. He didn't pass me, he just stayed beside me matching my pace, then glanced over at me and said, "Stay on it!" giving me an encouraging nod. Then he pulled in front of me but didn't speed off like he usually did. He biked just a few feet in front, leading me on. He arced his arm in a semicircle and pointed ahead as if to say *"Onward! Upward!"* I tailed him despite my fatigue and soon we were a bit past the halfway point.

The progress was slow but I refused to stop, especially now that Biker Dude was here to witness my defeat. I was standing on my pedals and every revolution was agony. With each foot in elevation gained, it felt as if the sun was getting exponentially hotter. Still I didn't stop. I went inward. The road disappeared, Biker Dude's ass disappeared, the mountain disappeared. I was still climbing but I no longer felt achy muscles or the blistering sun.

I had a vague sense of the scenery gliding past, of Biker Dude's rhythmic movements, but I was in the eye of the storm. I felt invincible. It seemed no time had passed since Biker Dude pushed me on, and then we were turning into Mount Baldy Village. I cruised in with my hands raised in victory above my head and Biker Dude was grinning from ear to ear. "Atta girl!"

I learned there was a place I can go to when my body and mind were pushed to their limit. A place within where I could draw strength to continue. I loved how I felt in that place. I was hooked.

By the end of the semester, biking to Mount Baldy Village was never easy but it was no longer a huge challenge. I returned from my ride pleasantly sore and emotionally high. I wanted something more. That summer I stayed on campus and took a job as a summer resident assistant with ten other students. The job entailed living on campus and cleaning out the dorm rooms and staffing campus summer programs, which included groups like Elderhostel and conferences. I became close with another RA named Heidi who also liked to bike. She was a petite blonde with skin and hair so fair it would be easy to mistake her for an albino if not for her striking blue eyes.

We began riding together on the weekends. On one of our rides I proposed a longer trip for the end of the summer: a two-hundred-fifty-mile bike ride from school to Santa Monica and on along the Pacific Coast Highway to Laurel Springs in Santa Barbara and back to Santa Monica. It was quite ambitious but we were both up for the challenge. We'd spend the first night at the Alta house and the second night at the Ranch. When I told Jane our plans, she gave the trip the OK with the exception of us biking up the last stretch of narrow road to the camp. "Too dangerous," she said, and made arrangements for someone to pick us up at a gas station at the base of the mountain.

Since I was about to embark on a real biking adventure, I decided it was time I looked like a real biker. So I went out and bought myself real biker gear: spandex shorts, a jersey, shoes. We trained daily, practiced changing tires and other minor bike repairs, and meticulously researched the best routes. We left campus early in the morning the day after our jobs ended. The first fifty miles from school to the Alta house was long but fairly straightforward. It was the first time either of us had biked fifty miles at once. We arrived at the Alta house well within the ten hours we scheduled. We rewarded our efforts with a spaghetti dinner, with ice cream for dessert. Then we watched a bit of TV before turning in early.

We were up bright and early the next day and made the short trek onto the Pacific Coast Highway to begin the next leg of the trip, a century (one hundred miles) to Laurel Springs. The ocean was spread out like a bejeweled blanket on our left as we pedaled along in the bike lane headed north. The weather was in our favor. We were pushed along with a wind at our backs.

My fear that the traffic would be a hazard, as it was known to speed along the highway recklessly, was unfounded. The problems arose when nearly every hour one or both of us got a flat from all the tiny sharp objects that accumulated in the bike lane along the highway. We got flats so many times we began to take pictures of ourselves repairing them.

On the way to Santa Barbara, our path left the highway and veered off into a hilly residential neighborhood before spitting us back onto a highway, then to the little gas station at the base of the mountain, where we were to use the pay phone to call our ride. I was a bit annoyed that Jane was against us biking up. I felt we were strong enough to make the climb. But when our ride came and I looked at the road for the first time through the eyes of a road biker, I knew Jane was right. The lack of guardrails and the blind turns and speeding vehicles made the road reckless for vehicles and doubly so for bikers.

When I look back at the many pictures we took on this trip repairing flats, standing with our arms around each other's shoulders and dressed in identical biking outfits, smiling like we owned the world, I see a girl being reborn. That trip would be the beginning of many challenges I would create for myself in order to recapture the feeling of being in control of my life.

CHAPTER 8

DURING A BREAK from college I flew to Mexico City for two weeks to join Jane on the set of *Old Gringo*, costarring Gregory Peck and Jimmy Smits, based on the best-selling novel by Carlos Fuentes. In the film, Jane plays an American spinster who travels to Mexico to tutor the children of a wealthy Mexican family only to find herself embroiled in a tempestuous love affair with a corrupt general, played by Jimmy Smits.

It was my first time on a movie set and my first time out of the country. A private car picked me up at the airport, and as we drove through the city I remember the sidewalks bustling with foot traffic in sharp contrast to the empty sidewalks of L.A., where walking is so despised people are willing to wait for twenty minutes for a parking space near the entrance of a building rather than walk a few hundred yards from a readily available spot farther away. The driver dropped me off in front of a beautiful traditional hacienda complete with a terracotta tile roof, whitewashed walls and a courtyard. Jane greeted me at the door and, after a light lunch, she showed me a schedule of activities she and her assistant had put together for me: Things we can do together and things I can do on my own when she's on set.

I was a bit embarrassed because I know she requested this schedule because of my propensity to loiter on couches if left to my own devices: "This is Mexico! I want you to get out there and explore!" On the schedule was lunch with the writer Carlos Fuentes and his son the following day. Ever since Jane introduced me to the classics as a way of improving my vocabulary, writers had displaced actors in the battle for my admiration. The combination of best-selling author and a movie adaptation of his work was enough to make me giddy.

The Fuentes's apartment was in a contemporary building with sweeping views of the city. Carlos's living room was lined with bookshelves and Mexican art hanging on the walls. He was a distinguished older man, welcoming but reserved in manner. His son, also named Carlos, looked to be ten or eleven years old, very thin and pale but with a lovely face—clear skin, big brown eyes and elfin features. Jane had told me beforehand that he was a hemophiliac. I'm good with kids, so while Jane talked with Fuentes senior, I tried to draw out the shy little boy. I asked him about his studies, what games he liked to play. He responded with one-word answers, avoiding eye contact. Rather than being charmed by me, I began to see he was extremely annoyed. I gave up and turned my attention to the adults' conversation. Jane and Carlos were discussing *Old Gringo* and Jane's character in particular. I was too intimidated to join in the conversation though content to listen.

The visit was a brief one. I shook Fuentes's hand and told his son good-bye, but the latter merely gave me a laconic stare. I left thinking I had just met the weirdest kid in all of Mexico only to find out later Carlos Junior was not eleven; he was seventeen, quite intelligent and had been winning awards for his writing since he was five years old. What an ass I made of myself inquiring about his schoolwork and favorite games! No wonder he was trying to brush me off. The up side was I now had a clear example I could draw upon that defined a new phrase I'd come across in my readings: faux pas.

The next day Jane went to the set and left me with a list of museums to explore. I started with the mother of all Mexican museums, the Museo Nacional de Antropología, at 100,000 square feet one of the largest museums in the world. I had a lot of poking around to do. I actually enjoyed the peaceful hours I spent strolling through this magnificent building as exhibits took me through every epoch of Mexican cultural history. I also checked out the Museo Rufino Tamayo and fell in love with the artist's deeply pigmented, textured paintings. I found his many works depicting watermelons charming. I thought now if I heard someone making a joke about black people and watermelons, I could debunk the stereotype and sound erudite too by referring them to Tamayo's obsession with the sweet fruit.

The next day Jane took me to the soundstage. I enjoyed sitting in the hair and makeup trailer listening to the ladies chat about life and work. Just like barber and beauty shops in the hood can be the best place to hear the latest gossip, so it is with the hair and makeup trailers on movie sets. Listening to the banter of the film crew over a catered lunch was also a good way to pass the time. But for me the best part of movie making was sitting in on the dailies, watching footage of what was shot that day along with the director, producers, actors and other key players. I enjoyed the intimacy of sitting in the dark with Jane and the crew, listening to them critique the performances, lighting, camera angles, et cetera.

The next movie set I visited was for *Stanley and Iris*, starring Jane and Robert De Niro, whom everyone on set called Bob. It was directed by the great Martin Ritt, known for his work on *Sounder, Norma Rae* and *Nuts*. I joined Jane on location in Toronto.

She'd warned me before I came that while on location in Waterbury, Connecticut, a group of Vietnam veterans showed up to picket the production and protest her anti-war activities. Since becoming a part of her family I learned there had been a few death threats made against her by people still angry about such activities. The more serious threats were met with a bit of heightened security, but Jane never seemed too fazed by it and never altered her routine as far as I could tell. I admired her fearlessness and her refusal to let her detractors disrupt her life.

My first day on set, Marty Ritt, the director, spotted me, introduced himself and personally welcomed me to his set. Whenever I was present he always took the time to say hello and inquire if I was enjoying my time in Toronto. There was a very homey closeness that existed among the cast members that was almost familial, even on the part of a big star like De Niro. He always spoke to me and inquired about my interests. I noticed he had a pretty bad fungal infection under his nails. He saw me staring and told me that he'd gotten the infection on the set of the film *Angel Heart*. In that film he played the devil, and as part of the character he was required to wear fake nails.

I was especially fond of his son Raphael, who was also visiting.

I spent a lot of down time on the set with Raphael, playing Frisbee and exploring the town. He was about eight or nine years old, a gregarious boy with olive skin and an expressive face. I enjoyed watching De Niro interact with him; it was reminiscent of the close, affectionate bond I witnessed between Troy and Tom. De Niro was always touching and holding his boy, who luxuriated in the attention like a contented cat.

Martha Plimpton, famous for her breakout role in the blockbuster *The Goonies*, played Jane's daughter. Martha was a few years younger than me but I found her extremely intimidating. She was a radical vegan who with the slightest of provocations would go on long tirades about the evils of factory farming and the moral ineptitude of anyone who ate animal products or wore fur or leather. Though I found her dedication to the cause of animal rights admirable, she was a little intense for me and I gave her a wide berth.

On days off from shooting, the entire cast would go on outings together. I remember an especially pleasant afternoon picnicking at Niagara Falls and a trip to see Cirque du Soleil. But Jane and I would also find time for just the two of us, and we spent several afternoons on long bike rides through Toronto parks.

For Martin Luther King Day in 1989, Jane, Tom and I had plans to attend the festivities in Atlanta. I had been looking forward to the trip for weeks. When the day of the trip arrived, I rushed to the Alta house to ride with Jane and Tom to the airport. I walked into the house to discover Jane carrying her bags downstairs, Tom nowhere to be seen. "Where's Tom?" I asked. "He isn't coming," Jane said, and quickly changed the subject.

During our stay in Atlanta we attended a solemn service at Ebenezer Baptist Church with the King family, celebrities, politicians and civil rights activists, including the Reverend Jesse Jackson. At a gathering after the service, Jane greeted her friends and signed autographs for fans. I didn't have a clue that she was agonizing over the end of her marriage to Tom. She told me after our return to Santa Monica that Tom had backed out of the trip after informing her that he was having an affair and wanted a divorce.

Jane told me then that her marriage to Tom had been unhappy for years. I was shocked. I never saw the discord, perhaps because I grew up in a house where one expressed unhappiness openly, vehemently and often violently. Whatever arguments Jane and Tom had must have occurred in whispered tones behind closed doors, because I never witnessed a moment of anger between them.

Though she tried to hide it, Jane was hurting and I hurt for her. I knew the pain of being rejected by someone who is supposed to be by your side no matter what. When I went back to school, I worried about her and checked in often. The divorce was bitter but neither one of them let it reach us children.

Troy seemed to hold up well and maintained a good relationship with both of his parents. I was much closer to Jane, so the fact that Tom had simply disappeared from my life was puzzling but not devastating. Vanessa didn't seem surprised at all by the breakup.

Jane didn't stay single long. Soon after the divorce she dated a handsome young actor for a while who Vanessa dubbed the Italian Stallion. Vanessa made it clear she was not pleased with Jane's new beau, but I felt differently. I saw that Jane's mood had lifted and that's all that mattered to me. Vanessa was thrilled when Jane tired of the Italian Stallion and sent him on his way.

One weekend I came home from college to find Jane, for the first time since the divorce, looking genuinely happy. The minute I walked through the front door she excitedly waved me over to join her on the big floral sofa. Her face was flushed and her eyes were bright. She grabbed both my hands, looked me in the face and in a conspiratorial tone with a grin as broad as the State of Montana she whispered, "I just went out on the best date!"

For the next half hour I listened as she told me about a man who had heard about her divorce and after waiting a respectful amount of time asked her out. She was hesitant to go out with him because after a bit of research she'd learned he was quite a ladies' man. In the end his persistence wore her down and they'd gone out.

"He's so handsome!" she cooed. "He kind of looks like Laurence Olivier!" She went on to tell me that he was some kind of media mogul who also sailed boats. I had no clue who this guy was but I was thrilled that he'd put a smile back on my mom's face. "Oh!" she said, giggling like a teenager. "He has a nickname. They call him 'The Mouth of the South'!"

This was my first introduction to my future stepfather, Ted Turner. A few months after our chat on the sofa, I knew the relationship was getting serious when Jane informed my siblings and me that her new boyfriend, Ted, was coming to town and wanted to meet us. "Don't be put off by how loud he talks," she warned us. "He's partially deaf."

These were the days before Google, so during the course of the next few weeks I was able to piece together a more complete picture of just who this guy was. I learned he was a twice-divorced, Southern billionaire philanthropist who owned a cable television network, several major league sports teams, lots of land and said whatever popped into his head. Loudly. He also wanted to colorize my beloved classic films. I didn't expect to like him.

When Troy, Vanessa, Nathalie (Jane's stepdaughter with Roger) and I showed up at the California Pizza Kitchen in Los Angeles for our dinner with Ted, I think we were all a bit surprised to find ourselves as enamored with him as Jane. He did not carry himself like a billionaire playboy. He dressed simply, was charming and very funny. What was most surprising was he actually seemed a bit intimidated by us. It was obvious he was doing his best to make a good impression. He asked lots of questions about our schools, our travels, our interests. Best of all, he doted on Jane. He made sure she was comfortable, kissed her frequently, and said endearing things to her every few minutes. Jane luxuriated in his affection. They were like a pair of lovesick teenagers. By the end of the evening I was confident that Ted was a good fit for our mom, and I could see that Vanessa didn't detest him, which was saying a lot since the men in Jane's life found it notoriously difficult to win her over.

Two years after our get-to-know-you dinner, Jane announced that they planned to marry. While I was sure that Ted and Jane were genuinely in love and that Ted would make a great stepdad, I had not yet met his kids. Ted had five children from two different marriages—two girls and three boys—who were about the same ages as we were.

Like their dad, the three boys loved to hunt and fish and were self-proclaimed rednecks, and the two girls from all accounts were the quintessential Southern belles who enjoyed the finer things in life. I couldn't imagine what we could possibly have in common.

The very first time I spent Thanksgiving at one of Ted's properties, I was the last of the Fonda kids to arrive at the airport in Tallahassee. Everyone else had reached Ted's place hours before. So it was the middle of the night when a chauffeured car whisked me onto the highway leading to Avalon Plantation. During the drive I couldn't help but wonder, *How in the world is our multicultural, granola-munching, radically liberal, highly opinionated crew going to blend with Ted's brood of Southern belles and rednecks?* As I thought about the upcoming week on the plantation, the famous line from one of my favorite movie classics *All About Eve* came to mind: "Fasten your seatbelts, it's going to be a bumpy night!"

The car turned off the highway and onto a long dirt road. All was pitch darkness except for the clouds of dust that swirled in the headlights like wayward spirits. The woods on either side of the road seemed thick and impenetrable. After a few minutes of riding in near complete darkness, I saw bright lights in the distance. It was a beautifully restored two-story antebellum mansion lit up with exterior lights. The house was white and trimmed in forest green, and the brick walkway leading to the large front door had two little figures of black stable boys cast in iron about three feet high guarding the entrance. A brief unease came over me. This mansion was nearly exactly like those I'd seen in films like *Roots* and *Gone with the Wind*. As a child of the Black Power movement, I'd never dreamed I'd one day call an old slave plantation home.

The driver helped me carry my bags inside. The door had been

left unlocked, which I soon learned was a common practice. After
the driver left and the sound of tires crunching on gravel faded, I
stood in a dimly lit entry hall with thirty-foot ceilings, a dazzling
chandelier and a spiral staircase. I stood quietly for a moment enveloped in the tranquil quiet of the sleeping house. I knew at least
eleven people were tucked away in various rooms fast asleep, but
all I heard were the shifting bones of the old house. I poked my
head into one of the two living rooms and was confronted by Scarlett O'Hara.

What looked like the original painting from *Gone with the Wind*
was mounted on the wall lit by a small overhead light. A haughty
Scarlett in an off-the-shoulder blue velvet gown and a white lace
shawl stared off to the left as if refusing to acknowledge my presence. I stepped closer for a better look. Jane had told me that *Gone
with the Wind* was one of Ted's favorite movies and he'd even
named one of his sons Rhett after the leading man played by Clark
Gable.

I squinted and rubbed my fingers lightly across the surface to
see if I could detect any sign of damage from when an angry Rhett
Butler threw a glass of liquor at the portrait. There was none. I
found out later it was a reproduction and that the original hangs in
the Margaret Mitchell House in Atlanta.

I wandered around the living room, checking out the interesting knickknacks and antiquated furniture. I wondered if I should
wake someone in order to find out where I was to sleep, or just
crash on the couch with Scarlett for the night. Just when I'd decided on the couch, a light at the top of the spiral staircase popped
on and there stood Ted in a terry-cloth bathrobe and slippers.
"Lulu!" he yelled down at me with his gap-toothed grin. "Welcome

home! I been waitin' up for ya! Let me show you where you're sleeping!" Since Ted doesn't know how to whisper, this greeting carried the decibel level of crashing cymbals. I cringed. He came down the stairs and embraced me before grabbing my suitcase and carrying it up the stairs, all the while telling me in his booming voice what a great week he had planned for us. Again I found myself moved by how much he genuinely wanted to make each of us welcome in his family. He showed me to my room and kissed me good night. He closed the door and I listened to the sound of his slippers swishing across the hardwood as he made his way toward the master bedroom directly across from mine. I fell asleep that night thinking here, in the most improbable place and in the most improbable person, I'd found a father.

Jane woke us up the next morning for breakfast at eight A.M. I was rested and anxious to meet my future stepbrothers and sisters. We filed into the formal dining room with views out the back to several acres of sloping manicured lawn running down toward a small lake ringed in long leaf pines dripping with Spanish moss. There were also several black labs belonging to Ted and his children standing and lying at a respectful distance from the table, feigning disinterest in the sumptuous aroma wafting in from the kitchen located down a long hallway at the rear of the house. These weren't just any labs. They were beautiful specimens with lustrous coats and were not just companions but well-trained and well-bred working dogs. Jane's golden retriever, Spencer, born and raised in Los Angeles, looked like a prince among a crew of construction workers. But within the year Jane would have him trained and hunting with the best of 'em.

The Turner kids were already seated when we Fonda kids (not

used to such an early rising, especially during vacation) wandered in. I took a spot next to Teddy Jr., Ted's oldest son. He greeted me warmly. He was a cuddly man with a boyish face and mischievous eyes. I couldn't stop staring at the bobbing lump his chewing tobacco made tucked in a fold between his lip and lower gum as he talked.

Beau, Ted's youngest son, sat to my left. He was tall, handsome and charming—the spitting image of his father. Rhett was quiet and uncharacteristically introverted for a Turner. I'd later learn he was the artist of the bunch. Within a few years I'd attend his graduation from the prestigious Rhode Island School of Design, where he'd earn a degree in photography. Across from me sat Jenny, Ted's youngest daughter. Blond, pretty and gregarious— what was not to love? But the true heart of the family was Laura, Ted's oldest. She was a beauty as well but didn't have the carefree attitude of her younger sister. Laura exuded an air of intelligence and a no-nonsense personality. Where Beau had Ted's charm, Laura had his outspokenness. She was protective of her family, especially of her younger sister, Jenny. Her fiancé, Rutherford, was a lawyer and he was the epitome of a Southern gentleman, with a bit of a frat boy thrown in to make things interesting. Beyond all expectations, our blended family got on well. Conversation flowed easily and naturally between us.

The table was dressed in the finest linens and silver cutlery. Once we were all seated, Jane rang a small silver bell in front of her and within minutes several African-American women came through the door carrying trays laden with cheese grits, bacon, eggs, hash browns, biscuits, pancakes, toast and freshly squeezed orange juice. I found the all-black staff a little too reminiscent of the antebellum South and so did my siblings. We also had to get used to our mom in the role of Southern mistress of the house.

The staff, I learned, had had family working on the plantation for generations. I got to know the entire crew but got especially close to a few. There was Edward, a butler of sorts, a kind, dignified, quiet fellow who moved around the house with the stealth of a cat. While working he was the consummate professional, but in his off-time he loved to joke, and to witness him smile was like beholding one of the world wonders. Viola and Etty Lee were the cooks, capable of churning out Southern dishes that made you want to thank Jesus for taste buds. I loved to sit out on the back porch or in the room off the kitchen and help them shell peas or shuck corn and listen to them gossip. Rounding out the house staff was the lovely Betty Jean, one of the maids, with her smooth dark skin and long flowing hair that she wore in two braids that reached down past her bosom. My mom was particularly enamored with her and usually prefaced her name with "beautiful," which she does even to this day.

I often stole moments away from the family to visit with the staff in the kitchen, where they taught me how to remove buckshot from and defeather quail, and how to make the perfect pitcher of sweet tea. I was happy to learn that Ted was a good boss and paid his staff well; in turn they genuinely liked the Turners. I grew especially close to Jimmy Brown, an older black gentleman from the South Carolina low country with a strong geechie accent. He'd originally worked for Ted's father and was like an older brother to a young Ted. When Ted grew up and took over his father's company, Jimmy became his closest ally and helped raise Ted's five children. Ted had made him a millionaire in his own right. Although he could afford to retire to some luxury resort on a tropical island, Jimmy chose to stay near the family where he could keep a close watch on them.

The Turner kids viewed Jimmy as a bona fide member of the family, and when they had children, Jimmy (who never married) became a grandfather too. Like Ted, Jimmy was hard-working and, despite a disability that limited the full use of one of his arms and left him with a limp, he was always on the move and enjoyed spending as much time as possible outdoors. His favorite activity was fishing, which he did remarkably well with one arm. When I met Jimmy, he was dating the much younger Joann, the sweet-natured and soft-spoken daughter of the cook, Viola. Some of my fondest memories of Jimmy Brown were traveling with him on road trips between Ted's plantations in Florida, Georgia and South Carolina. Jimmy didn't like to fly and if Joann was unable to travel with him, I volunteered.

Although our blended family got on remarkably well, there were a few things that would need to change. Ted insisted on structuring every aspect of the vacation. His idea of fun was not relaxing on the veranda with a hot chocolate or whiling away the afternoon in front of the television. He enjoyed spending nearly every minute doing something active and outdoorsy, and so he tended to run the vacation like he ran his businesses. We were expected to be on time for all activities and meals. Ted scheduled quail and deer hunts, and fishing for the predawn hours, breakfast at eight A.M., and more late-morning activities like skeet shooting and four-wheeling before lunch. After lunch there was horseback riding and nature walks. While his children were used to rising before the sun, formal meals and structured days (the Turner boys all attended The Citadel, a military college in South Carolina), we Fondas were wondering when we'd get a break from our vacation. The lull usually came in the evenings because Ted and Jane were blessedly in bed by 8:30 or 9 P.M., at which time we could count on being free and clear of Ted's schedule.

We spent the evenings in the Green Room, a masculine but cozy area off the dining room painted a deep forest green, with wainscoting and deep, leather armchairs. There was a large fireplace, which we kept roaring in the evenings. The walls were crowded with a virtual forest of mounted animal heads and more than a few prize fish, all bagged by Ted himself. In the midst of it all was a large TV and a library of the latest films. Under the empty gazes of dozens of herd animals, we Turner and Fonda kids bonded further watching films like *Edward Scissorhands*, *Dances with Wolves*, *The Grifters* and *Pretty Woman*.

It didn't take long for Vanessa and Nathalie to become representatives for us all and express our unhappiness with the scheduled fun. Ted took the criticism well and loosened the reins in terms of mandatory participation in activities, but maintained that meals together were not optional, though we would not have to dress up for them. We even got a few more healthy dishes included in the menu. Not only were we happy about the change but Ted also seemed less stressed, and I even think the Turner kids enjoyed the more relaxed atmosphere.

It was at Avalon that Jane and Ted married in 1991. My mom wore an antique white lace wedding dress and Ted sported a white linen suit. It was the third marriage for each. They'd originally planned to wed in a charming little one-room church on the property but plans changed at the last minute due to the paparazzi catching wind of the plan and descending on the site. Instead, the ceremony took place in the entry hall at the bottom of the spiral staircase, where I'd stood alone and uncertain just a little over a year before.

The holidays were my favorite family times. Best of all was Thanksgiving at Avalon. After a few years most of the Turner kids were dating seriously or married, and divided the holiday between two families. Nathalie, Vanessa and Troy were working or attending school. I was teaching English in Morocco and had several weeks of vacation time. So after nearly a week of a full house, by Thanksgiving morning all of the kids were gone, leaving just Ted, Jane, Ted's lab Blackie, my mom's golden, Spencer, and me.

We'd have a leisurely breakfast, after which Ted and I'd spend the morning fishing. We'd load up the old SUV with our gear and the dogs and head to the lake. The lake was less than three miles from the house but the short trip was elongated by frequent stops. Along the way Ted would pull over whenever he spotted a piece of trash, often left by poachers. Nothing escaped his notice. Not a beer can, a gum wrapper or a cigarette butt. He'd be in the middle of an interesting story when suddenly he'd brake hard and pull over at the same time. He'd hop out of the vehicle, retrieve the offending piece of trash, toss it in the vehicle and resume our conversation exactly where he'd left off.

At the lake we boarded one of the bass barges, a kind of motorized, floating platform with comfy seating. There was plenty of room for the both of us and the dogs. For the next couple of hours we cruised around the lake catching and releasing brim, crappie and bass. I often got my line snagged in the reeds no matter how many times Ted instructed me how to avoid it. He patiently disengaged my line every time. Sometimes we sat quietly enjoying the fine weather and the beautiful scenery, but mostly Ted was teaching me how to identify the various bird calls pouring out of the forest or quizzing me on the various wild plants. He also told me stories from his early years, stories about his beloved little sister, Mary Jane, who died from lupus at a young age. "I prayed to God every night to save her and when He didn't, I gave up believing in Him altogether." Ted wasn't melancholy very often. He was usually quite optimistic about most things, so those moments when he was emotional really stand out to me. Like the time we were watching one of his favorite films, the documentary series *Eyes on the Prize*, which chronicles the story of the civil rights movement. Whenever there were any scenes in which the protesters were being hosed or beaten or having dogs set upon them, Ted was reduced to a blubbering mess every time. With tissue in hand, he soldiered on through the entire segment. I also caught him crying during a screening of the Walt Disney animated film *Beauty and the Beast*. The scene where the beast was transformed into a handsome prince is what sends him reaching for the tissue.

After fishing, we'd return to the house and I'd spend the afternoon reading and after lunch head out on a hike. The staff didn't work Thanksgiving Day, so in the evening we'd all head into town for dinner at the only place open on Thanksgiving evening: Hooters. We'd enjoy our meal of buffalo wings and burgers served by nubile young women in tank tops and bright orange shorts before catching a movie at the local movie theater. Those last few days of solitary time with my parents always ended the holidays on a high note and I often returned to school or work feeling loved and quite lucky.

Being one of Ted's kids was like living in a whole new world. We flew around on Ted's private jet, sat front row center at Braves and Hawks games, attended black-tie fundraisers hosted in some of the finest homes and venues in Atlanta. But through it all we were connected as a family. We went to each other's birthdays, graduations and weddings. There were the Trumpet Awards, the Goodwill Games, fundraisers for the Captain Planet Foundation and for my mom's nonprofit, Georgia Campaign for Adolescent Pregnancy Prevention (GCAPP). When I had free time, I'd join Ted and Jane on speaking engagements, like an event in which Ted spoke to a crowd of Civil War enthusiasts. I loved to watch Ted speak. He is always unscripted, smart and absolutely hilarious. I had few friends during this time. I didn't need any, I had my family.

To give the Fonda side of our family something to work on together, for my mom's sixtieth birthday, Ted presented her with a $10 million gift to endow the Fonda Family Foundation, of which all the Fonda kids are trustees and Jane our head. It was Ted's intention that we enjoy the privilege of giving to a deserving organization, and also to experience serving on the board of a foundation, as his own children did for the Turner Foundation. There was a genuine camaraderie in working with each other for the greater good. We come together once a year to provide grants to dozens of nonprofits across the country.

Our family foundation's $10 million endowment was nothing compared to Ted's many foundations, which had combined endowments in excess of $1 billion.

So despite the vast wealth around me, it was the clear focus on giving that made the Turner kids so grounded and made it easy for everyone to get along so well. Both of my parents spent nearly all of their time engaged in some activity designed to help make the world a better place for others. My mom's groundbreaking work with teenage pregnancy prevention and Ted's work in protecting the environment made me immensely proud, and further strengthened my desire to do the same.

CHAPTER 9

THE BLACK PANTHERS, the Fondas and the Turners are as different as families can be, but they all had one crucial thing in common: they were not shy about acting on their political beliefs. For decades Jane made headlines for her controversial tours through conflict zones like North Vietnam, and Ted was quite vocal about his opposition to the proliferation of nuclear weapons. For them, the highest form of patriotism was dissent—all in the spirit of trying to make the world a better place.

As a college senior, I was enrolled in a sociology class run by an equally radical Hispanic professor born and raised in East Los Angeles. Field trips included activities like spending the night with the homeless on skid row in downtown Los Angeles in order to get a real-world understanding of the role the Reagan administration's policies played in increasing the nation's homelessness. From him I got a more detailed understanding of oppression of women and minorities and the misery derived from American foreign policy in other parts of the world, like Latin America, Asia and Africa.

In the early 1990s, my disdain for America's foreign and domestic policies was reaching a high point. Ronald Reagan had been president for eight years, and George H. W. Bush had just been elected for another four. I'd had enough. I started wearing dashikis, headwraps and a huge leather necklace shaped like the continent of Africa. The Michael Jackson poster came down and the Marcus Garvey poster went up. I took a course in African-American literature and started reading Eldridge Cleaver's *Soul on Ice*, *The Autobiography of Malcolm X*, Alice Walker's *The Color Purple*, the poetry of Langston Hughes and Chinua Achebe's masterpiece, *Things Fall Apart*. I began to think that a return to Africa would be the answer to my simmering disgust with the seemingly endless parade of privileged white dudes who had been riding roughshod over the White House since the founding of our nation.

At this point, I'd never traveled outside of North America and Mexico but I nonetheless held a crystal-clear image of Africa in my imagination that involved regal, ebony-skinned people carrying fresh mangoes and bananas in intricately woven baskets on their heads while garbed in exquisite robes of the finest cotton woven into colorful patterns of significant meaning. I envisioned myself hanging out with African poets and intellectuals, standing on the shoulders of their ancestors who reached back in time before maps, nations, language, race and Ronald Reagan. Back when the whole world was Africa.

My growing disillusionment with my country led to my decision to take a break from the United States altogether. I even entertained the notion of renouncing my U.S. citizenship and moving full-time to an African nation. It didn't matter to me which nation as long as it was African. So in my senior year of college I decided to do a little reconnaissance and signed up for a semester abroad. My first choice was Senegal, but I failed to meet the French language requirement. The only other African option I was qualified for was Morocco. While not technically black Africa, it would have to do.

My best friend at the time was a statuesque fly-girl from Inglewood, California, named Shawn. When I told her I was bound for the motherland, she was a bit worried: "Girl, don't come back with a bone in your nose!" I was undaunted. I played Tracy Chapman's "She's Got Her Ticket" over and over in the weeks leading up to my departure. I boarded the plane with the eager anticipation of a bride on her wedding day. A complex of incongruent emotions rushed through me when the plane touched down and I set foot on the continent: joy, gratitude, sadness and, maybe more than anything, the feeling that "I'm home."

From the moment I arrived in Morocco, I was charmed. Before I arrived, I knew next to nothing about Morocco or Islam. My perceptions of Arab people and culture had been shaped exclusively by what I saw in films and on the news, in which they were often pigeonholed as religious fanatics. The women were either covered from head to toe in black robes and veils or were fleshy *succubi*, belly dancing in pasties and jangly skirts. The men usually sported monobrows and were sweaty looking with cruel, pinched faces sprouting long beards or five o'clock shadow.

In reality I saw that the average Arab person I encountered in Morocco was far better looking than the average American by about a factor of ten. Lean-bodied, olive-toned skin, large dark eyes, long eyelashes, thick, shiny black hair. Moroccans both rich and poor were a great deal more curious about the world beyond the borders of their country. It was not uncommon to meet people who spoke two or more languages fluently. They also had a keen interest in world affairs. Perhaps because freedom of the press was not a fact of life in Morocco, the people went out of their way to gain access to news sources beyond what their government produced.

I fell hard for the Moorish architecture, the cobblestone streets, the quaint way grown men walked hand in hand. I especially loved the nose-tickling spices that permeated the air in the *souq* (open-air market). Nothing delighted like the brightly colored and multi-patterned *djellabas* worn by the women gliding down the streets like Christmas ornaments. No two alike.

During the first part of the program, nine other students and I traveled as a group to various cities throughout the country— Casablanca, Fez, Agadir, Ifrane, Oujda, Essaouira—where we stayed in hotels. In Marrakesh, however, we had our first home stay: a short weeklong visit before a return to Rabat for our long-term home stay.

When the Marrakesh families were invited to a small party to meet and greet the students they would be hosting, I saw that my family was rather large. It consisted of parents with five grown children, four boys and a girl my age. They all greeted me warmly, but I spent most of the luncheon speaking English with the daughter, who wanted to improve her language skills in order to study in the U.S. I was disheartened to learn the next day in class from a fellow student that my host mother had told her host mother that she was disappointed because she did not get "a real American." By real American she meant a white American. Despite the fact that they had to put up with hosting a "fake" American, I was relieved that the family did open their home to me and treated me like an honored guest during my brief stay.

I was the only black student. On the whole my skin color was not an issue because many Moroccans, including the royal family, have family members with sub-Saharan roots. I did get very weird comments, however, that were meant to be compliments but instead were just downright awkward. For example, often when I was introduced to Moroccans, some would greet me enthusiastically and then inevitably tell me I looked exactly like Tracy Chapman, Whoopi Goldberg, Whitney Houston or Oprah Winfrey.

During these strange encounters I always responded with "Thanks!" It was always one of these four women, I suspect not because I looked anything like them, but because during the late 1980s and early 1990s they were immensely famous, and commenting on some perceived likeness to them seemed to be a good conversation starter and a way to communicate to me that they knew something about African Americans.

To this day I still get such comparisons when I travel in other countries and even U.S. cities with few to no people of African descent. While traveling in Buenos Aires, Argentina (famous for being the whitest country in South America), I had a waiter tell me I resembled Serena Williams. This time I responded a bit differently. I said, "Thanks! You look like Che Guevara!" The tall, lanky, balding waiter looked at me quizzically for a few moments before switching the topic back to the menu.

There was a lot that I loved about my semester in Africa, but by the time the semester ended I was ready to go home. Witnessing firsthand the disparities between the United States and Morocco had reignited my patriotism. I was proud to be American again, which wasn't to say that I was ready to forget about Africa. I would miss many things. The friends I'd made, the food, the architecture, even the plaintive wail of the *muezzin* calling the faithful to prayer that blared through the city five times a day became soothing and familiar. What I'd miss most was my Rabat host family, the Benchekrouns.

While in Rabat, I lived with a middle-aged widow named Rachida and her daughter, Laila. Laila was my age and studying economics at the local university. The Benchekrouns were not your typical Moroccans in appearance or lifestyle. Rachida, like her daughter, was tall, fair-skinned and blond, unlike most Moroccans, who are medium to short in stature with dark features. It was also unusual that Rachida and Laila were not particularly religious. Like most of the country's privileged class, they were westernized. Though they were Muslim, they did not pray regularly, they ate pork, drank alcohol and celebrated Christmas. They rarely wore traditional Muslim clothes unless they were going to a wedding, at which point they'd wear the long jewel-toned and embroidered caftans required for such occasions. They loved to dress me up in these beautiful garments and take photos of me resting on *poufs*, leather-covered pillows, like a Moroccan princess. To which I happily obliged. Laila was educated in the finest schools; in addition to Arabic, she was fluent in French and English.

Rachida's husband had been a big deal in Moroccan politics and hailed from a very prestigious family. But after his death a decade before I met them, his widow had lost the income that maintained the lavish lifestyle they enjoyed when her husband was alive. They'd moved from a large house with many servants in a very fancy suburb, into a tiny one-bedroom apartment on a back street near the center of Rabat. Though they were no longer rich, Laila's father's family name and good reputation meant that they were able to continue to associate with people in high society.

They retained the daily services of a maid named Khadisha, who was not much older than Laila and me yet was already married with several children. She was a tiny woman with large callused hands. She had a perfect blend of Arab and sub-Saharan African features reflected in her café au lait skin tone, large almond-shaped eyes and tightly coiled hair, which she covered when she was not indoors. Being quite poor and religious, she wore traditional Muslim dress and the head covering called a *hijab*. I thought for many weeks that she did not like me because she never spoke to me or even looked at me. I later learned she was extremely shy and embarrassed to talk to strangers because her teeth were horribly rotted. But after a few weeks she grew used to me and even became comfortable enough to share her smiles with me. The third blond in the house was a small puff of a dog named Chloe.

I shared the one bedroom with Laila, and Rachida slept on the couch in the living room with Chloe. From the start Rachida and Laila embraced me wholeheartedly. With Laila and Rachida I did not have to suffer through an awkward adjustment. Rachida, who spoke no English, through the use of simple hand gestures communicated to me from the start, "You are my daughter no different from my own." She took my hand and put it in Laila's and took my other hand and placed it on her heart, smiling at me warmly. And that's how it was.

From the start Rachida and I shared a very close bond. Initially, we were not able to speak the same language—Rachida only spoke Arabic and some broken French—but when Laila went to school, I'd spend an entire day alone with Rachida in the little apartment watching Arab soap operas (Rachida would fill me in on the characters and plot lines) and gossiping about the neighbors. Rachida would often tell me detailed stories about her childhood, her marriage, her desire to go on the *hajj* to Mecca. Often her stories were hilarious, and we laughed so loud the neighbor's nosy maid would sometimes come by to see what was so funny.

Laila would come home from school and find us curled up on the couch like best friends, sipping mint tea and totally engrossed in a television program. When she would ask what we did all day, I'd recount the stories Rachida shared and Laila would stare at me gape-mouthed. "How'd you understand all that?" To this day I don't know what transpired between Rachida and me during those early, long companionable afternoons in the tiny apartment that enabled us to pass the time in complete understanding despite speaking very little of the other's language.

When Laila was not in school, we were inseparable. She spoke perfect English but also encouraged me to use my Arabic. I became the sister Laila never had. We went dancing nearly every weekend at the Cinquième Avenue, a little club down the street from our apartment in Place Bourgogne. Under the strobing lights we gyrated the night away to "Smells Like Teen Spirit" and "Losing My Religion."

Some weekends Laila and I'd go to dinner parties instead of out dancing. At these parties I enjoyed listening to the Moroccan dinner guests, all in their early to late twenties, engaging in very enlightened conversations about world politics, literature and even religion. Many knew as much if not more about U.S. history, geography, politics and popular culture than me.

I was stunned by the size and grandeur of the homes we visited. When Laila was invited to attend a party thrown in honor of Prince Moulay Rashid, one of King Hassan II's two heirs to the Moroccan throne, I happily tagged along. I was truly taken aback by what I saw. In the States I'd been in many beautiful homes and was privy to the lifestyle of some of our country's wealthiest, but I'd never been in a home where it would have been practical to have a golf cart on hand to get from one end of the house to the other. At least three of Ted's beloved Avalon could have fit into some of these homes, which in reality were more along the lines of palaces.

The first thing my eyes were drawn to upon entering the formal salon was how, despite the size of the room, it was cozy and inviting. Sultry lighting poured from Moorish globed, brass lanterns suspended from the ceilings and strategically placed candles in elaborate holders casting the room in shades of amber. Several areas contained upholstered banquette seating in rich fabrics and covered in embroidered, tasseled pillows in deep shades of red and blue. Each seating area had its own wide, low, polygonal dining table inlaid with geometric patterns.

There were columns partially covered in traditional terracotta tiles known as *zellige* decorated with Arabic calligraphy, which Laila told me were quotes from the Quran. The walls were covered in *tadelakt*, an ancient plastering technique, which made the walls reflect light and appear to glow. But the most beautiful aspect of the room was the carpets. Beautifully crafted antique Berber carpets.

I'm not talking about the modern, mass-produced Berber wall-to-wall carpet sold in the West. I'm talking brightly colored, intricately designed museum pieces woven by real Berber tribesmen. Carpets that were made within spitting distance of camels and sand dunes, not in some factory in China.

The wailing and crashing cymbals of traditional *Gnawa, malhun* and *chaabi* music could be clearly appreciated beneath the susurrations of conversation. There were about forty guests, the sons and daughters of the country's elite. I was the only foreigner. Soon after arriving, Laila introduced me to the prince. He was tall, athletic and baby-faced, just two years younger than me. He graciously welcomed me but struggled to make small talk. He held my hand and stroked it like a cat while smiling at me through unfocused eyes. This went on for nearly thirty seconds until another woman approached eager to greet him. I extricated my hand and stepped aside. And as with me, he began stroking her hand and staring into the near distance with a pleasant smile on his face. The fact that the prince was just your average, socially awkward twenty-something somehow put me at ease.

Later, I briefly found myself the life of the party. My fledgling Arabic was attracting a lot of attention from the other guests because it was quite rare for foreigners to speak the language. I was told an American accent in Arabic is quite pleasant, much like a French accent in English. After being seated at our table and before the meal began, I was asked to speak more Arabic. "Tell us your name and a little about yourself!" a guest asked, and everyone leaned in toward me with expectant faces. When I said it, they all laughed and clapped as if I'd just told a hysterical joke. I was prompted to say a few more things, which elicited a similar delighted response from the guests. Some patted Laila on the back, congratulating her for bringing along the night's entertainment.

I was saved by several servants who began to bring in huge platters of food. The meal began with copious amounts of bread being placed on the table along with several salads, my favorite of which was made of cooked eggplant and tomatoes and called *zaalouk*. Next were several varieties of stews prepared in traditional crockery known as *tagines*: slow-cooked stews of lamb and chicken with olives, dried fruit, nuts and fresh lemons. This was followed by several types of couscous. Among them was couscous with raisins and onions and couscous topped with chicken, peas, carrots and zucchini. The highlight of the meal was a seafood *pastille*, a flaky pastry stuffed with white fish, squid, shrimp and vermicelli. There were no utensils or plates. Bread was used to sweep up the food and we all ate from the large serving dishes placed in the middle of the table. Moroccan sweet mint tea, fresh fruit and several varieties of sticky, sweet pastries sprinkled with sesame seeds ended the meal.

After dinner we had refreshments by a large heated pool in the back garden, fragrant with the scent of orange blossoms. There was a bar with lots of wine and hard liquor. Just when the crowd started to get a little out of control—the prince was pushing fully clothed guests into the pool and others were pairing up for romantic interludes in secluded parts of the garden—Laila and I called it a night and headed out. Laila's friend who invited us to the party instructed his driver to return us to her apartment in the city center. We climbed into the car and leaned back into the soft leather seats and recounted the interesting moments of the evening, but as we pulled out of the gated compound the rose-colored glasses I'd been wearing all evening began to slip.

I noticed that interspersed between the walled compounds of Morocco's wealthy were the corrugated-roofed shacks of the poor, one-roomed hovels without running water or electricity. There were people sitting with small children bundled in their arms in the glow of campfires used to prepare their food and keep themselves warm. Unlike in the States, where the poor live out of sight of the rich, in Morocco they live side by side. Islam dictates that the poor not be forgotten. One of the pillars of Islam is for every Muslim to have concern for and to give to the needy. Though this was not always practiced, it did create a culture in which the wealthy and poor were able to live closely. I liked this aspect of Moroccan culture.

I've tried to never forget my impoverished roots but somehow during my semester in Morocco I'd found myself caught up in the party scene and running around with a group of spoiled rich kids. I assumed the family stay would be with an average Moroccan family, meaning more traditional and with no connections to the royal family. Those folks living in squalor just outside the walls of the fabulously wealthy made me realize I'd actually lost sight of the reason I'd come to Morocco in the first place. Seeing those families huddled in the glow of campfires watching me as I slid by in a chauffeured car was the wake-up call I needed. With just a few weeks left in Morocco, I decided I'd return and do something more than just club hop and go to dinner parties.

I was not done with Morocco. I had family there now. I had to return to the States to finish my degree, but during my tearful good-bye to Laila and Rachida at the airport, I promised them both that I would return—I just didn't know when or how.

My final semester of college after Morocco passed quickly. Unlike many of my friends, I was excited to leave school behind and begin my life as a bona fide adult. The weeks leading up to graduation were especially sweet because I'd already scored myself a position as a program counselor at a homeless shelter in Santa Monica. I'd been a full-time summer volunteer at the Ocean Park Community Center for several years, so when a position became available, the director basically handed me the job.

The shelter was a fifteen-bed facility that catered specifically to mentally ill homeless women. It was just a few blocks from our family home near the Santa Monica Pier and not very far from my new apartment. Jane was very proud that I'd found work so quickly. It was important to me to show her I could be self-sufficient.

My job entailed distributing medications, preparing evening meals, scheduling doctors' appointments, helping our clients apply for or maintain Supplemental Security Income (SSI), among other things. I also worked overnight shifts several days a week from seven P.M. to seven A.M.

The shelter was always full, as clients were allowed to stay a maximum of six months, supposedly plenty of time to stabilize on meds and find a job and housing. We saw many battered women and women struggling with addiction. Because the OPCC catered to mentally ill women, one of only a few places in the city, our clients felt safe and understood. The facility was located in a reno-vated warehouse with high ceilings and skylights. It was bright and open, with private rooms and meals often donated by some of the area's finest restaurants.

The women only had to refrain from using drugs and alcohol in the facility, take their meds, and seek employment and permanent low-income housing opportunities we scrounged up through part-nerships with sister agencies.

I enjoyed the work and getting to know the women. There was one woman in particular, Delores, a thirty-something immigrant from Brazil who I found particularly interesting. She was easy to overlook since she spent most of her time tucked away in an arm-chair in a corner of the living room. She never chatted with the other women or played cards or board games. She even avoided eating dinner at the dining room tables. She preferred to carry her plate to what was often referred to as Delores's chair in the corner, where she ate her meal in silence.

Delores suffered from depression and most of the clients and counselors gave up trying to draw her out of her shell. But I noticed that Delores often stared at me when she thought I wouldn't notice. When I asked her about it, I was surprised that she an-swered me and even more surprised with what she said. She simply told me she stared at me because I looked like her little sister, who she'd left behind in Brazil.

Delores and I did resemble each other, I realized. We could have easily passed for sisters. She asked if I had relatives from Bra-zil and seemed genuinely disappointed when I told her no. From that moment on she allowed me to sit quietly with her for a few moments each evening and even engaged in small talk when she could. I desperately wanted to know what had brought her so far from home but I knew opening herself up was painful, and whenever I tried to broach the subject she either shut down or changed the subject. During her six-month stay at the shelter, Delores would remain an enigma, but I secretly hoped that my resemblance to her beloved sister and the few quiet moments we shared freed her at least momentarily from the demons that tormented her.

Another client who was as different from Delores as could be was a vibrant, blond beach bunny named Karen. She was just in her mid-twenties and possessed the flawless skin and effervescent personality of a starlet. In fact she'd left her home somewhere in the Midwest to pursue a modeling and acting career in Los Angeles. Soon after arriving she developed a cocaine habit and was later diagnosed with bipolar disorder. Most of the time she was in a manic state, very animated and talkative. She'd often come over to my office and tell me about her day before giving me unsolicited hair, makeup and wardrobe advice.

Despite her larger-than-life personality that could be overbearing at times, she was often the life of the shelter. I worried about her when she left the shelter for the day—that her looks probably attracted the wrong kind of attention. We all suspected she engaged in prostitution to supplement her SSI. I couldn't help but feel maternal toward the ladies despite the fact that some were old enough to be my mother.

I spent two years at the center and in that time I burned myself out. Though I was attracted to social work, I didn't have what it takes to stay in such a position long term. My fault was I cared too much, I tried too hard and I expected too much. I saw a piece of my sister Deborah in each of the women who passed through the door. I took it personally when women I helped to secure housing and jobs, after a few months of self-sufficiency, only ended up right back in the shelter.

I decided it was time to move on. I'd kept in contact with Laila during the two years after I left Morocco. I'd even invited her to spend a few weeks with me in Los Angeles. It was her first trip to the U.S., and a big smile and wide eyes did not leave her face for most of the trip. I also learned she was inexplicably attracted to things that terrified her. We took a trip to an amusement park, where she rode a big loopy roller coaster. And though when she got off she was in tears and her legs too wobbly to stand on, she giggled madly and made her way back to the end of the line to experience it all over again. When I had overnight shifts at the shelter, she stayed up late watching true-life crime shows, which scared her so terribly she couldn't sleep until I came home the following morning. I told her to watch something more cheerful in the evening but she never would.

So when I called Laila to tell her I was planning to move back to Morocco, she was thrilled. I knew I'd have to have a solid plan for supporting myself before I got Jane's approval, so I started researching job opportunities and found I could probably get a position teaching English. I'd never taught before, so on my days off from the shelter I went down to my local library to see if I could get certified to help teach illiterate adults how to read.

Certification didn't take long and I spent a few days a month helping a middle-aged woman who worked as a cook at a local high school learn how to read. With a college degree in history and literature, my literacy certification and a few months' tutoring experience, I applied for a position as an English teacher at the American

Language School in Rabat. I was delighted and shocked when I was hired. I turned in my two weeks' resignation notice to the shelter and informed Jane of my decision to move back to Morocco. She was impressed with my ability to parlay volunteer opportunities into full-time employment and bragged about me to her friends. She gave me her blessings to move to Morocco but made me promise to write often and come home for the holidays and summer break. Then she asked me what I planned to do with my pet bunny, Bugs.

After I had graduated from college, Jane and I developed a fascination with bunnies. Miniature bunnies, to be precise. I don't know who purchased a bunny first but for a time we were both totally taken with the creatures. When I moved out of the Alta house and got my own place, I bought a little bunny to keep me company and named him Bugs. He was a tiny little ball of cottony gray fur with a white underbelly and ears that hung down along the side of his head like pigtails. Jane got two bunnies of her own, a miniature lop-eared like mine and a tiny white miniature with eyes ringed in black that gave it the appearance of wearing heavy eyeliner.

Jane had a hutch, which I called the bunny condo, custom built out on the patio behind the house, where she'd spend time playing with her bunnies. I chose not to cage my bunny after a little research revealed that bunnies could be trained to use a litter box. So Bugs ran freely throughout my apartment. He greeted me when I came home and even jumped in my lap and nudged my hand with his head to indicate that he was ready to have his ears scratched.

Some weekends Jane and I would go for long bike rides that led us past a bunny rescue sanctuary in Santa Monica. We'd always

This is my mama at
age sixteen.

My daddy holding my little
brother, Randy.

In the top row, fourth from the left, is my sweet maternal grandmother, Marie. The handsome gentleman in the suit next to her is my grandfather. They divorced before I was born, and though he lived in the Bay Area his whole life, I never met him. The baby in my grandfather's arms is my father.

One of my happiest memories is of visiting Daddy in prison. I was in my forties the first time I saw this photo of my little brother, Daddy and me. I was shocked how closely it matched my memory of the visit, right down to the nature mural behind us.

Me, three years old.

Uncle Landon, Aunt Jan and
cousin Thembi in1983.

Dress-up day at Aunt Jan and Uncle Landon's house. From the left: cousin
Thembi, me, cousin Kijana and cousin Ayaan. We are all sporting magenta
lipstick. I really resemble my mama at age sixteen with my poodle hair.

Tom Hayden, me and Jane at Laurel Springs.
This was the beginning of our beautiful friendship.

Twelve years old, and in my
first play at Laurel Springs.
I played a wicked nurse à la
Nurse Ratched in *One Flew
Over the Cuckoo's Nest*.

Me in my favorite striped
shirt, hugging Jane and a
friend in a summer-camp
group photo.

Me and Jane looking very eighties at
my high school graduation.

Shortly after my move to Santa Monica.
Me, Tom and Troy hamming it up in a tiny photo booth.

Me and Troy at Ted and Jane's wedding at Avalon Plantation in 1991.

The Turners and the Fondas celebrating Christmas at Avalon Plantation. There were so many presents, they nearly blocked out the tree!

Me, Troy, Vanessa and Jane at Ted's Avalon Plantation for our first Christmas together, in 1992.

With Jane at an
Atlanta Braves game.

1992: Jane took this
photo of me at Ted's
ranch in Montana.

Jane's sixtieth-birthday bash.
From the left: Peter Fonda, me, Jon Voight, Jane and dear family friend Jimmy Averitt.

Jane and me at her
sixtieth. Doesn't she
look fabulous?

Preparing for a canoe portage trip as part of my training as a summer environmental educator at the Kenai National Wildlife Refuge in Alaska. Once the trip began and I had to carry a ten-foot canoe more than half a mile, I lost my radiant smile.

Photo courtesy of Emily Sunblade

Hiking a section of the Colorado Trail in 2001.

Me with my neighbor in rural Shinyanga, Tanzania.

With Dave Eggers and members of the Lost Boys Foundation in 2002.

Jane and me surrounded by Lost Boys at a Thanksgiving
celebration thrown in their honor.

Sitting on top of Mount Katahdin, which is the terminus of the Appalachian Trail.
I was so exhausted when I finally got there that I cried.

Taking a photo opportunity on the Appalachian Trail.

A baby seal encounter while I'm out flagging roads.

Just another mind-blowing afternoon on the Ross Ice Shelf, Antarctica.

Me in Christchurch, New Zealand, suited up and prepared for a very long flight to my new job at McMurdo Station in Antarctica.

Christmastime at Jane's loft in Atlanta. From the left: Me, Santa Jane holding my nephew Malcolm, my sister Vanessa holding my niece Viva, and my sister Nathalie.

Mother's Day with Mama in Oakland. I cut her hair myself and
I think it looks quite chic.

My first meeting with Mama in her little house.

My very happy reunion with my uncle Landon.

A Williams family "Fun in the Forest" event at Samuel P. Taylor State Park. Uncle Landon took the photo.

Enjoying the moment in the belly of an ancient redwood tree.

Mama and me.

My mamas and me.

get off our bikes and stare at the hundreds of bunnies frolicking around on the other side of the fence. Most were ill-conceived Easter presents, unwanted after the novelty wore off and cages needed to be cleaned. People would bring their bunnies in the middle of the night and toss them over the fence. After a time, a group of concerned animal lovers started caring for the bunnies, feeding and playing with them—even raising donations for sterilizations, medical care and home placements. I'd sometimes volunteer at the bunny farm.

When I was getting ready to return to Morocco, I briefly thought of sending Bugs to live with my mom, but couldn't part with him. In the end, I bought a tiny traveling cage and Bugs made the transatlantic trip to Morocco with me, probably becoming the world's first intercontinental lop-eared bunny.

Bugs and I arrived safely in Morocco. The airport customs folks peeked into the carrier, chuckled when they saw my tiny bunny and waved me through. We moved in with Laila and Rachida temporarily while Laila helped me find an apartment nearby. Fairly quickly we found a bright, one-bedroom apartment with tiled floors and a large kitchen located a few blocks from their apartment in Place Bourgogne near our favorite nightclub.

On clear days I walked the two miles to school along the busy, vibrant sidewalks past street vendors selling roasted nuts, sips of water and cheaply made cleaning supplies. When the weather was foul I took a taxi, which I hated to do for several reasons. The cab drivers in Morocco drive like they are fleeing Satan himself. They weave in and out of traffic, through red lights, and are not averse to using the sidewalk to avoid having to wait in backed-up traffic. It didn't bolster my sense of security that there were no seatbelts in the taxis. I also hated taking cabs because the drivers almost always demanded more money than I owed simply because I was foreign.

I enjoyed my students but I hated teaching English. Contrary to what I thought, being a college grad and fluent in English doesn't make one a good English teacher. I was surprised to learn that all the stuff I didn't know about the language was more than I knew—by a multiple of ten. I knew my nouns, verbs and adjectives. I could speak intelligently about the past, present and future tenses. No problem. But my students were asking me about aspects of English way out in the hinterlands of my understanding. Holy hell! When did English get more than three tenses? Turns out a world existed beyond verbs and nouns. A big world that, for me at the time, seemed as deep and incomprehensible as quantum physics. Tenses like the past perfect, the subjunctive, the pluperfect, the present perfect, the future perfect continuous.

Often I used films to disguise my knowledge gap. While exposing students to film is a good way to get them familiar with hearing the language, I had ulterior motives. I wanted to show a film to eat up time I didn't want to spend telling my students that I was wrong in assuming that the future perfect progressive is what the children of liberal democrats aspire to be. On my very first movie night I made a huge mistake that could have cost me my job. I chose from the school video library the movie *A Clockwork Orange*. I read the synopsis and thought a film set in the future would interest my students. I did not bother to preview it. Later that evening I brought snacks for my small group of eight advanced students to enjoy during the screening, popped the cassette into the machine and pushed Play.

Just a few minutes into the film, all hell broke loose. It opened with a violent home invasion in which a husband and wife are sadistically beaten and tortured. When the wife was violently raped with a dildo, I jumped from my seat and switched off the film. I was terrified that I'd offended my students, in particular a pair of teen sisters who wore the *hijab*.

After switching off the film and switching the lights back on, I apologized profusely. They didn't seem to be fazed, not even the two girls. They thought I'd stopped the film not because it might offend them, but because it was offending me.

I finished up that first semester but did not sign on for another. Teaching wasn't my strong suit. Before I left Morocco, Jane helped me to get an internship at the United Nations Education, Scientific and Cultural Organization (UNESCO) in Rabat. I was relieved not to have to go back to teaching English, but working at UNESCO presented a whole new crop of issues and it didn't last long. Neither experience squashed my desire to work in Africa, however. Both made me want to get the skills necessary to get a job where I could be trusted to do the work. From Morocco I applied to graduate school and was accepted. I left believing I'd return, but life had other plans.

I invited Laila to spend the summer of 1993 with me, Ted and Jane at his Flying D Ranch in Montana. I wanted to share the experience of a home on the range where the buffalo really do roam.

In Montana we rode horses, square-danced in the barn, took fly fishing lessons and borrowed a ranch car to visit nearby Yellowstone National Park. We spent the days there exploring the hot springs and mud pots, and photographing wildlife. Laila could not get enough of Old Faithful.

Literally minutes after we returned to the ranch from our weekend at Yellowstone, Jane came into my room and hugged me fiercely before telling me my uncle Landon (who I had not heard from in years) had called her office to tell me that my sister Deborah had been killed. He'd also passed along the time and place of the funeral that was to be held within the week. I couldn't speak. Jane told me I did not have to go, but if I wanted to she would arrange everything. I struggled to comprehend it all.

I took a moment to myself to process it. I was going back. Back to Oakland and I'd see my mother, my father and bury my sister. I was numb but I knew I had to go. I asked Jane to make the arrangements and asked her to include Laila in my travel plans. The next day we flew out to the Bay Area.

We had a Moroccan friend who was attending college at San Francisco State, so we crashed at his place. I left Laila with him the following day and I took BART across the bay to meet with Uncle Landon and Aunt Jan. They still lived in the big, homey bungalow on Coolidge Avenue where I had spent many pleasant evenings. The mood of course was somber. Uncle Landon told me that Deborah had been killed but did not go into details. I didn't ask him to.

The funeral was the next day. There were lots of reporters and photographers, TV news cameras. My sister's murder had been particularly cold-blooded and had drawn a lot of media attention. I saw my mother. She was wailing and beating her chest. "Why? Why? My baby!" she cried and my heart was ice. I wanted to tell the reporters that my sister was dead because my mother, my grieving mother, gave up on her. But I was tired. My head felt as if it weighed a ton. My body could not support it.

I went to my sister's funeral full of anger at my mother for letting such a tragedy touch her child and convinced that my departure from her negligent care had spared me a similar fate. My big sister. If I could have shot flames from my eyes back then, my mother would have been a charcoal briquette. I sat at a distance observing her grief and thought, *What right does she have to her tears?* Her wails spiraled through the room like an ambulance racing toward a victim beyond saving.

I believed my sister dying like an animal in the gutter was all her fault. She failed my sister. She failed me. I spoke to Teresa and other family members at the funeral and at the wake. Polite conversations, brief and distant. With barely contained contempt I spoke briefly to my birth mother after the funeral and left the next day convinced that my choice to leave Oakland behind was a good one.

But I hadn't left really. For the next few decades, I'd carry a heavy bundle of anger that lived in the center of my chest. Though it was a burden to carry and it prevented me from making true connections to people, it also protected me by keeping me safe from feelings of sadness and loss. My anger was both prophylaxis and sickness—a pathogen that flowed freely through my mind, blocking my ability to mourn my sister's death or to see my mother as anything other than a monster for years.

I recall the rest of the day as if it were a series of snapshots, muted and dull around the edges. My grieving aunt and uncle. My brother a grown man holding the hand of a short, chubby, sweet-faced woman. His wife? My sister Teresa with a small girl. My niece?

After the funeral there was a gathering at the home of our paternal grandparents. Grandma Marie! Grandpa Rene! Kisses. Hugs. She gave me an old black-and-white photo of all six of my siblings. I was three in this photo. Deborah was nine and alive. Grandma told me to keep in touch. I kissed her soft cheek deeply. I did not linger.

I resurfaced back in Montana with Laila. I did not speak about the funeral. I had been there and at the same time I hadn't. It was like passing through the Underworld. I mustn't look back lest I get stuck there. In Montana everything was clear again. The colors were sharp; I was light in body and mind. I picked up where I left off as if I'd not gone back.

CHAPTER 10

AFTER MY PROFESSIONAL BLUNDERS in Morocco, I knew I had to improve myself academically if I had any hope of contributing anything useful to developing nations. This is what drove my decision to get a master's degree in public health from Boston University. I chose public health because it seemed to be a degree most sought after by international development agencies, large and small.

I enrolled in an accelerated program and had my master's in hand within a year. I then moved to Atlanta for a time to be near my family and to work for the Centers for Disease Control and Prevention in order to strengthen my résumé before applying for jobs abroad. Though I enjoyed my time at the CDC, I was frustrated by the government's apathy toward gun regulation, which I felt was contributing to our nation's death and injury rates, particularly in poor communities and communities of color.

After a year in Atlanta, I took a nine-month fellowship with the International Foundation for Education and Self-Help (IFESH), a nonprofit that places health and education professionals in service positions in developing countries. Through IFESH, I was assigned to a small mom-and-pop health NGO called Adventures in Health, Education and Agricultural Development (AHEAD). To go along with its big name, it also had a grandiose mission: to provide hands-on, people-to-people assistance and partnerships with rural catastrophically distressed communities to combat malnutrition, disease, extreme poverty, technological deprivation and other conditions that have an adverse impact on the health and welfare of people. My disenchantment with huge, bureaucratic multinational agencies like UNESCO had me primed to work with a "little engine that could" NGO like AHEAD.

I was thrilled that I would finally be living and working in sub-Saharan Africa. I would be the only expat working for the agency in Shinyanga, a city with a population close to ninety thousand located in northern Tanzania about three hundred miles from the country's capital, Dodoma. After accepting the fellowship, I attended an organizational orientation at IFESH's headquarters in Arizona and then was sent home with a month to prepare for my move. In that time I met and started dating an Atlanta native, a 6-foot-2 hottie named Andy. We met at one of Atlanta's many young black professional gatherings. There were plenty of red flags at the beginning of our romance to indicate that we were incompatible which, of course, I promptly ignored. Andy, a year older than me, was a high school dropout who had a hard time keeping a job and was living in a basement when we met. He was also a single father who struggled to make his child support payments. I knew this because his ex-wife made a point of letting him know this during heated phone conversations I overheard and whenever their two-year-old was picked up and dropped off for his visitation with Andy.

I moved out of my apartment and moved into Andy's rented basement apartment in order to save money for my move to Tanzania. Dating Andy was a sharp departure from what I was used to. Throughout graduate school I'd dated medical students and a sweet-natured Antiguan who was studying at the Berklee College of Music.

I found intimate relationships with men difficult because I found it hard to date and be myself at the same time. My relationships always started off intensely. I'd go from being a first date directly to being a serious girlfriend. I catered to my partners' every need, sexually and emotionally. So much so that Mario, one of my boyfriends, when describing me to a friend, said with a grin: "She's very Mario focused."

Unfortunately for Mario, there was only so long that I could keep up the façade, and eventually the relationship would slide from blissful into nonexistent, usually when I moved somewhere so far away my baffled boyfriends couldn't follow. Andy was the first boyfriend I let follow.

He managed to get time off from work and I booked both of us tickets to Tanzania two weeks before my assignment was to start in order to explore and enjoy the role of tourist before my real work began. Jane did not approve. Though she was kind to Andy and thought he was a nice person, she didn't think he was a good fit for me and told me so. I ignored her advice and insisted we were in love and our relationship would work. Despite his lack of a formal education and his economic woes, he was a loving father, a good person, and our chemistry was instantaneous and undeniable.

So despite our differences and Mom's disproval, the relationship deepened quickly. But events transpired just weeks before our departure that threatened to change everything.

In the afternoon of August 8, 1998, I received a call from IFESH informing me that the U.S. embassy in Dar es Salaam had been bombed and I was given the option of being posted to another country, but I told my country representative that I'd like some time to decide what I wanted to do. I hung up the phone and turned on the television. It turned out that two U.S. embassies had been bombed. The other was in Nairobi, in the neighboring country of Kenya. Over the next few days I learned that hundreds of people were killed and thousands injured in simultaneous truck bomb explosions. The vast majority of the victims were local people. Many of the injured were blinded by projectiles created in the explosions. These people were rendered unemployable and the impact of these lost wages on the locals would reverberate for decades. I was unnerved and unsure of what my next move should be, so I called my mom for advice.

"Hey, did you hear the news about the bombings in Africa?"

"Yes! It's horrible."

"So maybe I shouldn't go? I have the option of being reassigned."

"Why wouldn't you go?"

"Errrm . . . the bombings? The American-hating terrorists?"

"I think you should go."

"What?"

"If you don't go, then what about the people you were supposed to work with? The Tanzanians need support now more than ever."

What she told me made perfect sense. We talked for a few minutes longer and by the end of our conversation, I was 100 percent recommitted to my assignment. I could always count on my mom giving me the pep talk I needed whenever I was unsure of myself. Besides, traveling to a country in which an American embassy was bombed must have seemed a fairly low security risk to a woman who fearlessly toured throughout wartime Vietnam. If there was anyone who was qualified to counsel me in this situation it was her. My mom and Ted threw me a marvelous African-themed going away party at an Italian restaurant in Buckhead, and the following morning Andy and I were on a plane bound for Africa.

More than twenty-four hours later, we landed safely at Julius Nyerere International Airport in the middle of a night hotter and stickier than any I'd experienced. It sorely taxed the little bit of energy I'd held in reserve. We quickly exchanged some U.S. dollars for Tanzanian shillings, threw our bags in the cab of the most aggressive of the two dozen cabbies who swarmed us as we left the airport, and headed to the budget-conscious hotel recommended by my supervisor. It was a flophouse in the middle of the city, with hookers in the lobby. Our hotel room door did not lock, so we ended up barricading it with an armchair and our luggage. The bathroom was a microenvironment for several species of mold and mushrooms, many I suspected not yet classified. As for the bed, the pillows and sheets were covered with long blond hair. I wasn't too concerned because I figured you get what you pay for and the hotel was certainly dirt cheap. Andy, on the other hand, refused to enter the bathroom and would not lie on the bed without first covering it with his jacket and some towels he'd brought from the States.

The next morning I awoke to find Andy wide awake and rustling around in his suitcase. For the first time I saw its contents.

Andy's suitcase was nearly half full of cans of tuna and granola bars. When I asked him about it, he told me he was not going to eat any of the food in Africa. "I don't trust it," he said, never raising his eyes from his search. He went on to tell me that even when he visited his family in Jamaica he did not eat their food, preferring instead to eat at the local McDonald's or eat food he'd brought with him from the States. When I told him something was seriously wrong with a person who trusted the food at McDonald's more than a home-cooked meal prepared by his relatives, he dismissed me with a wave of his hand, still focused on finding something in his suitcase.

"You honestly expect to eat tuna fish and granola bars for two weeks?"

"Yep!" he replied, still rustling through his bag.

"What are you looking for?" I asked.

"I think I forgot my can opener."

I laughed until I nearly gave myself an ulcer. Andy, however, failed to see any humor in his situation. We wolfed down a couple of granola bars for breakfast then got dressed. As we exited the hotel and beheld Dar es Salaam in the full light of day, I did not experience the feelings of peace and homecoming I'd experienced in Morocco. Dar es Salaam is not a pretty city. My ears were assaulted by the blare of automobile horns, backfiring buses and the bleating calls of street vendors. The streets were a hive of activity, with people darting in and out of traffic. There were beggars, vagrants and the gainfully employed all bustling around in a swirl of organized chaos that I irrationally feared would pull us to its core.

I was particularly astounded by the city buses. They were packed beyond capacity. I could see the passengers on board with their faces pressed against the windows. On the same bus there were more passengers attached to the bumpers and the sides, hanging on for dear life as the bus wove in and out of traffic and braked hard at stoplights and for jaywalkers. Outside for less than five minutes, I was already sweating profusely and I imagined hanging from the side of a moving bus was more amenable than being packed inside in the hot and humid weather Dar es Salaam maintains nearly all year-round.

As we strolled along the sidewalk, I wanted to duck into the stores with smiling shopkeepers and lively traditional music pouring out onto the street. I wanted to practice my few phrases of Swahili and buy postcards for my friends and family at home, but Andy was in a sour mood and wouldn't let me linger long. As we approached another busy street, he was suddenly captivated by what he saw on the other side: a Sheraton hotel. It was a bright shiny spot in the middle of a grungy city. He dragged me across the street for a closer look. It was unlike any Sheraton hotel I'd ever seen in the U.S. The grounds were extensive, almost like a small park. The lobby was vast and air-conditioned and tiled in marble. Not a hooker in sight. We wandered over to the dining area and saw a delicious brunch buffet with fresh fruit, eggs, bacon, homemade bread, freshly squeezed orange juice. We sat down and ate a proper breakfast served by the most attentive and welcoming staff.

After we finished our breakfast, we rushed back to our hotel, grabbed our luggage, checked out of the fleabag and checked into the Sheraton. Andy's mood changed completely. He was grinning from ear to ear as he unpacked. He sang while he took a shower. While still naked and dripping wet from his shower, he threw open the curtains dramatically to behold a view of the golf course below before falling upon the gigantic bed that could easily accommodate a family of six. He writhed around under the freshly laundered sheets like a pig in mud before falling asleep with a smile on his face. Although I was happy to be away from our first hotel, I was distinctly uncomfortable with our newfound artificial bubble of western comforts. I did not come to Africa to look at a golf course and be waited on hand and foot by Africans. But, I rationalized, if it kept Andy happy, it was worth it.

A few days later we headed off for an overnight stay and safari in Mikumi National Park. Mikumi is a 47,000-square-mile tract of wilderness that stretches east almost as far as the Indian Ocean. It is home to elephants, lions, zebra, wildebeest, impala, hyenas, giraffes, baboons and buffalo herds. I hoped the trip to Mikumi would be a welcome respite from the crowded streets of Dar.

It was only after we left the kinetic chaos of Dar es Salaam to the horizon behind us that I felt truly wrapped in Africa. Gone were the bleating horns and the crowded humanity, in its place was profound silence and the infinite expanse of the savanna. Along the way, our guide, Joseph, told us that the landscape was similar to that of the Serengeti, which consisted of alluvial plains and savanna punctuated with acacia, baobab, tamarind and palm trees. We'd also see the flattened top of hundreds of towering termite mounds, some as tall as ten feet. He said we would also have great views of the Rubeho and Uluguru mountains.

I was enjoying the safari, but Andy was on edge most of the time. If the jeep stopped for us to view wildlife, Andy flinched visibly whenever an animal, whether it was herbivore or carnivore, got close to the vehicle. Several times during the game drive, he made his feelings known regarding his lack of confidence in the jeep's ability to outpace a determined lion or withstand the attack of an elephant. I didn't think he'd feel comfortable on this safari unless we were in an armored tank. His skittishness really started to embarrass me when he began to repeatedly ask the driver for updates on the fuel level and whether it would be sufficient to get us back to camp before dark. When we visited a lake to watch hippos and our guide told us they were the most dangerous animals in Africa, Andy retreated back to the jeep before Joseph could finish his sentence.

After a full-day safari, Joseph dropped us off at our lodging for the evening, a small, free-standing, single-story building with two bedrooms and a full bath. I thought it was charming. Andy thought it was a death trap.

Joseph had our dinner prepared for us on a table set in front of our little cabin. After setting up he joined the driver in their identical cabin a few hundred feet from ours. Andy refused to eat the food. Since we had left the Sheraton, he had reverted back to his granola bar diet. I wanted to eat dinner outside and enjoy the sunset, but Andy was terrified of the large troop of baboons foraging near camp. When I told him his concerns were exaggerated, he reminded me of Joseph's talk earlier in the day about black mambas. I rolled my eyes and wished Joseph had never brought up Andy's greatest fear: snakes. Now Joseph had kicked Andy's herpetophobia into warp drive by telling him he was deep within the territory of the baddest snake on the planet. Glancing repeatedly at the ground around us and sweating not just from the heat, he recounted Joseph's description of the mamba being the fastest and most aggressive snake with the most potent and fastest-acting venom.

"He also said they don't need a reason to attack, neither. They'll just roll up on you and Bam! You bit!"

"Yeah, but he also said the chances of that happening are slim to none. You're more likely to get killed by a hippo."

"Aha! Another reason why we should be inside!"

"Oh, brother!"

"What's that?" Andy shrieked, and rushed toward the cabin in a high-stepping fashion.

"What's what?" I asked, startled to my feet, causing my dinner plate to fall facedown in the dirt, attracting the attention of the foraging baboons.

"That!" Andy said, pointing at something under the table from the safety of the cabin. I cautiously squatted down to take a look.

"It's a rock, you dope!" I said, falling back in my seat waiting for the rush of adrenaline to clear my system. Joseph called over to us to ask if we were OK.

"It's OK, Joseph. Andy thought he saw something."

"OK," he said knowingly.

I let the baboons have my spilled dinner and joined Andy in the cabin. He climbed onto the bed and didn't utter another word, but I could see his mind fabricating all kinds of scenarios that could transpire after the sun had fully set. Scenarios that included us fending off venom-laced fangs, flailing hoofs, slathering jaws and eviscerating horns.

While I unpacked and Andy washed up, I learned that my big burly boyfriend's phobias weren't just limited to mammals and reptiles. He was also terrified of insects. He discovered ants in the bathroom and ran back into the bedroom to notify me of the situation. Resigned, I went to a small utility closet and grabbed a broom and swept the little beasts out the front door. To Andy's credit, they were pretty large for ants (nearly half the size of a thumb). I calmed him down and we turned in for the night. Neither one of us got any sleep. Our relaxing safari turned out to be an emotionally exhausting time for the both of us. So I was glad when the time came for Andy to board a plane back to the States, leaving me to explore more of Tanzania on my own terms.

The first thing I did after seeing Andy off was to return to the hotel and book a trip to Zanzibar Island, just off the coast of mainland Tanzania. With my tour book in hand, I bought a ticket on a high-speed ferry scheduled to leave the next morning at 7:30 A.M. The travel agent who arranged my trip suggested I also purchase Dramamine, as the ninety-minute crossing can be quite choppy. I ignored the suggestion. I'd been out on many boats fishing and never once experienced anything akin to motion sickness. It wouldn't be until I reached the Dar es Salaam port that I'd finally see that tooling around a lake on a bass barge and crossing the Indian Ocean on a high-speed ferry, standing room only, simply did not compare. I stood there on that heaving boat with my heaving guts, hot, soaked in my own and several other people's sweat, dehydrated and packed on board like an illegal stowaway, swallowing my own vomit for nearly ninety minutes that passed like centuries. If I had had a knife, I would have killed myself.

Luckily I had no knowledge of just what a risk I was taking. Boat crossings from Dar es Salaam to Zanzibar don't always get their passengers across safely. As recent as 2012, at least sixty-five passengers were confirmed dead and over two hundred missing after an overcrowded ferry traveling from Dar es Salaam to Zanzibar capsized. The year before that, another boat capsized, killing more than a thousand passengers.

It was a relief when we reached Stone Town, Zanzibar's main city. Its rich history and eclectic architecture dating back to the nineteenth century reflected the influences of Arab, Indian and African traditions. From the minute I stepped off of the boat, however, it was its Arab roots that screamed out to me. The great mosques, the narrow, winding streets, the outdoor markets and the elaborately carved doors all sent me back to my carefree days in Morocco. The use of coral stone as the primary construction material gave the buildings a reddish tint that lent the small city an even cozier vibe.

I wandered around taking in the wonders. I visited the small palace where Dr. David Livingston lived while preparing for his final expedition into Tanganyika in search of the source of the river Nile. Livingston must have been a pretty lovable guy, because the Africans that cared for him in his final days of malaria and dysentery bickered with Britain for his remains. The Africans, in the end, cut out Livingston's heart and sent the rest of his body back to Britain with a note attached, declaring, "You can have his body, but his heart belongs in Africa!"

I also visited the slave market and sat inside the tiny, dark cells where the slaves were held. I contemplated the possibility that my ancestors may have sat in this exact same spot under more unhappy circumstances. I whispered to their lingering spirits. I told them I was doing fine and that they were not forgotten.

Next I visited the Palace of Wonders, built in 1883. It got its whimsical name because it was the first building in Zanzibar to have electricity and the first in East Africa to have an elevator. The Old Fort was next door. Built in the seventeenth century by the Omanis to defend the town from the Portuguese, it was Stone Town's oldest building. I visited several other tourist sights, but I was most anxious to go on the much-hyped spice tour.

My guide ushered me into a vehicle and took me to the plantations outside the city where spices such as cloves, cinnamon, cardamom and lemongrass were grown. Our first stop was at a distillery where essential oils are processed. As we entered the space, the strong, sunshiny aroma of lemongrass greeted me. I bought several small bottles of it before my guide shuttled me on to a local spice farm. Small children played outside mud and grass huts in a world of neon green foliage and rich, dark earth.

Farmers walked us through their crops, identifying the various plants and their uses. In addition to spices and herbs, there were hundreds of fruit trees. Many were familiar like pineapples, mangoes, papayas and bananas. Some were totally alien, like breadfruit (the flesh has the texture of fresh-baked bread and taste similar to potato), jackfruit (the world's largest tree-borne fruit, which can weigh up to eighty pounds and with a taste similar to a tart banana) and custard apple (a sweet fruit that tastes, as the name suggests, like custard).

My guide waved a boy of about twelve over and spoke a few words of Swahili to him, which sent him scampering up a towering coconut tree with the blade of a machete clenched in his teeth. When he reached the fruit dangling just beneath the canopy, he used his machete to cut loose several green coconuts, sending them raining down to the ground. He scrambled back down the tree and with his machete whacked the top off of one of the coconuts and handed it to me, smiling broadly. After my long day trekking through the humidity, the fresh coconut milk revived mind, body and spirit.

As promised, my guide dropped me off safely back in Stone Town, where I wandered over to the Blues Restaurant overlooking the water. I grabbed a table on the deck and ordered lunch. I was charmed by a group of skinny, half-naked boys playing happily in the water. Their dark skin was as slippery and shiny as a seal's. I dragged my feet when the time approached for me to re-board the ferry back to the mainland. The minute I saw the ferry sitting there heaving up and down, the symptoms of seasickness washed over me. With a whimper I approached my destiny.

CHAPTER 11

I WAS LOOKING out the window of the plane as it made its final approach into Shinyanga and I did not like what I saw. Unlike the lush greenness of Zanzibar and the hustle and bustle of Dar, Shinyanga, from my lofty perspective, was a dust bowl in the middle of nowhere. We came to a skipping stop on the airport's unpaved only runway. My fellow passengers, all Tanzanian, broke out in applause for a safe landing. I joined them.

I stepped off the plane into a virtual furnace. I was surrounded by a dry, dusty landscape dotted here and there with thorny acacia trees. Historically, this area was densely forested with woodlands and bushland species of plants. The land has been degraded over the years, however, by drought, overgrazing, cash crop cultivation, destruction of the forests to wipe out *tsetse* fly infestations and an increase in population leading to a higher demand for firewood. This has transformed a once fertile area that sustained generations of agropastoral people into an area with low productivity and major soil erosion issues.

I dragged my suitcase through the dust and dry heat, following behind my fellow passengers, when a Tanzanian gentleman approached me and identified himself as an employee of the United Nations compound where I would be staying until I found permanent housing.

Like most of the Tanzanians I had met, he was extremely welcoming and well dressed in a blazer with a light-colored button-down shirt, polyester slacks and leather dress shoes despite the heat. Within the hour he deposited me at the compound, which was not as grandiose as the name might suggest. It was an underwhelming one-story, cinder-block complex with several bedrooms and a central kitchen, eating and living area. I was the only person living there at the moment, but there was a woman who worked at the compound who would be doing the cleaning and cooking. Her name was Amina, a soft-spoken, plump, older Tanzanian. She welcomed me inside and showed me to my room. It was neat and clean and contained a single bed, with a side table and a lamp. The thick tan curtains were pulled back and sunshine streamed into the room.

Outside my window was a large patch of dirt and, to my delight, a group of about fifteen banded mongooses were lounging in the shade of an acacia tree. Amina was puzzled by my excitement. I guess her response to my fascination with the mongoose would be similar to her visiting me in the States and becoming obsessed with watching tree squirrels. I felt vindicated, however, when a decade later the Animal Planet network aired their hit program *Meerkat Manor* that followed the day-to-day activities of Kalahari meerkats, which look and act very similar to the banded mongoose.

Amina pried me away from the window long enough to show me the bathroom across the hall and inform me that dinner was at eight P.M. This gave me plenty of time to unpack, shower, ogle the mongoose family and take a nap before dinner.

Shortly before eight, I joined Amina in the kitchen, which smelled pleasantly of a spicy vegetable stew. She was boiling a very large pot of water and told me I must never drink water straight from the tap. She made several days' worth of potable water at once in the big pot. She set the table and before she left, she told me she would come by in the morning to make me breakfast and show me around the town. Then she was gone.

I took a closer look at the meal she had left for me. The stew looked delicious. There were large pieces of potatoes, carrots and lentils. What I didn't recognize was a bowl of what looked like raw bread dough. I pinched off a piece and popped it in my mouth. Sure enough it tasted exactly like what it looked like: bread dough. I set it aside and devoured the stew, figuring I'd ask Amina about the raw dough in the morning.

The next day I was up early. Amina was already in the kitchen preparing breakfast: sweetened coffee with cream, toast and jam. After I sat myself at the table, Amina went to the kitchen and came back with the small bowl of dough that I did not eat from the night before. It turns out it was meant to be eaten as it was presented. The dish is called *ugali* and it is a staple food that could be found all over sub-Saharan Africa.

It is made from *cassava*, or corn flour mixed with water, and stirred in a pot over medium heat until it reaches the consistency of bread dough. More water can be added, making it into a porridge that many eat for breakfast. Amina told me how to eat the doughy version. The traditional way is to break off a piece and roll it into a ball and then make a depression in the middle of it with a thumb, effectively creating a spoon that is then dipped into a sauce or stew. One can also fold it around a piece of meat to keep the hands from getting covered in sauce. In essence *ugali* serves the dual purpose of being a food and a utensil, similar to how Moroccans use baked bread to eat their *tagines*. *Ugali* is cheap, easy to prepare and makes a very filling meal when combined with meat and stews, thereby sustaining millions of Africa's poor. For the uninitiated, *ugali* is an acquired taste, as it is flavorless and gummy in texture, though by the end of my stay in Tanzania I would be preparing it and eating it for dinner every night.

Seemingly about the size of a large village, Shinyanga served as the headquarters for the regional administration and the headquarters of the urban districts. It boasted a population in the tens of thousands and was home to several major nongovernmental agencies working on issues ranging from deforestation to HIV/AIDS prevention. There were no paved roads and almost no buildings over two stories, though the streets were crowded with people. Women, almost always beautifully dressed with hair and makeup done, strolled along with babies strapped to their backs. Some were shopping or gossiping in front of the many beauty salons. Men in grungier states of dress were hanging out on street corners watching the women or strolling hand in hand with their friends. Motorbikes and bicycles zipped by laden with entire families, carrying the week's shopping and a farm animal or two.

The streets were lined with barber shops, tiny one-room stores selling everything from sweets to small sachets of laundry detergent. There were many repair shops. Nothing was wasted in Shinyanga. In the States, when a radio stops working or a pair of shoes begins to wear thin, they are tossed in the trash. Not in Shinyanga. There were very clever repairmen and craftsmen who could fix anything and make a worn-out pair of shoes look new. There was sound everywhere: cars and motorbikes, barking dogs, boisterous conversations and music. Always music. Lively African music blared from every shop and passing car, reflecting the variety of music being enjoyed in the area. Traditional music from one shop blended with the hip-hop-inspired music from another, which was blending with Islamic tunes from another. The overall vibe was of a prolonged block party.

During my first week at the U.N. compound, I got a message from my supervisor in the States that he had delayed his trip to Shinyanga for two weeks. I was a bit annoyed because I was anxious to move out of the compound and into the community, as well as get to work. I was incredibly bored with having just two hours of Swahili classes a day and a group of mongooses for diversions. Luckily an unexpected visitor would change things for the better.

Not long after my supervisor's message, I got a visit from an African woman. Her name was Ruth. She came to see me when she heard that there was a newly arrived African-American woman in town. She was a beautiful, petite woman with skin best described as golden brown. She was originally from Ghana but several years ago immigrated to Norway with her Ghanaian-born husband named Emmanuel and their two young boys, Joshua and Derrick. They were in Shinyanga for her husband's work. He had a two-year contract working with the Tanzanian government on behalf of a Norwegian NGO on deforestation issues in the area. She told me that they had been in Shinyanga for several months and, as there was very little to do, she was bored out of her mind and in search of friends. We became inseparable.

Ruth introduced me to her neighbor, a local woman named Mercy. Mercy lived in one of the many corrugated-roofed mud houses in the neighborhood with her husband and four children. She was a tall, sturdy woman, kind and quick to laugh. When I visited her house for the first time, she showed me her new calf. It was honey blond with huge eyes and long eyelashes. Mercy told me to allow it to suck on my fingers. She giggled like a small girl when the force with which the calf latched onto my fingers startled me. From that moment on, I visited Mercy nearly every day to spend time with her and her family, and also to visit with the little calf.

Mercy helped me find a house to rent equidistant between her place and Ruth's house, which was very large, completely furnished and gated. Ruth also had several large shade trees in her yard and a chicken coop with a dozen chickens that produced fresh eggs daily. The three of us spent weekend afternoons and early evenings relaxing under the shade trees playing with her chickens, who allowed me to pick them up and even cuddle them.

My house was not as fancy as Ruth's but was considered extravagant in an area mostly comprising steel-roofed huts with outhouses and no electricity. My new home had a small used sofa for the living room and a full-sized bed with mosquito netting, a desk and chair for the bedroom. Ruth insisted that I hire a woman to cook and clean. I insisted I could do these things for myself, but Ruth explained that hiring the locals helps generate income for the community as well as makes life easy for us expats unaccustomed to handwashing clothes and scrubbing floors on our hands and knees. I saw her logic and hired the teenaged daughter of a family that lived in a little shack down the road from me.

Clara was shy and kept to herself no matter how much I tried to engage her in the hopes of using more of my Swahili. I'd hired her to come every day to make breakfast and lunch, do the shopping, clean the house and wash clothing as needed. I paid her three times what she asked, which didn't amount to much but elicited the first and only smile I could coax from her. She turned out to be an excellent cook. Every morning she made fresh fry bread, and for lunch she prepared a perfectly seasoned lentil stew that was so delicious I'd have her make it every day for the entire nine months I lived in Shinyanga.

I was thrilled to be out of the compound and in my own place. The first night in my new home I was awakened from a deep sleep by a strange noise. I turned on my flashlight, which I slept with, to discover to my horror that my mosquito net was covered with thousands of insects. Some were as long as my hand. Many I'd never seen before. The noise that woke me up was the buzzing of thousands of pairs of wings. I'd made the mistake of not closing my window completely before going to bed.

Since the hoard was not able to get past the netting, I simply turned off the light and went back to sleep. By morning the mosquito net was clear. The only evidence that the insects had been there at all were the dozens of crispy corpses ringing my bed.

Insects were not my only uninvited house guests. I also shared the premises with several geckos. They hung out primarily in my bathroom and bedroom, slithering across the floor and up the walls whenever I happened upon them. When I told Ruth about them, she surprised me by telling me I was lucky to have them. The geckos, she told me, eat insects and therefore will keep their numbers down in the house. From then on, I saw the slithering little beasties in a new light. Sealing the windows and hosting the geckos, however, did very little to mitigate my insect issue. Daily I found insects in my hair, in my shoes, in my food. I'd even occasionally find one or two in my underwear. I eventually had to come to terms with the fact that I was in rural Africa and simply had to get comfortable living up close and personal with wildlife.

It didn't take long for me to acclimate. After a few weeks I could blithely pick insects out of my hair and undergarments without first issuing a blood-curdling scream. I knew I had totally gone native, however, when after a hard rain millions of locusts swarmed the area, causing everyone to retreat indoors for at least an hour. I sat inside with Clara, listening to the sound of thousands of locusts slamming into the windows of the house like so many pebbles. After the majority of the swarm had passed, Clara grabbed a plastic tub and headed outdoors. I followed, curious. She started picking up the dead and injured locusts that covered the ground like a living, writhing carpet.

I could see other people up the road emerging from their homes and doing the same. Birds and small mammals were also about, snatching up the locusts as well. I thought, *"What the . . . ?"* Clara returned with the tub filled with the still wiggling locusts. It wasn't until she deposited the basket on the counter in the kitchen that I realized what was about to go down. I watched fascinated as she meticulously cleaned each insect, removing the legs, wings and head before placing them in a colander. She then rinsed them in cool water, fired up the propane stove and grabbed a frying pan. When the pan was hot, she poured in a heap of bugs, added a bit of salt and cooked them as if it were a stir fry. When they were done, she placed about a handful of them in a small bowl and handed it to me.

I daintily picked one up, irrationally expecting it to wiggle even after being dismembered and roasted. With Clara watching me closely, I closed my eyes and held my nose with one hand, as if I were about to jump into a pool, and popped the roasted locust into my mouth with the other. I chewed it slowly and deliberately. It was delicious—crunchy with a nutty flavor. Clara and I sat companionably on the kitchen floor and finished the first batch together. She made a second batch for me to eat later and carried the bulk of the still wiggling locusts home to her family.

My boss was a retired physician who, after a visit to Tanzania, decided to start a health-oriented nonprofit. I'd met briefly with him and his wife in the States and found them both to be open and sincere in their desire to help the people of Tanzania. I would be working solo to reopen an office in the town, and create and implement a health outreach program centered around conveying to the community the importance of childhood and maternal immunizations. I was worried that I wouldn't have the language skills or community ties to carry out the project, but he reassured me that my language would improve and he'd find local people for me to work with.

I tried to be optimistic about the project, but I felt as though

I'd entered into an experience similar to the months I wasted in the old U.N. office in Morocco. Within a few days, the doctor returned to the States. I was left alone again. As promised, I cleaned out the office, washed the floors, cleared away cobwebs, replaced the faded posters with shiny new ones the doctor had brought, using them to cover the larger holes in the walls. Workers from the surrounding offices would come over to chat while I cleaned. They wanted to know who I was and what I'd be doing in Shinyanga. They had no idea what our organization did and had never seen anyone occupy the office I claimed was our headquarters. I could tell they didn't know what to make of me. After several weeks, I decided I would not sit in the office any longer waiting for an opportunity to do something. Shinyanga is crawling with nonprofits doing amazing work. If the one I worked for wasn't going to give me work to do, I'd find one that would.

Though everything did not go as planned in Tanzania in terms of my job, I did make fantastic friends in Ruth and Mercy. I also made up for lost time by visiting with several local NGOs. One of the highlights was visiting the homes of local people who take in and care for children orphaned by AIDS. I visited local people making progress in their efforts to reverse the devastating impact of deforestation caused by decades of land misuse and mismanagement. I'll never forget the theater troop of young Tanzanians entertaining while educating their people about many public health issues and how keeping women illiterate only serves to amplify the nation's poverty levels and negative health outcomes.

In the end I came to believe that many of the world's ills cannot be solved solely by outsiders who believe that their wealth and degrees make them the most qualified. The most respectful, practical and efficacious approach to improving the lives of others is for wealthy nations and individuals to use their resources to empower people to help themselves. Years after leaving Tanzania, I would have the chance to put this theory into practice.

CHAPTER 12

I RETURNED TO ATLANTA in 2000 somewhat discouraged that I hadn't accomplished the work I'd signed on to do. I wasn't totally disheartened, however. By way of our family foundation, I was able to make a well-deserved grant to one of the local nonprofits to continue their good work in Tanzania.

While I was uncertain where my next professional step would lead me, I knew exactly where my romantic life was headed: long-term commitment. I'd spent most of my adult life running away from commitments, particularly professional and romantic ones. I usually kept jobs and boyfriends for an average of two years before moving on to something new. I thought it would be the same with Andy. But he showed more initiative than my old boyfriends, who were smart enough to see my cross-country or cross-Atlantic moves as a clear sign that the relationship was over.

Not Andy. Though we were separated for nearly nine months and by more than eighty-three hundred miles, our relationship had managed to progress, mostly because he e-mailed me daily and even made the occasional phone call while I was in Shinyanga. When I saw Andy off at the end of our stressful safari, I had no real plans to get serious with him, but I'd soon learn that the old adage about the heart and absence is not completely unfounded.

When he called one day to tell me he'd lost another job, instead of seeing it as yet another sign that I had no business getting serious with this guy, my savior complex kicked in and I saw him not as a loser but as someone who desperately needed me. My response to his firing was to ask a dear friend who worked at Turner Enterprises to help him get another job, which she was kind enough to do.

So by the time I returned to Atlanta, my boyfriend was gainfully employed. He picked me up at the airport and we returned to his basement apartment, where he proposed and I accepted. I was not in love. There were other factors that led to me accepting the proposal of marriage. I was in my thirties and living in the South, where women are usually well into their first decade of marriage with children by then. Also, I knew my parents' relationship was strained. Jane had written to me in Tanzania to tell me that she and Ted were talking about divorce. I had called the Turners family for nearly ten years. The thought of a split made me heartsick. The thought of creating a family of my own gave me a sense of stability in the midst of uncertainty.

The prospect of my mom divorcing was also troubling because I was very close to Ted. Unlike Tom and my birth father, he was a true father to me. When he learned of my engagement to Andy, he approached me and asked if he could give me away. The thought of that relationship being threatened by divorce was more than I could think about. So I didn't.

I was relieved upon returning to Atlanta to find my mom and Ted still together, married but clearly not the infatuated lovebirds I'd last seen. While Ted was his usual upbeat self, my mom was greatly diminished physically and emotionally. She'd lost a lot of weight from her already tiny frame. Though she continued to put up a front that screamed *"Everything's fine!"* I could see things were not. Emotionally, she was shutting down. Her marriage was eating her alive. There were times leading up to and even after the divorce when she wanted to share with me some of the things Ted was doing that destroyed their relationship, but I refused to listen. I knew that if she shared with me anything hurtful that he had done to her, my feelings for him would change. I didn't want that. I didn't want to be privy to the darkest inner workings of my parents' relationship and I told her so. She respected my request. Because we had shared everything in the past, I felt that by refusing to hear the details of their breakup I was somehow betraying her. But I didn't know how else to handle it.

Though they were discussing divorce, we continued to socialize as a family in public. Sometimes I'd watch my mom and Ted sitting together, looking shiny and powerful in their dress-up clothes and celebrity personas, and I knew. I knew but I refused to accept that our days as a family were numbered.

I began to occupy myself with my new life with Andy. My friends and family never understood my attraction to Andy. They didn't believe that being a decent person was enough to sustain a lifelong relationship. Though I knew we had very little in common, I was attracted to Andy because I felt physically safe around him. He was a big guy who if need be would defend me. He was also an amazing father to his child and I had no reason to believe he wouldn't be wonderful with our own child. Growing up without a father, and feeling vulnerable most of my life, I found these qualities in Andy extremely attractive. So when my mom offered to buy us a home, I accepted and Andy and I spent all of our free time searching for just the right place. And not surprisingly, Andy and I held very different opinions about what constituted the perfect house.

While Andy wanted something big and showy, I wanted something small and simple. I had my heart set on a renovated bungalow in one of Atlanta's older, diverse neighborhoods, which he called "the hood." Andy wanted a big home in as fancy a neighborhood as possible. In the end, we compromised on something big in the hood: a large, contemporary home on an acre in sketchy East Atlanta, which the folks in my mom's office quickly dubbed the Manse on Bouldercrest. I resented having to compromise at all.

After the purchase, my mom stepped in with an interior designer to help furnish and renovate. In the end, it was a beautiful home that I absolutely hated because it symbolized the beginning of the loss of me. After moving into the home, I found myself slowly morphing into what I thought Andy wanted me to be. On the weekends I was always up for a hike or a bike ride, but Andy was happier with a bowl of chips and the football game. So I stopped hiking and riding and joined him on the couch.

It annoyed him when I read while he watched TV, so I put my books aside. I started to drift away from the things I enjoyed and toward the things that interested him—particularly his number one obsession: television. The television went on from the moment we got home until we went to bed at night.

For Andy, when it came to television, the bigger the better.

Soon after we moved in, he purchased a huge television that had to be hoisted over the balcony in order to get it to his man cave located on the second floor. There was no such thing as too many channels, either. He was willing to pay for hundreds despite the fact that his taste fell toward ESPN and Jerry Springer. Oh, the hours of my life I have lost watching Jerry Springer! Over the course of our relationship, I gained about thirty pounds and lost an equal number of points off my IQ score.

Once settled into the house I directed my energies toward finding a job. I knew I wanted to remain in social services, and when I came across an opening for a program counselor working for the International Rescue Committee, a refugee resettlement agency in Atlanta, I could not have created a better position for myself. With my traveling days behind me, I thought working with refugees would feed my need to be with people of other cultures while utilizing my experience working in social service. I was ecstatic to get a position as the volunteer and resources coordinator, which tasked me with connecting newly arriving refugees with volunteers and essential items such as donated clothing, furnishings and other household items. I got to meet and assess the needs of nearly every refugee who passed through our office.

While my work with homeless women was intense, my new position was a lot more emotionally challenging. It's hard not to feel a personal connection to the extreme suffering of another. My clients came to me at their most vulnerable and confused, still healing from the physical and emotional scars left from experiences the average American could only imagine: human trafficking, war, genocide and persecution based on ethnicity, religion and gender. Though they came from diverse regions of the world, spoke different languages and believed different things, they all shared the title of "survivor," and it was my job to make sure they got the best shot possible to remake something of themselves.

They made my job remarkably easy. Having experienced what it's like to truly have nothing, they received the support from us as bounty and fully exploited it. Though it was mostly their hard work and determination that led to them prospering in the States, I couldn't help but take pride in learning that a client of mine got employee of the month or successfully completed a GED or was admitted to college. For the first time I was completely fulfilled professionally.

While work was going well, I began to develop a dislike for Atlanta. I had not lived in the same town as Jane since Los Angeles, where being the child of a celebrity is not a big deal to many people. In Atlanta, however, I often felt singled out. Atlanta was relatively new to being a place where celebrities lived and mingled, and I felt it difficult to make sincere friendships because of my parents. The circles I found myself in made Atlanta feel like a very small town, and in short order I felt I had no anonymity. To many, I was just an extension of Ted and Jane. Sometimes I was in the opposite position. When I attended sporting events at CNN Center or Turner Field with the entire family, I was often singled out by black security guards to show my ID or somehow prove that I was legitimately with my family and not some hanger-on trying to get access to the good seats (white security guards usually gave me the benefit of the doubt). Sometimes—but not always!—I could avoid being singled out and interrogated if I held my mother's hand. But woe unto me if I got distracted and found myself bringing up the rear.

Compounding this problem with the city was that many in the African-American community still held fast to a lot of ideas I found antiquated and offensive. Once I went to Piedmont Park with a young black woman I had met at an event; we got along fine and seemed to have a lot in common. I suggested we put a blanket down on the grass and relax in the sun; she looked at me stunned and said, "Let's go over to the shady spot instead. I don't want to leave here looking like a field slave!"

I threw myself into my work and my relationship, trying to convince myself that I'd be happy if I tamed my wandering spirit and molded myself into the perfect worker, the perfect fiancée. Though I had few examples of couples actually experiencing fulfilling careers and long-term matrimonial bliss, I couldn't help believing that I could achieve it. So I went to work early and left late. I began to tuck away all those aspects of myself Andy found annoying or intimidating like frayed cuffs on a fancy dinner jacket. And for a while it worked. I'd managed to work and tuck myself into a zombielike state where I became accustomed to feeling nothing. No matter that I'd given away my life in exchange for weekends, ten days a year vacation time and a warm body to sleep next to at night.

But something deep inside refused to allow me to give myself away completely. I could not bring myself to agree on a wedding date. No matter how much Andy pressed, I made excuses. One of the best was telling him we could set a date when he got himself out of debt. Andy was buried in so much debt I knew it would be a while before he could get out from under it. Months went by, then a year passed since our engagement. Then another and another.

Then, like a kiss from a prince, my trance was broken by two very interesting e-mails. The first came when I began having trouble with my laptop and Andy allowed me to use his computer to check my e-mails. He failed to close his e-mail account before I got on, and an exchange between him and a female caught my attention. They talked of twisted bed sheets and sweet kisses. Reading the explicit back-and-forth of their romantic romp made me realize that it had been months since Andy and I had been intimate. An intimacy I had not missed.

I was surprised that I was not angered by proof of Andy's infidelity. While we were far from satisfied with each other, we got along reasonably well and rarely fought. I didn't know how to break up with someone I was not fighting with and I wasn't the type to create drama where there was none. So I saw these steamy e-mails as a lifeline out of my dead-end relationship. I confronted Andy with the e-mails and, rather than admit to infidelity, he tried to make me the bad guy. His response was indignation at my invasion of his privacy. It was a masterful performance. But I stuck to my guns and proposed that we break off our engagement. Next came the tears. From him. While I wanted to end the entire relationship then and there, he convinced me to give the relationship more time. I knew Andy didn't have the money to move out so I suggested he move to another bedroom while he saved money to move out, and I returned his engagement ring.

We continued to live together but I no longer felt obligated to subjugate myself to him. I began to read again. To dream again. I read a book by Bill Bryson called *A Walk in the Woods*, about hiking the Appalachian Trail. I began to fantasize about walking the trail myself. I bought camping equipment, stashing it away in my downstairs office, and went on long training hikes at Kennesaw Mountain National Battlefield Park on the weekends.

Things got more interesting at work too. Over the past few months I'd become increasingly dissatisfied. It was a familiar cycle. I'd come onto a new job excited, only to work myself into the ground and take out my anger and frustration on my fellow coworkers. I went from being one of the most hardworking and optimistic folks in the office to a total grump full of nothing but criticism for everyone and everything. Things got so bad my boss told me she was considering letting me go. But before she could, I got an e-mail that changed everything.

One day in the summer of 2001, a coworker sent me an article in *The New York Times Magazine* about a group of refugees dubbed the Lost Boys of Sudan. The Lost Boys were a group of nearly twenty thousand Sudanese children orphaned during the second Sudanese civil war, which began in 1983. By 2001, with no end to the war in sight, the U.S. government was in the process of resettling about thirty-eight hundred Lost Boys in over thirty-eight cities in the U.S. Atlanta alone was getting three hundred Lost Boys. Many would be resettled by my office.

Like many people across the country, I was blown away by their story. While still children, these kids walked over a thousand miles through the wilds of Africa in search of safety. Many would die of starvation and be attacked by wild animals and soldiers along the way. They'd eventually turn up in a refugee camp in Kenya, where they'd spend the next decade waiting for an end to Africa's longest running civil war.

A few weeks after I'd read the article, a group of them were standing in my office. I did not expect that these young men would be so poised and hopeful. They had many questions about school. All had hopes of going to college and returning to Sudan to rebuild their country. Most of the refugees I'd worked with were individuals and families primarily looking to rebuild their lives. But these so-called Lost Boys were already talking about rebuilding their country.

They were tall and rail-thin, with clothes hanging from them like scarecrows. Their skin made me think of a line from the James Weldon Johnson poem "The Creation": "Blacker than a hundred midnights / Down in a cypress swamp." When they came into my office in small groups, they were polite and often deferred to some predesignated leader among them who asked most of the questions, which always centered on school.

I knew from having lived in Africa how the young people there dream of being educated like other kids dream of owning the latest sneakers or computer game. And unlike in the States, teachers are held in high regard. It took a while but my colleagues and I eventually convinced them that school could wait until we got them decent housing and jobs.

Over the next few weeks, more and more Lost Boys came through my door and shared their stories with me. One young man named Abraham talked of seeing his village burned by the horseback-riding Muslim *mujahideen* soldiers from the north. John talked of how frightened he was to have to walk at night to avoid the soldiers. He walked during the day anyway because he was more afraid of the soldiers than of Africa's big predators, which are most active at night. Emmanuel told me he lost friends when they were forced to cross a crocodile-infested river. Another spoke of being so thirsty he drank his own urine.

They also had inspiring stories as well. Joseph told me about the songs they sang to one another to keep their spirits up on the march. How they made little animals out of mud to keep the smaller boys entertained. Stories about an aid worker in the refugee camp who would bribe the boys with cookies to get them to come to school when longing for their lost parents made them too weary to leave their shelter some days. They often used a proverb to explain to me how they felt about the war in their country: "When two elephants fight, only the grass suffers." And when I asked one young man if they were called Lost Boys in the refugee camp, he told me, "No. We're not lost, because God knows where we are. In the camps, the elders called us the seeds."

"Why were you called the seeds?"

"Because like seeds we are expected to reach fertile soil. And now that we have, we must plant ourselves and grow strong. Then we must bear fruit. We must bear fruit for our country."

I was in awe of these young men. I wanted to do everything in my power to make sure they got more than the necessities. I wanted to help fulfill the hopes the elders back in the refugee camp had for them. So, soon after meeting the Lost Boys, I quit my job at the IRC and started the Lost Boys Foundation. With a grant from the Fonda Family Foundation I hired two women who had been mentoring Lost Boys and rented several small offices from my mom in the same building that housed her teen pregnancy prevention organization, GCAPP.

I created the Lost Boys Foundation to raise awareness about the plight of refugee children, the war in Sudan and as a vehicle to help secure scholarships, volunteer support and other needed resources for the guys. My ultimate goal was to build up the organization, and when the guys had gone through college, pass it on to them as a platform for them to help bring about change in Sudan. The worst thing I could envision was for these young men to survive all the horrors of war only to fall through the cracks in America.

Lucky for us there was a great deal of interest in their story. In fact, unbeknownst to them their greatest asset would be their stories. Their stories and their resilience. In a world where too many turn to drugs and alcohol and other self-destructive vices to lessen the pain of past traumas, here were the Lost Boys who somehow were able to look forward rather than backward. Local and national media were on the story, and I was optimistic that I would be able to quickly raise more funds for scholarships. Then everything changed on September 11, 2001.

I was at work on Tuesday morning prepping a young man acting as a spokesperson for the Lost Boys for a meeting I had arranged at Morehouse College, when I heard about the first plane hitting one of the towers. Someone turned a television on and I saw the second plane hit. At the first plane I thought, *What a devastating tragedy.* When the second plane hit I knew we were at war. I was stunned. I didn't know if we should go to our meeting. I asked Abraham what he thought. He looked at me puzzled and said, "Why would you let this stop our work? They have the towers, don't let them have this." That simple truth got me mobilized and off we went.

When we entered the building at Morehouse, I remember the receptionist was crying but she led us to the boardroom where our meeting would take place. To my surprise, everyone showed. Before we began, we said a prayer for the victims of the attack and in a solemn mood proceeded with our meeting. I gave my pitch requesting that the school match students to Lost Boys for mentoring and tutoring. They listened. The meeting ended early when people began to excuse themselves. They were interested in getting to their TVs as more information was coming in about the attacks. Unbelievably, the towers were collapsing.

Shortly after 9/11, another Lost Boy would arrive. His name was Valentino Achak Deng. He was scheduled to come to the States on 9/11. His flight was canceled. He got another flight a few days later. He told me he was afraid he would not be welcomed into America after what happened. Then he felt saddened that war had followed him all the way from Africa.

Valentino was particularly bright and, I soon learned, an excellent public speaker. I recruited him often to speak to church groups and schoolchildren about their story, and he never left a single person unmoved and unwilling to support us.

But a group of refugees from Sudan were no longer on the minds of a nation mourning their dead and looking for ways to help support the victims and their families. I thought our cause was lost, but I underestimated the generosity of Americans. There were many people who still wanted to support us, even in the midst of a national tragedy.

So while we continued to get support in the form of volunteers and donations, we still had to think of more creative ways to raise awareness and funds for the Lost Boys cause. So I reached out to the writer of a book I was reading about a young man who lost his parents to cancer and takes on the responsibility of raising his younger brother. The story struck me as a westernized version of the Lost Boys' tale. The book was *A Heartbreaking Work of Staggering Genius*, the author Dave Eggers.

I sent him a letter via his publisher asking him if he'd heard the story of the Lost Boys and if he'd be interested in writing a story about them. Dave responded and graciously agreed to come to Atlanta to meet with us. I invited him to attend a birthday party. A very large birthday party. Since many of the young men had no record of when they were born, they were all assigned the birth date of January 1 by U.S. Immigration.

So I invited Dave to attend a birthday party for three hundred Lost Boys at Philips Arena. The food and gifts were donated. My gifts to the guys, with help from Ted, were tickets for all of them to attend a professional basketball game and a surprise visit from a special guest: Sudan-born basketball player Manute Bol.

The boys crowded into the large room with thirty-foot ceilings and a wall of glass overlooking downtown Atlanta. They were dressed in their finest, hugging and slapping the backs of their brothers in greeting. The volunteers who had driven them were mostly upper-middle-class churchgoers, beaming at their adopted sons with maternal pride.

I'd recruited a DJ to play the latest rap and pop hits. There was an awkward moment when the boys circled the dance floor but didn't dance. There were no girls for them to dance with, I realized. Then all at once they paired up and hit the dance floor, grooving to Jay-Z's "Parking Lot Pimpin'."

They were joyous, tossed about by flow and beats, arms high and one foot tap, tap, tapping, thin hips swaying side to side. The volunteers stood around the dance floor clapping and cheering them on. When I thought they couldn't get any happier, Manute Bol entered the room. At 7-foot-6, he's hard to miss. Manute played for two colleges and four NBA teams over his career, where his shot-blocking ability was considered among the best in the history of professional basketball. Fame and money, however, did not make him forget where he came from.

Bol was a true activist who spent millions of his own money supporting organizations working for reconciliation and education in Sudan. Many of the boys knew him from the many visits he made to refugee camps. He gathered them all around him, and in the Dinka language gave, from what I could tell, a very heartfelt speech that I assumed was probably about staying focused on school and staying away from fast women and drugs.

Dave hung back, skirting the perimeter of the party with a little pen and pad taking notes. He's kind of a shy fellow with wild curly hair. I introduced him to Manute and Valentino. I hoped that he would use Valentino as the subject of a written piece. Dave and Val hit it off, and Dave did eventually write a book based on Valentino's life. They worked closely together to create *What Is the What.*

For a while I had something to be excited about. We were getting media attention from the *Oprah Winfrey Show, World News Tonight, People* magazine and other local and national media. We hosted a large gathering on Thanksgiving for the guys. I received a small donation from Angelina Jolie. Several of our guys were cast in films. I got a young man a speaking part in the Dustin Hoffman film *I Heart Huckabees,* and a volunteer managed to get several guys cast as extras in the Bruce Willis film *Tears of the Sun.* I was also working closely with Hollywood producer Robert Newmyer, who was interested in developing the story of the Lost Boys for the big screen. We had scholarships for several guys at a reputable junior college and volunteers lining up to help. Churches and school groups regularly requested talks. The only thing we didn't have was the tons of cash I thought we'd have after more than a year of nonstop work. And other problems were coming I never even suspected.

The Lost Boys community was not as united as I had once thought. From the very beginning, I had unknowingly been stepping on toes. Though the guys were all Sudanese, tribal divisions existed that I was not aware of. So when one guy got a movie part over another, the guys from a different tribe got their feathers ruffled. The same thing applied when someone got a scholarship, or sat next to me at a basketball game, or became the subject of a book.

There was a rift growing between several groups of Lost Boys. And I was becoming a target of intense scrutiny, accused of favoring one tribe over another and failing to meet the needs of all three hundred guys. Volunteers were pulled into the growing feud, as well as a local reporter who wrote a negative piece about the foundation. My staff and I defended ourselves and held several group meetings in order to answer questions and resolve issues. But the situation had gotten too far out of hand. Feuds between volunteers and one of my staff became personal, and it heralded the beginning of the end. My dear friend Valentino finally told me he had been targeted for a while. He and many other young men remained my staunch supporters, but in the end I got tired of being criticized by people I'd been trying to help and shut down the foundation.

But my work was not in vain. I had succeeded in helping a Sudanese become powerful enough to be an agent of change in his own country. The book Dave Eggers wrote about Valentino became a best-seller and Dave donated the proceeds to the Valentino Achak Deng Foundation, a nonprofit working to increase access to education in post-conflict South Sudan by building schools, libraries, teacher-training institutes and community centers. Like Ma-nute Bol before him, Val travels the world speaking on behalf of Sudan.

I was exhausted by my experience with the Lost Boys. I decided that my desire to save people was really my misdirected desire to save myself. I didn't know what to do with this revelation. I did know that I needed to get out of social services. I briefly took a position as the director of community development for the Atlanta hockey team, the Thrashers. I had become a workaholic and miserable, which made me very unpleasant to live and work with. I was quick to anger and overly sensitive to criticism. I began to get into tiffs with people at work over the smallest things: my missing stapler; So-and-So looked at me sideways; So-and-So left me waiting for ten minutes. I stopped greeting or even making eye contact with people I deemed my enemies. Slowly I began to isolate myself from everyone, including my family. Even the Lost Boys who I'd remained friends with were getting on my nerves. I was thirty-four and I knew I had to make a change, and soon. I didn't know what I needed to get me out of my rut, only that it had to be huge. I needed a new series of challenges to help me find the headstrong, happy person I had once been.

CHAPTER 13

CONVENTIONAL WISDOM would have it that it's unwise for a woman in her late thirties to walk away from a well-paying job and the prospect of marriage in order to hike the Appalachian Trail. But I did that, all of that. I told Andy we were over and moved him out of the house after months of him living in the spare room. The breakup was remarkably easy. We had months to process the end and we both knew it wasn't working. He left peaceably, and the sight of that humongous TV leaving my house brought an enormous sense of well-being. After Andy left, I quit my job, sold my house, packed a backpack and left.

The Appalachian Trail, or AT, is to many American hikers what Everest is to climbers: it's the thing they must do if they want to be taken seriously. I wanted to become what they call a "through hiker"—someone who does the whole trail in one season, all 2,175 miles of it, from Springer Mountain, Georgia, to Mount Katahdin, Maine. Thousands attempt it every year but only one in four succeeds. The hike usually takes about six months.

My family was cautiously supportive. I assured them that I knew what I was doing. I had, after all, traveled extensively and was no stranger to adventure. Apart from living in Morocco and Tanzania, I'd studied outdoor leadership and gone on several extended expeditions, including a month-long trek in the New Mexican backcountry and a cross-country bicycle ride. I assured them I could handle any of the possible ailments that might await me: septic blisters, giardiasis, injuries sustained in falls, the potentially disabling symptoms of Lyme disease and the pernicious effects of boredom and loneliness.

The afternoon before I planned to begin my hike, I walked into the office of a man I'll call Mr. North Georgia. Mr. North was a friend of Ted's and, given he lived near the trailhead, was familiar with the many things that could go wrong for hikers. Mr. North Georgia was a good ol' boy/country millionaire who made his money in real estate. He had the long, lanky body of Jimmy Stewart and a sticky Southern drawl that conjured mint juleps on the veranda of an antebellum mansion.

When I told him my plan to hike alone through the woods for half a year, he took a deep breath, exhaled slowly, and said, "Yer purty. You should carry a gun." He reached into his pocket to retrieve his business card and pressed it firmly into my palm. "If ya get out dair and find ya need help, just call me. I'll come gitchu. Ya hear?"

I was aware of female hikers being murdered on the trail, and friends and loved ones advised me against hiking alone. I wondered again if I was foolishly putting myself in harm's way. After all, I was a black woman who had chosen to go on a solo hike that would take me through very small, predominately white Southern towns and long, isolated stretches of forest. Maybe there was a damned good reason you rarely saw African Americans hiking the trail. That evening, I sat alone in my room and began to seriously doubt my sanity. But the last thing I wanted to do was go back home with my tail between my legs before I even set foot on the trail. I had difficulty falling asleep that night, and when I did it was fitful.

Luckily, by the time my alarm clock went off, my courage had returned and I quickly got myself ready for one of the biggest adventures of my life. On the morning of April 7, 2007, I stood at the AT trailhead on Springer Mountain. I hoisted my sixty-pound pack (I wasn't quite able to give up my books, two canisters of mace, a blank journal as thick as *Atlas Shrugged*, and other assorted unnecessaries) onto my back and walked down the trail like I owned it.

The day was clear and cold. I was decked out in three layers of clothing—everything I had. The forest loomed above me, utterly silent, the branches naked. I easily found the first of the thousands of white "blazes"—white rectangles painted onto a tree—that mark the trail, and set off.

I kept to myself the first few days, except for an overnight stay at the Walasi-Yi Center at Neels Gap, Georgia, located at mile 32. The Walasi-Yi Center is impossible to avoid; in fact, the trail goes through the building. The center is an outdoor store and hostel that employs experienced backpackers to advise hikers on how to reduce their pack weights. I spent most of my two-hour consultation defending what I brought. In the end I begrudgingly agreed to give up one pair of hiking sandals, one of three books, and a bottle of hair conditioner. I packed these items into a FedEx box and shipped them home.

Some lightweight backpackers manage to get their pack weights down to twelve pounds. Impressive, but there is a cost. It's not unusual to wake up in the middle of the night to the sound of a lightweight backpacker slapping out jumping jacks for warmth, all because he didn't want to carry a heavier sleeping bag. Fuck that. Long-distance hiking isn't just a test of physical endurance. It's a mental game as well. Books, an extra set of clothes and abundant toiletries make me happy. And if you're not happy, you're not likely to finish.

I spent the evening in the Walasi-Yi hiker hostel, sharing a dark, stinky bunk room with about ten guys. The following morning, my fifth day on the trail, I was out the door at six A.M. The temperature remained chilly, and the air was damp. I spent mornings in a shroud of mist thick enough to drench my clothes and pack. I kept warm by marching.

Fourteen miles later, preparing to eat dinner, I realized that I'd inadvertently packed my camp stove in the FedEx box I'd sent home. This sounds as though it would be hard to do, but it isn't. Camp stoves are tiny enough to fit into the palm of your hand. Also, I'd stored it in one of the many little nylon sacks into which I'd organized all my various gear (it's easy to mistake one sack for another). I settled for a peanut-butter bagel. Then, like all good backpackers, I hung my food bag safely out of reach in a nearby tree. I lay in my sleeping bag reading, as rain pattered on the tent. Outside, I heard branches rustling in the tree where I'd hung my food bag. I yelled through my tent to frighten the animal intruder away. It worked . . . for about ten minutes. I yelled again, but was too scared and tired and cold to leave the safety of my tent.

When dawn broke I crawled out of my tent and into the rain. I was anxious to inspect what was left of my food bag. The animal had kindly left me a bagel, a bag of couscous I'd have a hard time eating given my lack of a camp stove, and some partially gnawed dried apricots.

I had to make this food last two days, roughly twenty-four miles, until my next resupply. I ate half of my soggy bagel and drank a pint of spring water.

I headed out at 7:30. At noon I nibbled from the remaining half of my bagel. Hours passed without seeing another hiker. I had envisioned my hike as not only a physical challenge but also a spiritual quest. I wanted to experience a quiet mind, but by noon on the sixth day I found myself wondering how Paris Hilton's latest romance was holding up. It was humbling to plumb the hidden recesses of my mind and find not a wellspring of wisdom, but a wasteland of pop culture and a Pandora's box of annoying songs. I hadn't realized I knew all the words to Madonna's "Lucky Star." (I love Madonna, but I've just never liked that song.)

It was nearly dark when I entered the clearing around Low Gap shelter, one of hundreds of shelters along the AT. The shelters are three-sided lean-tos on platforms. They generally sleep about six people. The Low Gap lean-to already held six hikers: all male, all white, all smelling like ass. To my relief, they squeezed together to make room for me. As I settled in, we introduced ourselves using our trail names.

The tradition of taking a trail name goes back to the early 1970s, and nearly all hikers use one. If you don't name yourself, someone will name you. I met a guy named Cum Shot (after a crowd gathered to watch him lance an infected boil with explosive results) and a cute sixteen-year-old girl who was christened Trail Bait.

Wolverine, a friendly thirty-something guy with the belly of a woman six months pregnant, loaned me his camp stove so I could cook my couscous dinner. My new friends couldn't understand how I'd lost something as vital as a camp stove. I tried to save face by telling them that it was totally out of character. After all, I told them, I'm a National Outdoor Leadership School graduate. They were unimpressed. I ate my couscous in silence.

After dinner I crawled into my sleeping bag fully dressed to ward off the cold. Three of my other shelter mates were prepschool graduates with the collective trail name of The Hobbits. I told them a friend from home had given me the trail name Rosie, in honor of Rosie Cotton, the only prominent female hobbit in the Lord of the Rings trilogy. They promised to check my progress in the shelter logs. Each shelter has a log: a spiral notebook in which hikers write poems, draw pictures or pass messages. We turned in early because Wolverine and his hiking partner, Hong Kong Phooey, were planning a forty-mile hike in the morning. I lay in the cramped, dark shelter listening to the rain dance on the tin roof. I enjoyed the body heat radiating from my fellow hikers. In the darkness I grinned. I finally felt like I belonged; also, for the first time I was absolutely sure I would complete this hike.

On April 14, as I crossed the North Carolina border, I noticed the first clear evidence that spring was on its way: budding flowers. Also changing was the terrain. Overnight, Georgia's rolling hills had transformed into steep rises and knee-biting descents.

I almost cried (twice) while ascending the North Carolina Grind, a steep, four-mile stretch of trail. My double-digit-mile days were starting to take their toll on my body. I had hyperextended my knee, but that pain was nothing compared to the screaming in my feet caused by an excruciating case of plantar fasciitis, an inflammation of the tissue that connects the heel to the toes.

The pain was particularly intense in the mornings and at the end of the day. Endorphins pumped through my system when I hiked, but once I unshouldered my pack, my body shut off the drugs. It was the worst pain I've ever felt. Experienced hikers assured me the pain was temporary: it should only last for the first three to four months. In my case, I endured this excruciating condition most of my hike and for several months after my hike ended.

The weather had improved from cold drizzle to cold sunshine when I arrived, on April 19, at the Nantahala Outdoor Center (NOC). Located at mile 134.1, at the bottom of a slick rock gorge, this compound of buildings (including restaurants, an outfitter, a general store, hotels and hostels) is a much-anticipated stop for hikers.

I was a physical and emotional wreck when I checked in. I'd slept poorly the night before and was weary from the long, bone-jarring hike down from Cold Spring shelter. I assured the receptionist that I didn't want kayak lessons. Word was that the climb down to the NOC was nothing compared to the steep climb out. I wanted to be well rested.

I peeled off my filthy gear. I washed all my clothes in the washing machine while I showered. A hot shower after ten days on the trail is, and I do not exaggerate, better than sex.

On my way back to the bunkhouse, a young woman intercepted me to ask if I was hiking the trail. She walked without a limp, no infected bug bites marred her legs, and she looked well fed. Telltale signs she wasn't a through-hiker. I told her that I was. Through-hikers are rock stars on the trail. Locals buy us meals, offer us rides and even open their homes to us.

She was a social worker supervising a group of twenty foster children, all girls, staying at the NOC. She asked me to talk to them about through-hiking.

I met the girls in a common room with big bay windows that revealed a forested hillside. The girls were tall, short, chunky, thin, black, white, Asian and Hispanic. Each was fiercely beautiful in the way of young girls made to witness the harsher side of life at an early age.

I told them that I, too, was raised in a dysfunctional home. When I was their age, I was frightened of everything. I couldn't sleep in a room alone if I didn't wedge a chair under the doorknob. But I was lucky. I was adopted by people who loved me. I got better and now I was strong enough to go on a six-month hike all by myself.

I asked how many of them would like to hike the trail one day. They all raised their hands. "Well, since you are all gonna hike the trail, you have to pick a trail name for yourself. It's best to pick something that will let people know what kind of person you are." They took turns telling me their trail names: Panther, Waterfall, Moon Dancer, Queenie, Buttercup. Each name provided a clue to the secret selves these girls nurtured. Despite their tough-luck lives, they still had the dreams and ambitions of girls raised under more innocent circumstances. If they were fortunate, they'd be adopted by loving people who could help them realize these dreams.

Those first thousand miles I endured alone, I suffered from insomnia, excruciating hip pain, several twisted ankles and plantar fasciitis. I scared off a black bear in Shenandoah National Park. I taught myself to safely read and hike at the same time. (The trick is to read only on uphills.) I volunteered on trail maintenance crews and I pushed myself to hike thirty miles in one day.

I was more than halfway through the AT before I allowed myself to accept hiking partners. I wanted first to prove to myself that I could survive on my own. I met Walker and Mellow a few days after I left Harpers Ferry, West Virginia, the AT's unofficial halfway point. We kept passing each other on the trail, mostly because Walker was faster but had to stop every twenty minutes to pee. I told him that he should get his prostate checked. He said, "Why don't you check it for me?" They soon invited me to join them.

Walker was a gangly, balding white guy from Austin, Texas, whose wife had begrudgingly allowed him to attempt his second through-hike. Mellow was an uptight Korean guy from Chicago. They were both in their late thirties. They fought often and had a pretty intense love/hate hiking partnership. Walker hoped my estrogen might cool their hostilities.

We ended up hiking Maryland, Pennsylvania, New York, New Jersey, Connecticut, Massachusetts and part of Vermont together. I thought of them as my boys. They were fun to hike with, but I was hiking more on their terms than my own. Before I met them, I was a White Blazer, trail lingo for hikers who rigidly follow the trail and refrain from taking short cuts or skipping sections. While

I hiked with the boys (inveterate Yellow Blazers, the opposite of a White Blazer), we skipped about a hundred miles of the trail.

In Vermont I left them, and briefly left the trail, to attend Troy's wedding in New York City. It was an intense shock to my system, after 134 days on the trail, to find myself battling my way through throngs of people on the streets of New York.

At the wedding, I was surprised to learn how much my time on the trail had changed me. I felt like a fish out of water as I watched the celebrity guests looking gorgeous in their designer gowns. Though I was squeaky clean and well dressed, I couldn't shake my laidback, grungy hiker state of mind. I loved being with my family but I also missed the trail.

After the wedding, I decided to pick up the trail on Mount Katahdin, in Maine (5,267 feet), and hike back toward Vermont. This is called flip-flopping, and is a great alternative when you find yourself hiking late in the season. I wanted to relax and enjoy my last weeks on the trail. I didn't want the pressure of hiking long days to reach Mount Katahdin before mid-October, when bad weather closes in.

But Katahdin, I learned, is tricky to climb no matter the season. The 5.2-mile climb to the summit began uneventfully enough. The first three miles meandered through a dense spruce forest. Birds sang, the sun shone. I passed streams and rivers, and even a cascading waterfall. Then the ground transformed to bare granite, with brutal gains in elevation. Huge boulders blocked the trail. Soon I realized the boulders *were* the trail. I was nearly rock climbing. The temperature began to drop and the wind picked up. I hadn't believed the ranger when he told me that the summit had its own weather.

At the crowded peak, I took my photo with the sign that marks the northern terminus of the AT. I was cold, tired and pissed off. I wasn't alone. I overheard several novice hikers asking if there was some other way to get down besides on foot.

At the bottom, I found a shelter and slept like the dead. I woke up refreshed and ready to take on Maine's hundred-mile wilderness, the most isolated section of the trail.

Most hikers get through this section in ten days or fewer, but I spent two weeks there. I saw moose every day and slept near glassy ponds. I nearly ran out of food twice, but I met northbound hikers who were happy to feed me.

It was during this time that I realized, after months of hiking, I'd only seen one other black person on the trail. A bearded, smelly fellow who I believed was a myth until I ran into him eating alone in a McDonald's during a quick foray into town. We chatted about how unfortunate it was that more people of color didn't get out to enjoy the great outdoors. After I had finished the trail and was back home, I found myself donating money to organizations whose missions included getting more people of color and women involved in wilderness activities.

Two weeks was the longest I had gone without access to modern comforts and world news. When I emerged from the wilderness in Monson, Maine, I checked into Shaw's hiker hostel, cleaned up, ate and planted myself among my fellow hikers on the couch. They were watching the film *300*. I had seen it, so I reached for a newspaper. A headline struck me dumb. There was a story about a young African-American woman named Megan Williams. Six people in West Virginia had kidnapped Megan, raped her and tortured her. They held her captive for a month. Finally, the police mounted a rescue. The details were shocking. In addition to sexually assaulting her, the kidnappers forced her to eat dog feces, to drink from a toilet and stabbed her multiple times. She was lucky to be alive.

In the following weeks I could not forget Megan Williams. I wondered what would make people want to treat another human so cruelly. I also wondered if I were being sent some kind of a message—an African-American woman with the same last name as mine had met the fate I'd cavalierly decided couldn't befall me. Whenever I got off-trail to resupply, I collected newspapers and searched for coverage of the story. I realized there was another reason Megan's story affected me so deeply. Megan reminded me of Deborah.

I could see my sister's beautiful caramel-colored skin, white teeth and large brown eyes, the spitting image of our handsome father. She was physically perfect except for a mass of melted skin that spread from below her right buttock to just above the crook of her knee. She got the burn before I was born, when her nightgown caught fire on a space heater. She was never ashamed of her scars, and wore shorts and bathing suits every summer. As a child, she loved to play the trombone. She was a member of the first graduating class of the Black Panther elementary school. When asked by a reporter on graduation day what she had learned, she proudly said, "One of the most important things I have learned . . . is what freedom means."

Deborah had been the mother of three children. She spent years as a prostitute and developed an addiction to crack. Through it all, she carried a yellowing, tattered copy of that newspaper article with her quote about freedom. Through years of homelessness, it stayed carefully wrapped in plastic.

I went online to research the exact circumstances of my sister's death. I found several newspaper articles. One night she was doing drugs in the hallway of an apartment building. One of the tenants, a nineteen-year-old woman named Stacey Lee, got angry and demanded she leave. When Deborah refused, they fought. Stacey drove Deborah out into the street and pursued her, wielding a kitchen knife. Fifteen bystanders on a nearby corner saw Deborah running toward them. They knocked her to the ground, taunted her, stomped on her, kicked her and hit her in the head with a wine bottle. She lay curled in a fetal position over the grate of a storm drain. Stacey Lee attacked Deborah again while the bystanders cheered her on. To shouts of "Kill her! Kill her!" Lee stabbed my sister three times in the chest, ending her life.

A street-hardened homicide detective said that he had never, in his long career, witnessed such a callous and cold-hearted slaying.

Deborah and Megan weighed heavily on my thoughts during the final weeks of my hike. I carried them through the White Mountains and to the peak of Mount Washington. I was more exhausted than I had ever been. I also had a chance to rethink why I'd come out here in the first place.

I thought I hiked the Appalachian Trail because I wanted adventure. I knew then that I hiked it for other reasons as well. I did it because my mother stopped loving me. Not because she was a bad person but because she was tired. I did it because my adoptive mother saw greatness in me. Not because it was there but because it could be. I hiked the trail because my sister's life was taken. Not because she deserved it but because she lost her way. I hiked the trail in order to free myself from those things in the world that made me tired, overwhelmed me and led me astray, in order to see clearly these women to whom I owed so much. This in turn helped me clearly see myself.

I chose to end my hike in Crawford Notch, New Hampshire, in a beautiful valley at the entrance to the White Mountain National Forest, just as the leaves were beginning to turn colors. I sat in a deck chair and watched the sun set, the clouds spilling over the mountains. I wished Deborah could have been there to share it with me. I felt her presence as strongly as I did when we were girls, crammed into a little green car, looking up at the blank screen, waiting for a story to begin.

CHAPTER 14

AFTER COMPLETING THE AT in early 2008, my relationship with Jane was strained. She had become, unfairly, the reason for everything that was wrong in my life, for my growing feelings of disconnect that filled me with anxiety. I began to reject her advice and support. I pulled away from her even as she struggled to reel me in. At the same time, my Oakland family was weighing heavily on my mind. A small, newly discovered place in my heart believed I needed to reconnect with my Oakland family; a much bigger place was as opposed to the idea as ever. I had already invested so much energy in becoming a badass who didn't need anybody. I didn't need my family in Oakland, nor my family in Atlanta. And in my mind there's only one place real badasses went when they wanted to leave everything and everyone behind: Antarctica.

My love affair with Antarctica began unexpectedly some years before in an IMAX theater in Atlanta, watching *Shackleton's Antarctic Adventure*, a film about Captain Ernest Shackleton, one of the greatest figures of the Heroic Age of Antarctic exploration. He set sail on the vessel *Endurance* with a crew of twenty-seven to attempt the first crossing of Antarctica from sea to sea via the South Pole. But an early spring brought icy seas that froze his ship fast for ten months in the frigid waters of the Southern Ocean.

With the advent of spring, the men were hopeful that the climbing temperatures would release the sea's grip on their vessel. But the spring brought heartache not hope. Instead of releasing them, the fracturing ice put tremendous pressure on the hull of the ship, eventually crushing it and leaving the men stranded on an ice floe. And so began a two-year, seemingly insurmountable struggle that would end with all the men rescued and Captain Ernest Shackleton being hailed as one of the greatest leaders under hardship the world had ever seen.

I sat in the dark, mesmerized by the grand, otherworldly beauty of Antarctica rolling off the screen like so much confection. How could a place be so beautiful yet so alien? So peaceful yet foreboding? I completely understood Shackleton's desire to insinuate himself into Antarctica's good graces despite the fact that to nestle close to such a place, for many in his day, was to welcome in heartache, hardship and often death.

In my eyes, Shackleton was the ultimate badass. And what girl doesn't love a badass? Sure he could use a bit of a makeover. The greasy slicked-back hair with a part down the middle reminiscent of Alfalfa from *The Little Rascals* did little to highlight his hotness, but still I was smitten. After the film, I headed to my local bookstore and bought everything I could find about Shackleton and Antarctica.

The opportunity to visit the continent did not present itself for several years. It was during some random Internet surfing that I stumbled across a Web site looking for people interested in working in Antarctica. I applied immediately. Several months later, I was hired, pending a very intense physical qualification process in which I would have every orifice poked, prodded and critiqued like a baked squab at the judges' table on *Top Chef*. In the end I passed with flying colors.

I was hired as a general assistant. A GA, in addition to being one of the lowest-paid positions, is a jack-of-all-trades post that also has the added perk of lots of travel on the continent. Antarctic jobs are very competitive and I couldn't believe I'd made the cut on my first try. I had done it. I was now a participant in the United States Antarctic Program.

As with my decision to through-hike the Appalachian Trail a few years before, some of my friends and family were a bit baffled by my decision to work in Antarctica. While it is true I am not a fan of the biting cold (biting cold being anything below 50 degrees), I was willing to endure the hardships of Antarctic weather in order to walk in the steps of my hero.

I stepped out of the secure confines of the C-17 Globemaster III, a large military transport aircraft operated by the United States Air Force, into the tail end of winter on the world's highest, driest, windiest and coldest continent.

The day was clear and sunny but a marrow-freezing -28 degrees in September. Brutal. My forehead and ears felt like high-powered blowtorches were burning them. My lungs rebelled against the chilled air, and within seconds I was wheezing and coughing like a two-pack-a-day asthmatic. It had been 110 degrees when I left my apartment in Tucson, Arizona, over a week earlier.

My first steps onto the frozen continent brought to mind something I'd read somewhere about hell. Turns out the prophets' original depiction of hell was not fire and brimstone. It was a frozen wasteland. A place where a snowball would feel right at home.

Despite being dressed from head to toe in specialized extreme cold weather gear (ECW), I was still cold. I took a few obligatory photos, then made a beeline for the large orange (unheated) bus that was waiting to take us to McMurdo Station, which would be our home on the ice for the next five months.

McMurdo Station, also known as Mactown, looked like a small, rundown mining town—not the space-age research base I'd envisioned. There was a fire station, a small hospital, a power plant, dormitories and many other utility buildings in dire need of fresh coats of paint, scattered around in a seemingly haphazard fashion. The roads were unpaved.

Soon after arriving, I met my new boss, Jesse, a funny, sweet-faced young beauty with long brown hair. Our workplace was easy-going and a lot of fun. We listened to music all day as we went about our duties. Our workspace was in an old building that looked like a funky New York loft inside. Our second-story window provided a majestic view of the sea ice and the Royal Society mountain range.

My job involved preparing gear packages and survival bags for the scientists and workers to use in the field. I also scheduled training sessions for them on topics such as how to safely drive across a crack in the ice. I learned that safety in the field all boils down to the Boy Scouts' credo: Be Prepared. The gear packages we prepared consisted of tents, sleeping bags, stoves, survival bags, first aid kits, tools, extra clothing and food. The survival bags had enough food for two people to survive for three days. There was also reading material in each bag. My coworkers competed to imagine the most twisted books to include: *Alive*, *The Donner Party Chronicles* and *Into Thin Air*. In reality we stuffed bags with Sudoku puzzles and Larry McMurtry westerns.

The most important piece of gear issued to every United States Antarctic Program participant is Big Red: a seven-pound, goose-down-insulated parka with a fur-lined hood, thirteen pockets and a gray patch on the back that reflects radar. The patch comes in handy should Search and Rescue need to find you (or your corpse) in a whiteout.

Big Red's *raison d'être* is to keep you alive. But after a few weeks on ice, you quickly learn its limitations and advantages. Physically overexert yourself in the field in Big Red, on days that are relatively warm, and you are in danger of overheating and committing one of the cardinal sins of cold weather survival: sweating. Sweating in cold weather can be deadly because it can quickly lead to hypothermia.

These ubiquitous coats are reused every season, and many show the wear and tear of years of hard use: torn cuffs, frayed collars, stains, patches, faded color. But as with a good lover with a wild past, you quickly come to overlook these imperfections.

Since everyone wears the same coat nearly every day, a Velcro name tag is adhered to the front pocket in order to distinguish one from another. But in Antarctica, opportunities for entertainment are limited. Thus some folks took great joy in switching the name tags on the coats. So every once in a while someone goes to retrieve their coat from the coatroom after lunch only to find that they have either lost twenty pounds or Big Red has gone through a miraculous growth spurt. And with over a thousand coats on base, it will be a bitch to track your coat down. Ha. Ha. Hee-fucking-larious.

So how did one improve the odds of not losing one's coat? You must bond with it. You must become intimately familiar with the myriad characteristics that make your coat unique. Scent, texture, battle scars. Everything. Some became so bonded with their coat that they could walk into a full coatroom and in seconds, like a mother penguin searching for her lost chick among thousands, distinguish their coat from dozens of others.

I had such a relationship with my Big Red. My coat was one of a few in nearly pristine condition, its only issue being a sticky zipper. Such coats are highly sought after by some Antarcticans. I loved my coat. It got me through Happy Camper hell and any number of forays into the field relatively unscathed.

One afternoon, I decided to wash my beloved coat. While it was in the dryer, I made the foolish mistake of leaving the laundry room for ten minutes to go to the restroom. When I returned, the dryer was empty and placed on top of it, like some sort of sick offering, was a strange, mangy Big Red. I had fallen victim to the switcheroo. It's a harsh continent.

The work of the first month centered on getting the station ready for main body. Main body is the group of contract workers and scientists that descend on McMurdo Station a month after the early birds. The season began with 320 of us. It felt fairly crowded at that number. When main body arrived, our ranks swelled to 1,100. Gone were the days of long showers, short lines for meals and relative quiet in the dorms.

McMurdo Station felt like a big polar summer camp or frat house. Many rooms even had bunkbeds. Most of the residents were outdoor types who had climbed mountains and traveled the world. Many were social outsiders who found it difficult functioning in the rat race.

Every day the air was charged with excitement as we adjusted to the fact that we were actually "living the dream." But walking around in a state of wonder is not the safest state of mind for life on the ice. There was a spate of injuries that first month. We were all trained and given the proper gear to work with and live safely, but accidents happened. A friend of mine broke her wrist after flipping a snowmobile. Another sprained an ankle playing soccer; another sprained a wrist after slipping on an ice patch. And yours truly strained her back while shoveling snow. I was promptly put on muscle relaxants and painkillers. I was back to work in a day or so.

A lot of the injuries can be directly attributed to the cold. Muscles are tenser in cold environments and, when injured, heal slower. Because I often worked outdoors, I suffered from some new ache or pain each day I was on the ice. My knees swelled up for no apparent reason. My neck decided the weight of my head was just too much to support. Some days I felt as if my body had been switched out with that of an eighty-year-old ex-football player with arthritis.

I held on to the advice from others that my body would eventually acclimate. I had serious doubts. The cold is relentless in its assault. It envelops you like Saran wrap. Insinuates itself into any opening in your clothing. It is like a hungry vampire, but instead of blood it wants to suck all the warmth from your body. All the vitality from your muscles. All the swagger in your step.

Luckily our station was nice and warm inside. This wonderfully warm space can make you forget you are on the coldest continent in the world. Like the time I wanted to go to the library, which was housed next to my dorm. I grabbed my coat and strolled outside without a hat or gloves. It felt like an invisible ice giant was trying to kill me by strangulation. Within less than a minute my forehead, ears and fingers were screaming for mercy. I had to turn back.

During the worst of the cold in those early days, I spent all my free time indoors. Those days while I sat on the couch I was perfectly happy to acknowledge my defeat and watch a DVD on my laptop. I was Antarctica's bitch!

When I initially told Jane of my desire to work in Antarctica, her first question was a very baffled, "Why?" I told her that, among other things, it would give me the chance to confront my fear of the cold. I promised I'd stay in touch via e-mail, which I did. I wrote lengthy missives each month, entitled "Soul on Ice," which tickled Jane immensely.

Despite Antarctica's claim to fame as the highest, coldest, driest and windiest continent, it is surprisingly rich in wildlife. There are seals, penguins, birds and whales. There is nothing living on the continent that doesn't have the ability to swim or fly away when the katabatic winds start blowing and the temperature begins to drop.

A katabatic wind, as defined by Wikipedia, is "an Antarctic wind that carries high-density air from a higher elevation down a slope under the force of gravity. The density of cold air over the ice sheets and the elevation of the ice sheets brings into play enormous gravitational energy, propelling the winds well over hurricane force."

In Antarctica, it's all about the weather.

We were all interested in what the weather was doing. A good day and a bad day can mean more than just being cold. It could determine if we worked or not. Recreated or not. Got trapped in buildings. Got physically cut off from the outside world. We learned quickly that we were at its mercy.

So we all became obsessed with the weather. We wanted to know more than if it's cold. We asked questions about wind chill. Because if the temperature was a balmy -3 degrees, wind chill could make it feel like -50. Was it snowing and if so what was the visibility? If visibility was less than a hundred feet, you could get disoriented and lose your way. What was the wind speed? Was it strong enough to blow doors off vehicles, blow in windows or blow you across the sea ice like a lost rag doll? Enquiring minds wanted to know.

Throughout the day we were kept updated on the weather. McMurdo Station categorized the weather into three Conditions.

CONDITION 3 is observed when all of the following is true:
wind speed < 48 knots
visibility > ¼ mile

wind chill temperature > -75F

There are no restrictions. You are free to travel around and outside of town. You can work outside and recreate.

CONDITION 2 is observed when any of the following is true:

48 knots > wind speed ≤ 55 knots

100 feet < visibility < a quarter mile

-100F < wind chill temperature ≤ -75F

Recreation is limited and travel outside is restricted to town.

CONDITION 1 is observed when any of the following is true:

wind speed > 55 knots

visibility ≤ 100 feet

wind chill temperature ≤ -100F

You cannot go outside for any reason.

The McMurdo weather categories were fine, but after nearly two months on the ice I had been able to pseudoscientifically categorize the weather into five distinct categories that the average person can understand:

CONDITION COLD: You can wear that cute REI down jacket you brought from home, jeans and a pair of light gloves. It feels like a chilly but pleasant mid-December afternoon in New York or Boston.

CONDITION REALLY COLD: It's time to break out Big Red, the huge down-filled parka assigned to all visitors to Antarctica. You have a fleece on under Big Red, a pair of wind pants, a warm hat and mittens. Dressed like this you feel pretty insulated from the worst of the cold.

CONDITION DAMN COLD: Big Red is zipped up to your nose and the hood is fitted around your head, depriving you of peripheral vision (not that there's anything to see but blowing snow mixed with black volcanic sand). You must start wearing your extreme cold weather (ECW) gear, which includes glove liners and gloves, wind pants, long underwear, a fully engaged balaclava, polar sun goggles and special foot protection called "bunny boots" made for extreme weather in Antarctica. Most people have never experienced weather like this and may ponder if it is similar to a blustery winter day in Alaska, right after pondering why in the hell you thought working in Antarctica was such a great idea.

CONDITION NO. WAIT! SERIOUSLY?: You need all the ECW gear the National Science Foundation has to offer, plus that scarf Grandma made for you last Christmas and a strong belief in a higher power. The wind seems to be coming at you from all directions, battering you like a piece of Alabama catfish. Despite your ECW you are still cold. When you're caught in this, it doesn't take a Ph.D. in Adverse Atmospheric Dynamics to know that it's time to seek shelter.

CONDITION UNCLE!: If you are not an emperor penguin with an egg nestled between your gut and your little clawed feet, you have no business being outdoors. All the ECW gear in the world will avail you nothing. In fact, nothing short of the McMurdo building is going to protect you from the big bad katabatic that keeps blowing and blowing and blowing.

After the main body had arrived, I learned that I was scheduled to attend the season's first Happy Camper training. All employees and scientists who do work that takes them out of Mactown and/ or into the deep field have to go through Happy Camper training. Happy Camper is a euphemism for Survival Training. I asked a veteran for any advice she could give me regarding Happy Camper. She cackled and said, "Get right with God."

Happy Camper began in earnest on the sea ice about four miles outside of Mactown and one mile from New Zealand's Scott Base. Scott Base is a lot smaller than Mactown and sits on the edge of the sea. The total population is under thirty. Its small modular buildings are elevated on stilts. They are all the same shade of green that resembles the flesh of kiwi fruit. From the barren patch of ice that was our home for twenty-four long hours, we could see Scott Base.

After being dropped off on the sea ice with our gear, we walked a mile and a half along a flagged route to the instructor's hut. It's a large, solid, semipermanent structure where the instructors slept and some were courses taught. It was rustic but heated.

It was Condition Damn Cold. Our instructors continued the course outdoors. As we stood close together listening to our instructors, every inch of our bodies was covered, including our faces. It would be nearly impossible to distinguish one person from another if not for the name tags we wore on the front of our Big Reds.

Our first task was to go to an unheated shed and assemble sleep kits: two ground pads, a sleeping bag liner and a sleeping bag. We then unpacked and assembled two Scott tents (ten-foot-tall cloth tents) and five regular tents. Then we built a three-foot-high, forty-foot-long wind wall around our camp from snowpack. We actually sawed square chunks of snow from the ground and built a wind wall! We were doing all of this while trying to stay warm, which wasn't easy. We were not allowed to go to the instructor hut to warm up and have a hot cup of tea. The right to take breaks was suspended. I began to miss my easy days working at the Berg Field Center with my filthy-mouthed but break-loving supervisor, Jesse.

We started Happy Camper at nine A.M. It was closing in on six P.M., and we had still not had a break. We ate lunch standing up outside. Our instructors were telling us we must build a Quonset hut—a shelter similar to an igloo—made of snowpack. After that we must construct a trench shelter. This is a deep hole that has a sleeping compartment dug out horizontally at the bottom. It looked like a grave.

Around nine P.M., I couldn't feel my fingers or toes. We were told the virtues of each shelter. The Quonset hut was the warmest, followed by the trench (grave), the Scott tents and lastly the regular tents. I (like nineteen other folks) got my mind set on the Quonset hut. But there were a few housekeeping chores that needed to be done before we would be left to decide among ourselves where we would sleep. The only instruction we got was that there must be at least three people to each structure. However, before all the work was done, some stealthy cocksuckers started moving their gear into the Quonset and the Scott tents. I unfortunately was not one of those stealthy cocksuckers. I ended up sleeping in a regular tent.

Around 9:30 P.M., we were done setting up camp and the instructors left us to cook dinner and turn in. Though it was nearly ten P.M., the sun was still shining. People were boiling water for dinner and hot drinks, others were planning short hikes before bed, and others were socializing. I was pissed off because I was cold and had to sleep in a regular tent, so I crawled into my tent and wrapped myself in my liner and bag fully clothed. I figured I'd take a short nap before dinner, and within minutes I was dead to the world.

I woke up to absolute silence and there was no one else in my tent. I looked at my watch—it was 3:30 A.M.! I missed dinner and the others must have thought this tent was full. My feet and hands were as cold as they were before I turned in, despite the chemical hand and foot warmers under my gloves. Worst of all, I heard the wind howling outside and my bladder was about to burst. I spent the next three hours rationing my power bars and trying to use mind control to will my bladder to hang in there until 8:30 A.M., when we would be allowed to make contact with our instructors.

I finally broke around 6:30 A.M. and made a mad dash for the outhouse. Of course it was freezing. The snow wind wall we spent so much time and effort building was oriented toward the south, the direction from which most wind comes. We also oriented the openings to our sleeping structures in the opposite direction:

north. However, the wind decided to blow in from the north. As I walked back to my tent from the outhouse, I noticed that the entrance to the Quonset hut was completely snowed in. The folks who slept there would have to crawl up through the freezing snow to get out. I grinned the grin of the vindicated as I passed the snowed-in Quonset on the way back to my humble tent that luckily had entrances on opposite ends.

When 8:30 A.M. rolled around, we deconstructed all tents, ate and repacked all tools and sleeping kits. The graves were also filled in.

I learned later at our debriefing that I was one of only a few people who actually slept. The two guys who slept in the graves seemed to have had it the worst. The folks in the Quonset were blown on by the north wind and had trouble breathing because our instructor forgot to tell them to make air holes. Most everyone said they were cold or uncomfortable. But the purpose of the exercise was not to find a way to survive the night with the comforts you'd find spending an evening at The Four Seasons. The purpose was to get through the night alive and with all your digits. That we did.

It wasn't until I was safely back in my room in Mactown that I noticed I had frostnip on all of my finger tips, most of my toes and the tip of my nose. After my Happy Camper ordeal, there were days when I hoped and prayed that my next assignment would be doing data entry at the Science Support Center or the Chalet, civilized assignments that meant I would be indoors, in front of a computer, surfing the Internet, taking breaks, drinking tea, staying warm.

Because I have office skills, I had had a fair number of such days. But inevitably my job did take me outside. One morning I found out I was getting an assignment that I had been dreading for a while: flagging roads. This entails going out on the sea ice on Ski-Doos with a sled loaded down with an ice drill and flags attached to bamboo poles. Every hundred feet, we would drill a hole and set a flag in order to create a discernible road in an expanse of white.

This sounds really exciting except for the fact that it was incredibly cold and the task would take all day. The fact that we were flagging the road leading from Mactown to Penguin Ranch, a field camp devoted to emperor penguin research, did little to brighten my mood. I had heard from other support staff assigned to Penguin Ranch that the scientists had not captured any penguins yet. I fully expected to be disappointed as well.

But my mood brightened when I discovered that I'd be wearing a bright red bunny suit for my Ski-Doo ride. Red is my favorite color. When we got out on the ice and began flagging, the work went by quickly. We started at nine A.M. and were done flagging by noon.

As we pulled into Penguin Ranch, I spied seven beautiful emperor penguins hanging out in a fenced-in pen. We were told by Dr. Paul Pagonis, the head of the project, that they had just brought them in an hour ago. They seemed pretty calm for birds that had just recently been chased down by an old college professor and several grad students, dumped and sealed into large trash cans, put on a helicopter and flown to this little pen far out on the sea ice. Dr. Pagonis said he had to chase one for half a mile before he caught it.

He then asked us if we wanted to check out his dive hole. No, he's not a dirty old man. He was talking about what looks like a manhole cover in the ice. When you lift the top off, you are looking straight down a Plexiglas tube that goes about twenty feet beneath the ice.

You climb down rebar steps to a small room at the bottom just big enough for two people. The room is encased in shatterproof glass and affords you a beautiful, indescribable view of the ocean and the bottom of the sea ice above. I got an added surprise when I was below and saw a Weddell seal swim by. It was very peaceful and surprisingly warm inside the dive hole.

When I climbed back out, I met Dr. Pagonis's wife, Mrs. Dr. Pagonis. She is a doctor too. We talked for a while about penguins and seals. She shared that she had also been to East Africa, and so I found myself speaking Swahili to a penguin expert on the Ross Ice Shelf. I think that might be a first.

Since we were done with work early, we decided to go by the Weddell seal nursery to see the new seal pups. On the way we saw a group of ten Adélie penguins in the wild. We pulled over our Ski-Doos and the curious penguins began to run toward us. I guessed they didn't see well and it took them awhile to notice that, though we were standing upright, we weren't penguins, because they suddenly stopped, about-faced and slid off on their bellies in the opposite direction.

So we hopped back on the Ski-Doos and went to see the seals. The scientists there led us to the moms and babies. We stood about ten feet from them! The babies were very cute but thin. They were born with almost no blubber. Instead, they had thick fur called "seal pajamas." For them it's like being wrapped in five fur coats.

My day got progressively better. The only thing that could have sent me over the edge was if we were to see a killer whale poke its head up through the sea ice just as we were about to pull into

Mactown. But if that had happened, my head would have exploded with joy.

When I found out that I'd be going to the West Antarctic Ice Sheet Divide (WAIS) for three weeks, I was less than thrilled. The bitter cold of my Happy Camper experience was still fresh in my mind. I wasn't looking forward to weeks of living out of a tent, relieving myself in pee bottles and unheated outhouses, shoveling snow in order to make enough water for a two-minute shower in a co-ed bathroom, in addition to other field camp hardships.

Little did I know that these things would pale in comparison to my adjustment to the sheer emotional magnitude of living in such an alien environment and my sudden insertion into the off-beat camp community.

When I first arrived in McMurdo, it was strange but there were still familiar sights. There were beautiful mountains every-where, there was the sea. It was frozen, yes, but it was still plainly a sea. There were animals. There were permanent buildings.

But WAIS was different. It was completely flat, white, no ani-mals; the sighting of the occasional lost skua or snowy white petrel was cause for excitement. You won't find dirt or rocks because the earth is buried under thousands of feet of ice. Nothing but snow stretching out to the horizon in all directions. There were no per-manent buildings. We lived in mountain tents for sleeping and sev-eral larger tents for medical, recreation, eating, et cetera.

WAIS is a place unlike the rest of the world, which is ruled by biology. In the rest of the world, things are mating, birthing, living, dying. WAIS, on the other hand, is ruled by cold, hard physics: pressure, friction, speed, drift. Only dead things grow and fade here: the ice sheet, the cloud cover, the wind, the temperature. Even the sun is alien. In this flat, barren place, it is easier to see that the sun never touches the horizon. It circles overhead like a great unblinking eye. It is a stingy sun. Hardly ever does its warmth reach us. It floats above us, a stark reminder of a familiar comfort hopelessly out of reach.

The never-setting sun had a strange side effect. I would wake up several times during the "night," perhaps because the presence of the sun shining through the thin walls of my tent was telling my body it was time to wake up. I woke up on average every two to three hours, every day for the entire three weeks. Once, I left my watch in the galley while washing dishes and went to bed without it. When I woke up, I didn't have it to let me know what time it was. It's useless to peek outside because midnight and eight A.M. look exactly the same. I had the choice of crawling out of my tent into the cold and trudging the quarter mile from tent city to the galley only to find it deserted because it was midnight. Or I could go back to sleep, potentially missing breakfast and being late to work. That was a stressful evening. I made the right choice, however, by opting to go back to sleep.

WAIS is known for its bad weather. This far into the continent, it is quite common to be "treated" to some of the coldest temperatures, strongest winds and heaviest snows Antarctica has to offer. Sometimes a bigger problem occurs when the weather is simply overcast. When the sky is overcast, the contrast between the ground snow and sky is almost zero. You are suddenly unable to orient yourself. A dark hat someone has dropped on the ground twenty feet in front of you looks like a huge building somewhere off in the distance. You stumble around because you step into depressions in the snow that are suddenly undetectable. People liken these weather conditions to being trapped inside a giant white ball. For safety reasons, no outside work can be done on days like this. In short, you never forget for a second where you are. WAIS won't allow it.

After I was at WAIS for almost a week, the camp supervisor decided to treat me to a boondoggle. A boondoggle is a morale-boosting field trip or experience to release the boredom and frustration of monotonous camp life. A boondoggle in McMurdo can mean a trip to see seals at the pressure ridges, a trip up Mount Erebus or a trip to Cape Royds to see a penguin rookery. Boondoggles weren't so exciting at WAIS. My boondoggle was on an old Twin Otter plane carrying eight hundred pounds of explosives, several 55-gallon drums of fuel and some kind of compressed gas in large canisters. I was squeezed in the back of this plane with this menacing cargo. The only other people on the plane were the two pilots up front.

The mission of the flight was to deliver these supplies to another deep-field research team called CReSIS. CReSIS is the Center for Remote Sensing of Ice Sheets. Its mission is to develop new technologies and computer models to measure and predict the response of sea level change to the mass balance of ice sheets in Greenland and Antarctica. I had briefly met some members of this small crew (ten folks at most) before they took an overland traverse from WAIS to their research site. The land traverse took several days. It took forty-five minutes in the Twin Otter.

During the flight, to keep my mind off thoughts of the plane crashing to earth, leaving behind nothing but a smoking crater and a mushroom cloud, I focused on the single track left by the traverse vehicles, which was still visible in the snow days after they left. There was nothing else to see. Once the WAIS camp was out of sight, there was nothing but a flat, white, featureless expanse with a track across it. Twenty minutes into the flight, I smiled when I noticed the perfectly straight line left by the traverse vehicles suddenly turn into loop-the-loops and a doughnut. I could imagine the driver not being able to stand the monotony any longer and deciding to shake things up. Though the vehicles they used on the traverse can barely break thirty miles an hour, I'm sure the loop-making must have been exhilarating.

I was happy to see little dots on the horizon. CReSIS. As we approached, I got a lump in my throat. The camp from the air looked so insubstantial in the vastness of Antarctica. It was just a few mountain tents. They looked so vulnerable. Forget that these are experienced field researchers and contractors who had been working in places like this for decades. From my perspective on the plane, they looked as formidable as a splattered bug on a windshield. What chance would they have against a really brutal storm, or if someone got hurt? Help was at least an hour away by air, days by land.

Several CReSIS team members were on hand to greet the plane. I rushed out of the plane into the arms of my friends. Though it had only been days since our last meeting, it felt like much longer. I made sure to hug each of them at least twice. I'm sure they thought I was just being nice but it was more than that. I was giving them a proper good-bye should anything horrible happen to them. When the plane took off for the return to WAIS, I had the irrational feeling that I was abandoning them.

That night I didn't feel so well. There was this heaviness in my chest. The next day I was lethargic, couldn't eat dinner and had trouble getting to sleep. Somewhere around three in the morning I was able to diagnose my problem. I thought, *Could I . . . ? Could this possibly be . . . homesickness?* I'm never homesick. Never. Not when I picked up and moved to Morocco or Tanzania. Not once biking across the United States, through-hiking the Appalachian Trail, relocating to Tucson, Arizona. Never. Somehow Antarctica managed to get me. Subconsciously I had translated the vulnerability of CReSIS into a reflection of my situation in WAIS, in the world. I had an epiphany that no matter how fit, hardy and capable we think we are, from the right perspective we are all vulnerable. I'd stayed in contact with my family and friends via e-mail, even the limited access to e-mail at WAIS, but it was not enough to fend off my crushing loneliness.

Leaving WAIS was bittersweet. What I thought would be a challenging experience (it was) was also one of the most rewarding of my life. I would have liked to stay longer. But I was needed back in Mactown, so off I went. By the time I returned to Mactown from WAIS, my five months in Antarctica were coming to an end. The thought of leaving was unpleasant. I wasn't ready. I began to look into staying on and working the winter season, all the time wondering how I'd fare living on a base reduced to a hundred souls. What would it be like to spend months in the winter darkness? I began to covet bragging rights to spending a solid year on the ice. So I reapplied for several winter jobs, and when my summer assignment officially ended, I began the required physical qualification process all over again. But because I was over forty, I was required to receive a mammogram, which could not be done on ice. Arrangements were made for me to fly to Christchurch, New Zealand, for the screening.

It was early January 2008 when I got off the plane in New Zealand and walked into a world pleasantly basting in 90 degrees. The smells! The colors! Your sense of smell atrophies in the cold. The eyes grow used to only seeing white and the earth tones of the buildings and the dirt roads of Mactown. But New Zealand in January? My God! And so just like that, the spell was broken. Broken by the beauty of wildflowers, rolling green hills, butterflies, a radiant sun and the complex scent of a busy city. I suddenly became acutely aware of all the aches and pains my body had been hoarding all that time on the ice. I thought of other adventures not yet had. I let go. I let Antarctica go. It was time to make room for others. I'd already gotten what I wanted. What I needed. There was nothing left to prove. But I was bringing something away with me. The ice opened up a space in me that I was now ready to fill with family. Again.

CHAPTER 15

AND YET I DIDN'T GO straight home. I took an assignment at a wildlife refuge in Alaska, thus fulfilling my dream to be bipolar. Then I took several more temporary positions in North Dakota, California and Oregon. It was while living in the caldera of a volcano in central Oregon in 2011 that I finally decided it was time to go home. After spending years obsessively traveling everywhere, except Oakland, the pull of home became a little too strong to resist. I'd made half-hearted attempts in the past, like an ill-prepared alpinist pushing for the summit of Everest, but each time I noticed that at even the faintest signs of trouble, I hightailed it back to base camp.

My first attempt was after a colleague at an Alaskan wildlife refuge introduced me to Facebook. She thought the social network was tailor-made for folks like me who led reclusive and transient lives. She hailed it as the ideal way to stay in touch with friends and family. I never dreamed it'd be the vehicle that would propel me home.

Soon after I set up my Facebook account, I found myself a bit embarrassed that after a little more than four decades of life I'd only managed to amass eighty or so friends, family and acquaintances that I could list as Facebook friends, compared to the hundreds, sometimes thousands that some of my friends, barely into the second decade of life, could boast. Out of a sense of inadequacy, I trekked deeper into the landscape of Facebook, and thus into my past, in search of more people I could lay claim to. That's how I found Neome Banks, someone I hadn't seen since childhood.

Neome and I grew up as the children of Black Panthers. Like me, Neome was the baby girl of her family, raised by a single mother. As small children we spent most of our time at the Panther-run school, starting each day with a hot breakfast followed by calisthenics, classes and afterschool activities. After leaving the Party, we hung out in the tiny bedroom she shared with her two older sisters in her family's apartment down the street. We listened to cassette tapes of Michael Jackson, Marvin Gaye, the Pointer Sisters and the Commodores while gossiping about the goings-on in the neighborhood. She was my first true friend.

In her Facebook photo, Neome still closely resembled the young girl I once knew. I clicked on "Add as friend," and, across space and time, she accepted my friendship. Again. Through our correspondence I learned that Neome was still in touch with one of my birth sisters, Teresa, who was also on Facebook. And so, after typing in Teresa's name and seeing her picture pop up, I friended my sister too.

Just like that, we closed the void. After high school, Teresa went on to college and graduate school to become a college professor. When our sister Deborah was killed, she had really stepped up, along with my mother, to help raise her two children.

Teresa and I began sending each other Facebook messages and e-mails. She told me she'd recently divorced but was happy, and lived alone in a modest apartment by the sea; her daughter was now a tall young woman with long black hair and severe bangs. Then we reminisced about our family—a great-aunt who covered her sofas in thick plastic and kept hard candy in little crystal dishes on the coffee table in her living room. We coveted those brightly colored sweets but were admonished to only take one each. We recalled another great-aunt whose house always smelled of boiling chitterlings, and our mother's father, China, who with his bald head and chubby body resembled the Buddha at birth and in old age. She told me our mother had stopped drinking and that they took a cruise together. She e-mailed a photo of them on the deck of a cruise ship. Our mother was plump, dressed in a purple pants suit paired with a loose pink blouse, sitting on a red mobility scooter. Her close-cropped hair was now gray, but her face was unlined. Though she wasn't smiling, she looked fiercely happy sitting there in the sun on the deck of a ship headed for Mexico. My sister knelt next to her smiling a smile not unlike my own. Her hand rested on our mother's arm.

Seeing this picture made me weep. My mother looked vulnerable but regal, so different from the woman I remembered. Out of nowhere I fantasized about forging a new relationship with her and Teresa. We could travel together. We could recapture the good times before our family fell apart. I wanted to visit, I told my sister. Considering the lives they led now, and how they appeared so unlike the childhood snapshots in my head, I opened my mind to the possibility of a reunion. I bought a ticket to Oakland and Teresa invited me to stay with her. I couldn't believe how fast and stress-free things were moving. Teresa gave me our mama's phone number and told me to give her a call. "She'll be happy to hear from you. You don't know how many times she has cried missing her baby daughter."

Instead of warming my heart, this statement reignited my anger. "Misses me?" If she missed me, she would have reached out to me well before three decades slid by. I told my sister I didn't believe I was missed. I told her I remembered well the abuse, the neglect. We argued.

The possibility of a reunion fell to ruin in the wake of my rekindled anger. Defiantly, she withdrew her invitation of a place to stay. She told me that she was angry too. Angry with me for turning my back on our family. A few days after the fight I reached out to her again. I told her I was still coming and if she wanted to meet, I was open. She let me know she was no longer interested in seeing me. The night before I caught my plane to Oakland, I sent her one last e-mail, letting her know the dates of my trip and giving her my cell phone number in case she changed her mind. She didn't respond. I thought that, at the very least, I'd get to see my old friend Neome.

The clear, warm beauty of the Oakland weather belied the storm brewing in me. I was waiting to meet Neome at the train station when I saw her approaching on foot with a small boy. She recognized me instantly and we embraced. She was tiny, thin and not much taller than she was as a young teen. She still possessed flawless ebony skin and a radiant smile.

Her seven-year-old son, Josael, was biracial, with caramel skin and thick, curly black hair. He stared at me with his mother's almond-shaped eyes, shyly hiding behind her. Neome and I had very difficult family dynamics growing up. Yet Neome still lives near her mother. They spend holidays together, visit often and are fiercely loyal to each other. Neome even left her children with their grandmother so we could spend a few hours alone. How did two girls so alike end up so different? I wanted to ask Neome if she would have accepted the opportunity of a better life, if one had come along, even if it meant leaving her family behind. But I was afraid of how she might answer.

Teresa waited until the last day of my trip to call, which pissed me off.

"Hello?" I said.

"You sound like me," she said.

"Who is this?"

"Teresa. Funny how our voices sound alike."

"No, they don't."

"So, how are you?"

"Fine."

"Well, I was just checking in."

"Great. I'm kind of busy. So . . ."

"OK."

"OK."

Click.

It was an awkward and unfulfilled end to my first real attempt to reconnect with my family. Though it stung, I was also relieved. There was obviously still a great deal of pain and unresolved anger that needed to be aired. I wasn't sure I wanted to wade into that particular cesspool. So I chalked up the experience as a valiant effort on my part that was not realized through no fault of my own. I figured it would have to do as the closure and validation I needed to support my decision to stay away.

I went back to the Bay Area the following spring to work as an environmental education teacher at the San Francisco Bay National Wildlife Refuge. The refuge was less than an hour by public transportation from Oakland. Though I would be in the Bay Area for the next four months, I had no intention of trying again to reconnect with my birth family. I did make a few stealthy trips into San Francisco and Berkeley to visit friends and a few museums, always praying that I wouldn't run into anyone I was related to.

So there I was. Again. So close and yet so far, and totally cool with that. I was still licking my wounds from being shut out by my sister. Instead I wrote about my ill-fated reunion, a piece that was published in O, *The Oprah Magazine*, and by means of that writing, I felt I had, for the most part, processed decades of trauma in eight thousand words.

When I first went to live with Jane, one of the first heart-to-heart talks we had was about anger. I had a hard time dealing with the emotion. My coping strategy was to completely repress it. The problem with this was that when I did get upset, my anger was way out of proportion to the situation. A stranger inadvertently nudging me on a busy street or a perceived snub from a waiter in a restaurant would have me seething with anger that I'd immediately wrestle back into the little cage within I'd created for it. While I was often bubbling with barely contained anger, I was good at keeping it concealed behind a façade of equanimity. Jane knew this about me and encouraged me to deal with my anger rather than repress it. She even went as far as to tell me that it was OK to be angry with her. "No matter how angry you get, let it out. Even if it is at me. I can take it." I believed she was underestimating just how angry I could get and I vowed that I'd never turn my anger on her.

Throughout my teens, twenties and thirties, I was able to keep the beast caged, but as I entered my forties I found it more and more difficult to cloak my anger. I dubbed this period my Terrible Forties. I was an emotional chimera of a two-year-old and a sulking teenager, extremely sensitive to even the most benign criticism or perceived insult. Even Jane was not exempt. Where previously I had been open to any and every bit of advice and constructive criticism she had, now her advice and even the sound of her voice grated. I'd never missed our family holidays, and now I began to boycott them. And when Jane failed to invite me to her seventieth birthday party in Argentina, I became so enraged I partially lost my vision for a few hours and suffered a massive migraine that lasted for days. When I recovered enough to respond to this slight, I sent her an e-mail informing her that she was no longer my mother. And I meant it. I was thoroughly ready to throw away my relationship with Jane and be completely motherless.

Jane responded by e-mailing and calling repeatedly to say, "I am your mom!" I deleted all of the messages and consigned any messages from her and her office to junk mail. She continued to e-mail and call. It was weeks later before I agreed to meet with her. She flew out to Arizona to talk. When I saw her, she looked so worn out and confused I immediately felt bad for my behavior, but my anger quickly overrode those feelings. We were both in tears and she apologized for not inviting me to her party. I told her I accepted her apology but it would be another two years before I truly let it go. I remained contrary, passive-aggressive and distant whenever we were together. She remained patient, open and loving. Every waking moment of those years, I was angry, sometimes openly, though most times it hummed through my body like a low-grade fever. But it was always there until I realized that I wasn't mad at Jane. I was really mad at my birth mother. I was torching Jane in effigy of my mother.

CHAPTER 16

IN THE FALL OF 2011, I was sitting in bed at three A.M. reading Mary Karr's memoir *The Liars' Club*, which chronicles the author's experiences growing up in a family struggling with alcoholism but also incorporates wonderful moments of humor and familial warmth. As I read, thoughts from my own childhood began to intrude. Not dark memories but pleasant snippets, mostly about my mother. The memories carried me from my bed and deposited me in a chair at the kitchen table in the little yellow house. Mama was at the stove stirring a huge pot of gumbo. The memory was so vivid I could smell the spices, sausage and shellfish. She was wearing her royal blue muumuu with yellow hibiscuses. She was still young, tall, powerfully built, thick-legged, wide-hipped and busty.

I smiled, put my book aside and powered up my laptop. I retrieved the picture Teresa sent me over a year earlier of our mother and her on the Mexican cruise ship. Though I had looked at the picture dozens of times, it struck me for the first time how old and frail my mother looked and how little time she had. How little time we all had.

It took years for my pent-up anger to drain away enough to free me to reconnect with my birth mother. I was for the first time able to remember her clearly and not through the haze of my pain and anger. My birth mother was not a monster who failed me but a woman who did her best in the face of poverty, addiction and social injustice to raise her children. My anger was gone and in its place a newfound respect for the woman I'd hated for most of my life. I was finally ready to go back.

For fun I decided to Google her to see what popped up. I typed in her full name and poked the Enter key. My heart stopped when Google slapped me with an obituary for Mary Nell Kennedy. In a panic I opened the link and was relieved to see, instead of a photo of my mother, a picture of a bespectacled, gray-haired white woman in a plaid jacket with a huge red bow around her neck. Definitely not my mama. But the thought that it could have easily been her unsettled me.

I e-mailed my sister Teresa. It'd been nearly a year since my last awkward phone chat with her. I was tired of fighting. I needed to let her know where my heart lay and I wrote:

Hello Teresa,

I'm writing to let you know that I will be in the Bay Area in early 2012 and would love to try and meet again. I've carried a lot of anger and regret and I'm proud that I am at a point where I no longer feel the need to carry it anymore. I know that our mother did the best she could with what she had and in retrospect she did an amazing job. While life was far from rosy she made sure we were fed and clothed and had a roof over our heads. About a year ago I visited our old house in Oakland and I thought it would stir up bad memories. But the opposite happened. I remembered us playing Monopoly, making rock candy by heating water and sugar in a spoon over the stove, playing Pac-Man.

I'd forgotten the good times we had. I've also been thinking that our mother is getting older and I would hate to lose the opportunity to see her and get to know her. And to let her know I have thought of her and truly appreciate the struggles she faced in trying to raise us.

I would love to meet with you, Mama, Randy, Deborah's children, everyone eventually, and try to rebuild a positive relationship.

Best,
Mary

The minute I sent the e-mail, my anxiety lowered. I placed my laptop on my nightstand and picked up my book again, not expecting to hear back from my sister until the following afternoon if at all. A few days later she responded. I sat staring at her e-mail in disbelief but unable to open it, scared that she'd reject my offer. Scared that she wouldn't. In the end I decided to shut my computer down without opening her e-mail. It felt like slamming the lid shut on a box of vipers.

When I mustered up the courage later that day to read her response, I found an open invitation. She gave me our mother's phone number and suggested I give her a call on Christmas Day, which was a few weeks away.

"She'll like hearing from you. You don't have to talk long if you aren't able. Just say hello."

I got a sheet of copy paper and wrote "Mama," "Christmas Day" and the phone number on it in big block letters with a black Sharpie and stuck it to the refrigerator. Not because I was afraid I'd forget to call but to get used to a daily reminder over the next few weeks that I was finally going to hear my mother's voice.

When Christmas arrived, I waited until the early afternoon to call. I dialed the number and was relieved when an automated voice told me to leave a message. I hung up before the beep. I called back a half an hour later and after three rings was about to hang up again when I heard,

"Hello?"

Other than sounding a bit crackly and out of breath, her voice was the same.

"Hey! It's Lawanna."

"Lawanna?"

"Yeah. It's me."

"You sound like Deborah's daughter. I thought this was Deborah's daughter. You sound just like her!" she said with a chuckle.

"No. It's me. I got your number from Teresa. I wanted to wish you a Merry Christmas."

"Merry Christmas to you too!"

"I also wanted to let you know I'll be in the Bay Area in the New Year. I was thinking I'd come and see you."

"You gonna come by?"

"Yeah."

"OK! If you got a pen I'll give you my address!"

"No. I don't need it right now. When the time comes I'll call again and get it from you."

"Oh. OK."

"Well, I just wanted to say Happy Holidays and I'll see you soon."

"OK."

"OK."

(Awkward pause.)

"Well, I have to go but I'll see you soon."

"Lawanna?"

"Yeah?"

"I love you."

"Uh . . . love you too."

"Bye."

"Bye."

I hung up the phone completely dazed. That was the first time I ever remember my mama saying she loved me. I said I loved her too because that's the appropriate response, but I didn't completely believe that. I said it because a part of me did love her. Never stopped loving her.

The lady I had just spoken to sounded like my mama, but the sweetness and openness that the voice carried was new. The overall impression I got was . . . cuteness. A cute little old lady taking a holiday call from her middle-aged daughter as if they had never spent more than a few days apart.

Was it possible that the drunk, angry, depressed mama had mellowed into a sweet-hearted granny? My rational mind was not easily convinced, but my heart had softened. The weeks leading up to my Bay Area trip suddenly seemed less daunting.

CHAPTER 17

I ARRIVED at the oakland airport in late March. From the moment the plane landed on a day as gray as tepid dishwater, my main objective was to get out of Oakland as soon as possible. Within minutes of snatching my luggage from the carousel, I boarded a train for San Francisco. From the train window, the city's despair oozed from the shabby houses, the struggling residents, even the graffiti was sad and pathetically executed.

While many things languish in Oakland, some things have always thrived. Oakland, like any ghetto worth its salt, can boast robust exponential growth in several businesses: organized crime, churches, liquor stores and fast-food joints. It is a rare block that is not inhabited by one. Many host all four.

The sense of gloom didn't lift until the train left Oakland, slid under the bay and emerged in San Francisco, where I booked a hotel room perched precariously on the boundary between the affluent shopping and residences of Union Square and the squalor of the Tenderloin. One could literally stand on the corner where the hotel sits, look to the right and be face to face with dozens of the city's underclass gathered for the social services offered by my hotel's neighbor, Glide Memorial Church. If you looked to the left you'd see scores of tourists toting huge shopping bags emblazoned with the logos of upscale department stores like Macy's, Nordstrom's and Bloomingdale's.

Standing on that corner where these two worlds meet, I couldn't help but think how for the past two years I'd also been standing on a similar line of demarcation that runs between my birth family and my adopted family. Though a narrow strip of metaphorical macadam separated these two worlds, crossing between them was no easy feat. Once one has crossed from one to the other, re-entry was as hazardous as a rocketship's fall through the upper atmosphere. The potential to crash and burn was great.

I settled into my hotel room and slept for twelve hours. Then I called my mama. We made plans to meet. I took the train back across the bay and hailed a taxi back to our old neighborhood. She had not strayed more than half a dozen blocks from the little yellow house.

During the taxi ride, I struggled to keep pessimistic thoughts at bay. My mood lifted when my big, burly Nigerian cab driver unself-consciously started singing along to Celine Dion's "The Power of Love," which blared from the radio. As a huge Celine Dion fan who gets berated by my friends for my predilection, I found his unabashed enjoyment of the song charming and a mood booster. When he pulled up in front of my mama's house, in a show of support I joined him in belting out a verse before I got out:

Lost is how I'm feeling lying in your arms
When the world outside's too much to take

He grinned at me in the rearview mirror. I grinned back.

My mother lived in a little beige house with dark green trim, with a tiny yard out front teeming with overgrown grass and weeds. Four steps led me onto her concrete porch and past a picture window. I tapped solidly on the black wrought-iron security door. I waited. I tapped again.

"I'm coming!" my mother said through the closed door. I could hear her fumbling with the lock. When the door opened, I had a hard time seeing her because her house was dark inside and the black iron mesh of the security door was obscuring.

"I can't move fast. It takes me a minute. Whew!" she said as she swung open the security door. I noticed right away that she had shrunk. At least a foot. Contributing to her short stature was the fact that she had a back problem that prevented her from standing fully erect. Her hair was a wild, white cotton ball and her eyes twinkled with a combination of mischief and glee. She was wearing an oversized T-shirt and cotton pants with an elastic waistband and brown Ugg boots. She reached for me and we hugged. It was a hug I had been waiting for for a very long time. There was no emotional preamble. In my imaginings this hug took place in slow motion accompanied by a sound track worthy of a 1940s melodrama. In reality it felt more like two acquaintances meeting after a brief absence as I rested briefly in Mama's arms.

She invited me in. Her living room was dark, warm and close. The curtains were drawn and streaks of cigarette smoke drifted throughout the room like cloud cover. She told me to relock the security door.

"You can't forget to lock up around here." She chuckled and walked in a slow, plodding way back to her overstuffed chair that sat facing a flat-screen TV tuned to *The People's Court*.

"Wow! You have a lot of pictures!" I said, noticing dozens of family photos, many I'd never seen, ranging from large 8x10's to tiny wallet-sized, lining the walls and resting in frames on bookshelves. We never displayed photos in my childhood home. There were old photos of my siblings: Deborah as an infant, a large photo of my mama in her twenties holding my baby brother. A photo of me and my brother sitting on the floor at Soledad with Daddy in front of a mural. Louise as a smiley little girl. My paternal grandmother, my mother's great-aunts. Several photos of Deborah, Donna and Teresa as little girls before the other siblings came along.

All of my siblings in various life stages were represented, including pictures of me from elementary school. In one photo I was smiling brightly into the camera with a perfect sphere of an afro. I was wearing a heavy coat, which was my custom even on warm days to mask my growing bosom. I recognized childhood photos of Donna's daughter Latasha and Teresa's daughter Atraui. My brother, Randy, now a husky full-grown man with wife and child. There was an adult picture of my sister Louise with her children. She lives in Las Vegas. Mama told me her firstborn were twins, which made me smile because when we were kids and played the board game Life, she always wanted to have twins in her car token as it rounded the board.

There were many children I did not recognize. Nieces and

nephews conceived, born and grown up in my absence. Mama instructed me to show her the photos of the people I did not know.

"My blood pressure acts funny if I stand up and sit down too much."

I showed her a family portrait of a young light-skinned woman surrounded by five children. "Oh, that's your niece Latasha and her kids. She live in Houston." I pointed to a dark-skinned little boy. "That's Donna's other child, Bruce." I showed her another photo of a beautiful brown-skinned little girl with thick, long braids standing with a handsome, slim boy. "These are two of Deborah's children. Teresa and I raised them after Deborah died."

"Where are they now?" I asked.

"Oh, they around. They was the sweetest little thangs when they was little. But because Deborah was using crack when they was in her, they went kinda wild when they got older. We couldn't handle them. They grown now, living they lives." She told me Deborah's firstborn, a boy, was born with severe birth defects from his mother's drug use and remained in the hospital for a year after his birth. He was adopted by a caring family after he was well enough to leave the hospital. He would never learn to walk or speak. Mama showed me pictures in a photo album of my sister looking thin and sickly in the hospital, holding the baby she'd never raise.

"She visited him a lot when he was in there. Because he was born with so many problems, she made sure she didn't use as much crack when she was pregnant with her other kids."

I stared at all these faces staring at me from the wall. I didn't know how they could bring my mother comfort. All I could think about when I stared into these faces was how much many of them suffered.

"Hey!" my mother said. "Get me that photo album over there on that shelf." She pointed to a book resting on a shelf to the right of the TV.

"This?" I asked, touching it.

"Yeah. Bring it here," she said, gesturing for me to sit in the overstuffed chair next to hers.

I sat down and began to pass the photo album to her. "No. You open it." I took it onto my lap and opened it and saw photos of me. Photos taken after I went to live with Jane. There was a photo of me graduating from high school, pictures of me hiking the Appalachian Trail. There were enough photos to fill half the book. Many of the photos I recognized as ones I posted on Facebook. Someone (probably Teresa) had downloaded them and had prints made.

"I've been following you," my mother said, staring at me intently.

"So I see," I said. This collection of photos made me feel as if I'd just discovered I had a stalker for several decades. I returned the photo album to its place on the shelf.

"So you live here alone?" I asked.

"Well, me and Marsellus."

"Marsellus?"

"My Rottweiler!"

"Your Rottweiler?"

"I got him when he was a puppy. His full name is Marsellus Wallace, after that tough guy in that movie *Pulp Fiction*."

"Oh." I thought: *Who is this woman? She never showed the least interest in dogs before, and now here she is with a Rottweiler as a companion?*

"He out there in the backyard. You can go look at him but don't go out, he don't like strangers. The only people he like is me and Atraui. Teresa and Randy scared of him 'cause he's so big."

I walked a few feet toward the back of the house and pulled the drapes back, exposing a sliding glass door. Lying in the middle of the yard was indeed a big Rottweiler. He stared at me through the glass, mildly curious. I was a dog lover, so to me Marsellus didn't inspire fear. I thought he looked downright cuddly.

"He's so cute!" I cooed.

"Yeah, he's a good boy. He's normally in here with me but I put him out for you."

I took my seat next to her and noticed the various prescription bottles on the little end table between us.

"What are all these for?"

"Lawanna, I got a lot of thangs going on. High blood pressure, COPD, arthritis, sleep apnea, asthma . . ." she said as she lit up another cigarette.

Like most old people, she went into a detailed description of her medical history over the past decades. I sat across from her, riveted.

"I have an appointment with the doctor to get my own oxygen tank soon," she said proudly. In that warm, smoke-filled room with disgruntled litigants screaming at one another on the television, I was thinking I could benefit from an oxygen tank myself. Though I was feeling a bit queasy from the cigarette fumes and the too-warm room, I couldn't imagine any other place I'd rather be than right there listening to Mama telling me about how much she hates wearing her dentures.

I spent a couple of hours catching up on that first visit, and

when we embraced to say good-bye, I felt an unexpected closeness. When she called out "Love you!" as I descended her porch
for the waiting cab, I paused to tell her I loved her too. And I
meant it.

Uncle Landon was coming to pick me up at the BART station near
his home. He still lived in the Fruitvale neighborhood, which was
just one BART stop from Eastmont, but the two neighborhoods
couldn't have been more different. As I exited the Fruitvale BART
station, I reflected on how the Fruitvale neighborhood had always
been a step up from Eastmont, but while Eastmont had slid farther
downward over the years, it looked to me as if Fruitvale had held
steady and in some respects improved.

When Uncle Landon pulled up and stepped out of his car, I was
surprised to see he had not aged much at all. He was sixty-eight
and still tall and fit. He told me I was heavier but wore it well. As
we drove along, Uncle Landon told me about his recent return to
the Bay Area. A lifelong community activist, he left for several
years to do community organizing in post-Katrina New Orleans.
He and his current wife had returned to Oakland almost a year
previously—he and Jan had been divorced for over a decade—and
were still in the process of unpacking.

We pulled up in front of the always welcoming two-story bungalow with the large tree out front, and I was flooded with pleasant
memories of hanging out with Uncle Landon, Aunt Jan and my
cousins. I remembered taking my then two-year-old cousin Thembi
to a yard sale next door and how the homeowner greeted my cousin

with baby talk and she responded in full sentences and how impressed the woman was. I remembered setting the table for dinner and playing with my cousins. I spent a lot of time in this house. I was sure that without my uncle and the sanctuary he provided, my life would have been a lot more hazardous.

When we went inside, the house enveloped me in its familiar woodsy scent. They had done some renovating over the years, expanded the house to create a beautiful family room, but for the most part it was the same: bright, clean and welcoming.

I asked about Daddy, and Uncle Landon said that Daddy went back to prison for five years for domestic violence. He didn't seem to want to tell me much more about him. I got the feeling he didn't want to talk about Daddy because he didn't want to tell me that he wasn't interested in seeing me. Though I would welcome a visit from my father, I was not troubled by his continuing absence. Uncle Landon showed me some recent photos of Daddy and it looked as if life had not been treating him so kindly. My once vibrant, handsome father stared back at me from a photo as a shrunken old man with a hard, weathered face. I have a hard time missing him because I never truly knew him.

Uncle Landon wanted to know what I'd been up to professionally, and I spent the next hour and a half telling him about my travels and my work history with the homeless, African refugees and the environment. He seemed to swell with pride at each revelation. I could see that more than anything, he was proud to know that I, like him, did work that benefitted others.

Next he got out the photo albums and caught me up on my four cousins who, unbelievably, were all grown women. One cousin was married and lived in the Pacific Northwest, another was in college in San Francisco, another lived up the street with my Aunt Jan and had a small daughter. Another also lived in Oakland and had two grown sons, one of whom got into some scrapes with the law and was living with Landon. I told him I was glad to see he was continuing to be a shelter in a storm. That made him smile.

Mama and I took a trip to see her aunt Nell, my great-aunt, whom we visited occasionally when I was growing up. Aunt Nell was one of twelve children. At ninety-five years old, she was one of the remaining two. My aunt Nell had one of the few homes in the neighborhood in which the front and back yards were perfectly manicured. Her lawn was like a neon green shag carpet, and it seemed colorful flowers were always in bloom. As we pulled up to her house, this fact has not changed in a neighborhood where many houses fall into neglect. Aunt Nell's little house was still a showpiece.

She didn't have small children in her home often, so it had a cream-colored carpet and was decorated with lots of little breakable porcelain and glass figurines. There was a crystal figure of a seal balancing a ball on the tip of its nose that I was particularly attracted to as a kid, but I never got to do more to it than stare and dream. While at Aunt Nell's, Mama watched us like a hawk to ensure we didn't destroy anything.

"Don't touch that!"

"Get away from there!"

"What did I just say?"

With dark looks and threats, Mama was usually able to keep us under control. Unlike our house where anything goes or Uncle Landon's house, which was child-friendly, Aunt Nell favored French colonial reproduction furniture with the cushions sealed in thick plastic and glass-topped coffee tables. We had to be on our best behavior. If we were good, Aunt Nell would reward us by allowing us to take a piece of candy from one of the candy dishes she kept on the coffee and end tables. We had our choice of a mint, toffee or Jolly Rancher. I always chose the toffee, which I'd promptly pop in my mouth, and spend the next few minutes savoring the sweetness until it was a distant memory on my tongue.

When we entered Aunt Nell's house that morning, everything, including the crystal seal and the candy dishes, was in its rightful place. But the gleam was gone. After more than twenty years, the plastic was no longer hermetically sealing the couch, which was finally showing a bit of frayed edges. The cream-colored carpet had dark tracks in the high-traffic areas, reminding me that we were in another time.

Aunt Nell, who had been a heavy woman, was now rail-thin but sprightly. She hugged and kissed me enthusiastically. She used a walker to get around and was a bit hard of hearing, but aside from that she was as well preserved as her furniture. I can only hope to be as fit in mind and body at ninety-five years old.

We spent the afternoon looking through photo albums. Aunt Nell had really old photos I'd never seen of my mother's mother. There was a photo Mama was proud of. It showed her mother as an infant in a frilly white gown with a small ring on her finger.

"My mother's family was from Texas and dirt poor, but look

how rich she look in this picture! She even got a ring on her finger. Most kids ain't got rings but my mama had one," she said, staring at the photo.

There were also photos of Aunt Nell and her sister, Aunt Dilly, as young women and newly arrived in Oakland from Texas. They were sitting near the water with their hair done up and wearing pretty dresses. My favorite was a picture of Mama as a girl of five or six years old. She is alone and stares at the camera solemnly. Even at that young age she seemed not quite sure of her surroundings but ready for anything.

When we finished reminiscing and prepared to leave, Aunt Nell told me I could have a piece of candy if I liked. I reached over and plucked a toffee from the candy dish on the end table. I unwrapped it and popped it in my mouth, anticipating the rich creaminess. What I got instead was a mouthful of stale candy. This piece tasted as if it had been sitting in that bowl since the last time I was there, decades ago. I didn't want to insult my aunt so I tried to eat it even though it tasted like I was sucking on a glob of crystallized crazy glue.

Before we left, I asked Aunt Nell to tell me the secret to her longevity. She laughed and said, "I really don't know. I ate soul food my whole life. The stuff they say is real bad for you too! I can't cook so much now, so I like to eat the fast food now. I really like pizza."

We all chuckled at this. I gave Aunt Nell a big hug and told her I loved her.

"I love you too! Will you remember to call me?"

"Yes, Aunt Nell. I'll remember."

———————

Mama told me she went to bed around six P.M., so if I wanted to visit or call I should do so before then. It was a few weeks before I learned she wasn't exactly telling the truth.

One evening I called her shortly before six P.M. trying to catch her before she went to bed to see how her day went. When she answered the phone and said hello, I could tell she was sloppy drunk.

"Hey, Mama. I won't keep you. I just wanted to check in with you before you go to bed."

"Check in?" she said with a sarcastic slur.

Here we go, I think. I knew this moment was coming. The moment I would be reintroduced to the ugly Mama who ran me off years ago. I didn't know when or where, but I knew she'd crawl out of her lair sooner or later.

"It doesn't sound like it's a good time so I'll let you go."

"No, Lawanna. I got thangs on my mind. I want to talk about the lies you wrote about me."

"That's fine, but let's do it in person."

"No! I want to talk about it now!"

"I don't want to talk to you when you're drunk!"

I could feel myself losing my temper, but she ignored what I said and my tone, and continued on.

"Why did you write those nasty things about me and your sisters? You talked about us like we was dogs."

"Did you even read what I wrote?"

"I don't want to read them lies! You not the only one who can write! We can write nasty lies about you too!"

"Did I lie when I wrote you were an alcoholic?"

She paused on the other end of the phone. I could hear her television blaring in the background.

"I hurt my knee!"

"What?"

"I drank because I hurt my knee. I was in pain."

"Well, that doesn't change the fact that your drinking got in the way of you taking care of us!"

"How did my drinking hurt you? What did I do wrong?"

"You checked out!"

"I kept you fed. I kept you clothed."

"It wasn't enough!"

I was so pissed at this point that, like a demented David Letterman, I ran down for her the Top Ten list of ways her drinking hurt our family, starting with the physical and verbal abuse and ending with her indifference to my leaving with Jane. She denied it all. Denied whipping me with an extension cord despite the fact that I bear the scars on my body.

"I never beat y'all with extension cords! That's how I got whipped when I was little, I never did that to y'all."

So that was where she got it from. In her booze-addled state, she insisted we were an idyllic family and held up my college-educated sister as proof of her good parenting. I had to really hold my tongue to keep from telling her that Teresa's success was despite her, not because of her. I wanted to ask her why only two of her remaining children wanted anything to do with her.

"You got a selective memory!" she yelled.

"No. I remember the good times. I remember when you were an awesome mother. And I remember when you changed."

"You're lying!"

"You're in denial!"

This was exactly where I didn't want to be, out of control, angry and yelling like a crazy woman at a crazy woman on the phone. My rational mind was wondering when someone would call the hotel front desk to complain about the noise.

Then I realized that this was the moment I'd been waiting for. This was my Everest base camp and I had to choose if I was going to continue climbing upward or retreat. It was time to make my stand. I decided to do the most difficult thing I could have possibly done. I stopped yelling, blaming, raging. Instead I listened. I'd open my heart and listen.

"You lie! I never hurt you. I was a good mother! You were the bad one. You were a bad child."

She recounted a time when I was eight and my little brother was seven and she sent us to the store to buy cigarettes for her. But instead of going straight to the store, we stopped by the laundromat to troll for leftover change in the slots. One of the washing machines was emptied before finishing the spin cycle and I stuck my arm in to stop it spinning. When I couldn't, my brother tried and his arm got tugged along by the centripetal force, which injured his arm.

"If I was a bad mother, I would have beat you for what you did to your brother. Because of you he couldn't play professional baseball. He could have been a great baseball player. You were an awful child."

She also told me how much my brother loved me and felt abandoned when I left, thus also emotionally scarring him.

"I'm the only one here who wants to see you 'cause I'm your mother, not Jane Fonda!"

After a while I thought my silence had a soothing effect on her. She told me I must understand that she started having kids early. She had three kids before she was twenty-one years old. "We was all growing up together."

She talked of the physical and psychological abuse she and my older siblings experienced from Daddy. How she came home one day and found my older sister Donna, just a few months old, with swollen lips from where Daddy thumped her over and over again to keep her from crying. How he scheduled her life right down to what meal should be cooked on what evening. How he came home one day, ate his dinner, looked at the schedule and saw the wrong meal had been cooked and beat her savagely. How she ran to the neighbors for help many times. One evening the neighbors called the police to report a bloodied woman running through the neighborhood. That's when the Panthers intervened and put Mama and her kids in Panther housing to give Daddy less opportunity to beat her and draw the attention of the police. She talked about how scared and depressed she got. How she'd dream about her mother comforting her, telling her she'd be all right, and how those visitations gave her the will to keep going.

"He beat every woman he was with. When I heard his last wife turned him in and he got five years in prison, I was so happy I didn't know what to do. To this day if I ever run into that woman, I'd shake her hand for what she did. I'd thank her for doing what I couldn't do."

I was beginning to understand why my mother lived like a teenager, spending her days listening to rap music, playing video games and hanging out with her friends at the mall. She was enjoying her freedom. Better late than never.

"I really did my best but it was hard. I didn't know a lot of things. I lost my mama too early. I didn't have no one to help me. I had a lot of things I wanted to do but I knew after I started having kids I'd never get to do them. Did you know I wanted to be a scientist?"

"No. I didn't know that."

Suddenly her tone changed and she was angry again. "No, you didn't! I saw how you looked at me when you first came over. I saw in your eyes how you thought I was ugly and old! Nobody!"

"No! Don't tell me what I thought! I didn't think that at all."

My heart was breaking for her. Breaking for the young girl living her life saddled with so much abuse and responsibility. Straining under the stress of being marginalized because of her sex, race and class. I finally had a crystal-clear view of the woman who was more than just my mama. She was a woman with hopes and dreams of her own. An amazing, flawed and spirited survivor born into circumstances that deprived her of being something even more extraordinary. I tried to reassure her that I was not judging her, but her anger was rekindled and she was dismissing me.

If she wanted to remember her child-rearing years as all sunshine and lollipops, who was I to deny her? I didn't want to make her see things as I experienced them. I came to Oakland to share the future with her, not the past. I told her I didn't want to fight. If she wanted to talk more, we could do it another time. We hung up.

The next day she called as if nothing had happened. She chatted about the latest episode of *True Blood* and the trouble she was having cracking a video game. "So we still going to the flea market tomorrow?" she asked. "Of course," I said, willing to pretend with her that we had not just angrily yelled at each other the night before. And, surprisingly, the next day we had a wonderful time at the flea market.

CHAPTER 18

THE WILLIAMS FAMILY was hosting "Fun in the Forest," a weekend camping trip at Samuel P. Taylor State Park across the bay in Marin County. The Williamses in attendance were my Uncle Landon, his current wife, Ora, my cousins and their friends. There were about twenty folks in all. The fact that Uncle Landon was getting everyone together for a camping trip was not surprising. I remember him always being a lover of the outdoors. One of my earliest memories is of him taking me and my sister Louise, his young daughters Thembi and Ayaan, and Aunt Jan on a trip to a California beach where we spent the day eating pizza, playing, swimming and watching the sunset before packing up the car and heading back to East Oakland.

This camping trip gave me the opportunity to reconnect with Uncle Landon's two oldest daughters, Kim and Kijana, from an earlier relationship with his current wife, Ora. I spent a lot of my early childhood with Kim and Kijana, especially during the period my father was in prison. Kijana was flying down from Seattle with her husband, and Kim was coming with one of her two grown sons. I was especially excited to see my cousin Petik, the only child of my paternal aunt, Virginia.

Though I didn't see her often, the times we did spend together were memorable. Part of the reason I didn't see much of Petik was because her parents were not heavily involved in the Party. As a small child, I identified strongly as a Panther before anything else, before being American or even female. So to have a family member not in the Party was puzzling. I thought of Petik as a tragic princess. Tragic mainly because she was an only child. I couldn't fathom how she occupied herself without any brothers or sisters to play and fight with, and she didn't have any friends over that I ever saw. Aunt Virginia and Uncle Al didn't seem to be the type of parents who'd let her just go play in the street, either. Also Aunt Virginia was an amputee who needed a wheelchair to get around. She was always well dressed and sweet-natured (she invited us all over and bought each of us Easter baskets one year when Mama didn't have the money), but I couldn't help feeling sorry for her.

Petik also had the aura of a princess. She lived in a beautiful apartment (well out of my neighborhood), and had her own room complete with a girly bed with frilly bedclothes and stuffed animals. Her toys weren't broken or abused. Her bedroom was like a real-life representation of the bedrooms of kids I'd seen on TV. When I tuned in to watch *Leave It to Beaver* or *The Brady Bunch*, no matter how many episodes I saw, the kids' beds, like cousin Petik's, were always made as if they'd never been slept in. There were never toys, clothing or dirty dishes strewn around the room, like at my house.

Kim and Kijana and Kim's twenty-one-year-old son, John,

picked me up from my hotel. When I went down to the parking lot to meet them lugging an oversized duffel bag, they took one look at me and burst out laughing and I knew perfectly well why. From the look of my bag, it looked like I was about to rehike the Appalachian Trail instead of spending a weekend in the forest. I really had not brought much. What was bulking up my bag were several full-sized blankets I was bringing to supplement a sleeping bag in case the evenings got really cold. I was not quite sure what Kim and Kijana had packed. The entire rear of Kim's SUV was nearly stuffed to capacity with just their things.

Before we worked out how we would get my bag into an already overpacked vehicle, I greeted my cousins. Kim was petite, with neat dreadlocks, and had the striking hazel eyes that I had coveted for as long as I can remember. Her son, John, was well over six feet tall, broad-shouldered, with thick curly hair and rich brown skin that was a perfect blend of his mother's African-American and his father's Mexican bloodlines. His looks were swoonable. Kijana was well built and had the baby face and radiant smile typical of the females in our family.

There were embraces all around. John crammed my bag into the rear of the vehicle, leaving Kim barely a sliver of space to see out the back window. He chastised us for our decadence and pointed out the fact that he had only brought a small tote bag to get him through the weekend. We pooh-poohed him and set off chatting a mile a minute as we scrambled to get caught up with each other's lives.

As we crossed over the Richmond–San Rafael Bridge into Marin County, John pointed out Quentin Prison, which occupies a very picturesque position on primo waterfront real estate overlooking the north side of San Francisco Bay. I thought how ironic it was that one must go to prison to get to live in such a beautiful spot but without the benefit of seeing the views. I thought about the many Panther members who had been locked up here and in places like Soledad. I felt a hollow ache in my chest for my daddy. I asked my cousins when was the last time they saw my father. There was a long pause while they tried to recall the last sighting. They conferred with each other, then told me they had not seen him since they were children and each of them was now in their forties. John had never met him. This news made me give up any hope of seeing him during that visit. It saddened me that the best memory I may ever have of him was within the walls of a prison, the only place that kept him from running away from me.

As we passed by the sweeping seascapes along the bay, through the idyllic streets of Marin and into the cool shade of towering redwoods, I could feel my body tingle with anticipation of a new beginning with my family in a primeval forest.

I stared out the window, admiring the towering hulk of the redwoods and the smaller flora like redwood sorrel, elk clover, giant trillium and mountain lilac. We pulled into the campground and drove over a little bridge that spans Paper Mill Creek, which an interpretive sign informed us is " . . . one of the last natural spawning corridors for coho salmon and steelhead trout." A hard right brought us to our three reserved campsites.

I saw two Asian fellows and a woman already parked near our campsite. Kijana pointed to one of the men and told me he was her husband, Yupo. Her face was aglow at the sight of him and I felt happy for my cousin. The other two people with him were his brother and sister. I could also see Thembi's daughter, Indigo, playing with a group of friends whom she had invited to camp with us. One of them was a white boy. I was really digging the multicultural vibe of our campsite. There were other members of our group milling around the site getting things set up before dusk. We began to unload the car, leaving most of the heavy lifting to John, who seemed resigned to the role of pack mule.

We were among the last to arrive at camp and I could see a group of women sitting in camp chairs around a crackling fire. One of the women was my cousin Petik. She jumped from her seat at the sight of me and gave me a big hug. She was a tall, beautiful woman and bore a striking resemblance to Cousin Ayaan and I told her so. This set off a round of discussion about who looked like whom, an exercise that we never seemed to tire of as we all looked so damned similar. Petik grabbed my hand and informed me that we would be tenting together.

I could see that there were several large tents already erected. They were the Cadillac of tents, multichambered and tall enough to accommodate a standing person. When I was a hardcore backpacker, my friends and I used to make fun of the kinds of people who used tents like those. To us they were "glampers," a despised hybrid of camper unwilling to leave the glamorous aspects of city living out of camping. My camping friends would be horrified to see me at a campsite harboring mega tents and a picnic table laden with three kerosene-burning stoves, a set of kitchen knives, chopping boards, saucepans, stacks of plastic cups and more food and beverages than many African villages see in a month.

I was the kind of camper fond of cowboy camping, which meant sleeping on the ground without benefit of a tent or tarp. If I did bring a tent, it was portable and about as roomy as a coffin. I cooked on hand-sized camp stoves and subsisted on Ramen noodles, couscous and trail mix. Although I am proud of my camping prowess, it had been a long day, the forest was damp and chilly and my back was aching, so I wasn't feeling very judgmental at that moment about sleeping in a two-room tent. Uncle Landon, Aunt Ora and their little dog would be in the second room, which I jokingly referred to as the master suite. I also did not feel an inkling of shame when I got excited to learn that there were hot showers to be had for fifty cents.

Petik and I ducked into our tent to get set up. I laid out my yoga mat, which would be doubling as a sleeping pad, then unfurled a spare sleeping bag Uncle Landon was lending me and laid it on the pad, along with a pillow and the extra blankets from my hotel for added warmth and comfort. I was pretty pleased with my posh accommodations. Then Petik brought out the biggest air mattress I'd ever seen. Upon being fully inflated, it was at least the height of a bed with box spring and mattress and towered above my setup. Petik smiled sheepishly when she saw me eyeing it.

"I know it's big. Sorry."

"Don't be embarrassed!" I said. "If I had an air mattress like that, I'd be using it too!" I chuckled, pointing at my suddenly not-so-comfy-looking pallet.

As evening fell, we all gathered around the fire pit. It was a chilly night but the warmth of the fire and good food kept everyone in good spirits. Cups of booze and hot chocolate and plates of turkey sausage, burgers, chips and salad settled into waiting laps. Kijana's husband, Yupo, sat a little apart from the group, surrounded by the children. He was telling scary stories. He must have been very good at it because they stared up into his face with fierce interest.

As the firewood and conversation began to wane and the cold crept in, folks started to turn from the glowing embers into the dark that blanketed the tents and waiting sleeping bags. Petik and I made our way to our tent. Uncle Landon and Aunt Ora had turned in hours before, so we tried to be as quiet as possible. It was freezing and we both opted to sleep in our clothes. Once we were tucked in, we had a whispered conversation in the cold darkness.

"I'm glad you came back, cousin."

"Me too!"

"Have you seen your mother?"

I told her I had and that the visits had gone better than I expected. She told me her father lived in Los Angeles and was doing well, but her mother died years ago. Though I couldn't see her, I could hear the sadness in her voice. Aunt Virginia was loved by everyone. Despite her disabilities, she continued to work as a rehabilitation counselor. I shared with Petik how grateful I was when her mother bought us those Easter baskets years ago. She told me that she saw my mother recently. She went over to her house with Teresa and they played cards together.

"Your mother is so funny!" she said.

"I know," I said, smiling in the darkness.

I woke up refreshed the next morning. Dappled sunshine pierced through the tent walls and I could hear the muffled voices of my aunt and uncle outside. Petik's bed was empty. I didn't know what time it was and feared I had overslept. I grabbed my toiletry bag and headed for the washroom. I ran into Petik on the way, who informed me it was only 7:30 A.M. She told me she fled the tent just before dawn for the warmth of her car. She was not the only one who was cold. Kim had gotten up in the early morning darkness, driven from her tent by cold. Petik told me she had driven back across the bay to her house to retrieve warmer clothes and extra blankets. As more and more of our group woke, the unifying complaint was how cold it was last night. Uncle Landon and I seemed to be the only two who slept well.

When I returned from washing up, I saw that another campfire was lit and surrounded by sleep-puffed faces and outstretched hands. Uncle Landon prepared pancakes he had made from scratch, while Aunt Ora whipped up scrambled eggs and sausage. Hot tea, cocoa and coffee were also on hand. The women recounted the horrors of the previous evening that mostly involved hearing raccoons invading the campsite and fighting each other over scraps of food carelessly left out overnight. A friend of Cousin Thembi's was convinced she would have been torn limb from limb had she so much as poked her head out of the tent. Another talked of having to brave the cold and beasts in the middle of the night when a swollen bladder could no longer be ignored.

Around ten A.M., Kim came back from her mission laden with blankets and a toasty looking pair of Uggs, beaming with as much satisfaction as Moses returning from the mount. Now that all our members were present and accounted for, the conversation turned to plans for the day's activities. I was looking forward to a hike but it seemed that everyone else was interested in spending the day at a nearby beach. Everyone except Uncle Landon and Aunt Ora, who were convinced that if left unattended our campsite would be looted and raided by other campers whom they eyed suspiciously.

I quickly saw that my decision to stay behind—despite a last-minute appeal from Petik—was a good one when I watched the mayhem that ensued as more than a dozen adults and four children tried to reach consensus on when and how they would get their caravan to the beach. It took an hour for them to gather an afternoon's worth of food, water, blankets and other gear. Another hour went into finding missing children and locating errant sunglasses and pullovers. What would have been an exercise in frustration for me made for great entertainment since I wasn't involved. After much fanfare they managed to get everything and everyone loaded up and on the road.

Left in the wake of the group clearing out of the campsite was a feeling of having narrowly avoided a stampede of wild horses. I could now hear my own thoughts, the songbirds and the gurgling creek. Uncle Landon and Aunt Ora were enjoying the quiet as well, as they relaxed in camp chairs and admired the view of the creek below.

I said good-bye to them and headed out into the forest to explore some nearby trails. I decided to hike the Ox Trail over to the site of Old Man Taylor's paper mill. The day had certainly warmed up since that morning, making for a beautiful day for a walk in the woods. Despite the noise from the nearby highway, I was enjoying this easy hike along the creek accompanied by a few robins and dark-eyed juncos. I was a bit underwhelmed when I reached the site of the paper mill because all that remained were a few crumbly blocks of concrete. I looped around and headed back past the campsite and jumped on the Old Pioneer Tree Trail just past the bridge and entrance station.

It was another short loop that meanders through laurel, Douglas fir, madrone and oak. The trail promised to lead me to one of the remaining old growth redwood stands in that section of the forest, which is mostly second-generation. A little over a mile in, I spotted the Old Pioneer, which easily dwarfed the younger redwoods in girth and height.

The Old Pioneer was not one tree but a cluster of trees whose bark had fused together over time. creating this towering ancient that still stands despite evidence of fire damage that has hollowed out about thirty feet of the trunk. I stepped into the crevice at the base of the tree and stared up into the darkness of the Pioneer's hollowed innards. I sat cross-legged in the shadows, closed my eyes and lost myself in the quiet and the terrene emanations of my refuge. When I emerged about a half an hour later, I was ready to shed the solitude for the comfort of kinship.

CHAPTER 19

IT WAS MOTHER'S DAY, and I was thinking of pushing Mama from a moving vehicle for backseat driving me like Miss Daisy. Her logic was that she hasn't seen me since I was a teenager, pre-driver's license, and therefore wasn't totally convinced that I knew how to safely drive the car I'd rented specifically to take her out that day. If she didn't let up soon, I would be forced to fake the sudden onset of a disabling bowel condition to get out of this.

"You have to slow down if you want to make that left."

"I know, Mama."

"Ain't that the exit? You betta get over to it before we pass it."

"I'm on it!"

Despite all the effort I had put into compiling meticulous directions to get us from her house in East Oakland to an IMAX theater in Emeryville and then to a toney soul food restaurant in downtown Oakland, she insists on trying to offer alternative routes.

I wanted her to relax and let me worry about getting us around and she wanted to show off her knowledge of the only city she had ever lived in. Things nearly reached the breaking point for me when she tried to direct me out of a Target parking lot where she had shopped for video games to blow some time in between watching *The Avengers* movie (her choice) and brunch.

"Turn right to get back to the street."

"Thanks, Mama, but I think I know how to get out of this parking lot."

She's also showing me behavior I've never even heard of, like *passenger* road rage.

"Did you see that motherfucker almost cut you off?"

"I saw him. No worries."

"Watch out for that asshole over there in the blue car, he don't look like he know what the fuck he doing!"

At least it's clear where I get my love of cursing. I tried to diffuse her anger by getting her focus off the road.

"When I went to visit Uncle Landon, I was impressed by how much the Fruitvale neighborhood is being built up."

Instead of diffusing her anger, she seamlessly redirected it and went on a rant about how little public officials have done to serve the East Oakland neighborhood.

"You know the Mexicans took over Fruitvale. It used to be black now it's damn near all Mexican!"

To Mama, Mexicans were all people south of the border, from Mexico to the tip of Chile.

She continued, "They were able to get politicians elected who gave a damn! Our representatives ain't worth shit because niggers don't vote for who's good, they vote by race! That's why we ain't got shit in East Oakland! Just churches and liquor stores! Black politicians in Oakland ain't done a motherfucking thang for us, Lawanna!"

While I sympathized with her concerns, her tone of voice and her anger made me think of the times when I was a kid and it was directed at me. My head was starting to throb but I stayed quiet, keeping my face blank and my eyes on the road, feeling like a back-country hiker playing dead in the hopes of avoiding a grizzly bear attack.

Luckily her anger ran its course just as we pulled up to the restaurant. Because of her COPD, she couldn't walk more than a few feet before getting out of breath, so I dropped her off at the curb in front of the restaurant, instructing her to go inside and wait for me at the table while I searched for a parking spot.

I took several tours around the block not because parking is scarce but to decompress from my stressful time in the car with Mama, which felt akin to Chinese water torture. Ten minutes later, after regaining my equilibrium, I got a parking spot on a side street and made my way back to Picán Restaurant.

I had scrambled to get reservations because I hadn't planned on spending Mother's Day with Mama. It had never occurred to me back in March that things would go as well as they had. So just a week before, I had found myself spending the whole day on the Internet searching for just the right restaurant that still had open reservations for Mother's Day brunch.

Picán (which serves upscale Southern food) is a black-owned business and one of Oakland's few quality restaurants. The online reviews were highly favorable and I was able to snag the last reservation. After a peek at the online menu, I knew Mama would appreciate the offerings that included biscuits and gravy, catfish, buttermilk fried chicken and slow-cooked collards—some of the foods she used to cook for us growing up.

I entered the restaurant and I was pleased to find towering ceilings, a rich décor and dramatic lighting. There was an air of homey elegance that was complemented by Michael Jackson music wafting through the main dining room filled with a multicultural crowd of large families at long tables and in booths, and mother-daughter duos at two-tops scattered throughout.

It was easy to spot Mama sitting alone and looking a bit forlorn at a small table in the middle of the dining room. I paused to take in the scene. There was a red rose on the table in front of her, given to her by the hostess. She looked adorable in one of her new outfits: a patterned top, black slacks and silken black ballerina flats. I gave her a haircut the week before, so her wild white afro was gone, replaced by a sophisticated cropped do. She looked as good as any of the women in there, but I could tell she felt out of place in this upscale crowd.

As I approached the table, I could see her slyly sizing up a sophisticated older woman who was sitting at a two-top next to ours with her daughter, who was a bit younger than me. When Mama saw me, she looked relieved. "I was wondering what happened to you."

"Yeah. I'm sorry that took so long."

While we perused the menu, we enjoyed the cream biscuits, coffee cake and maple butter our server left for us. We complimented the surroundings and peeked over to see what the couple next to us was having. The sophisticated black woman and her daughter recommended we try the ribs and shrimp and grits. Then the older woman engaged Mama in a bit of small talk and soon they were laughing and discussing recipes and stories about the welcome revitalization of downtown.

I could tell Mama was starting to feel like she belonged. The tension had left her face and body, and she was no longer glancing furtively around the room like Cinderella newly arrived at the ball.

A friendly waitress came by and took our order. While we waited for our food, we rehashed *The Avengers* movie, which we both enjoyed. We cracked each other up quoting funny lines from the movie, like when the Thor character defends his evil brother against the critiques of his fellow Avengers, then quickly points out that the brother was adopted when he is told his brother recently massacred a large number of people.

Mama also loved the scene where Thor and the Hulk, fighting side by side, succeed in defeating a behemoth from another dimension. After the beast is conquered, they stand together in victory when out of nowhere the Hulk punches the daylights out of Thor, sending him soaring out of frame.

We were nearly in tears with laughter. We discussed who our top three favorite Avengers are. We both selected Iron Man as our favorite but differed on the remaining two. Mama picked Thor and the Hulk. I chose the Black Widow and Captain America. We both agreed the Hawkeye character was a waste of screen time. Hawkeye from the old TV series *M*A*S*H* would have made a better impression.

Then before I knew it, Mama and I were deeply engrossed in a debate regarding who was the *ultimate* superhero badass, the Hulk or Superman. We go back and forth for a while. I'm standing firmly behind Superman and Mama's going with the Hulk. I pointed out that Superman could reverse the rotation of the planet. Mama countered with Superman not being as intellectually strong as the Hulk's alter ego, Dr. Banner, thus giving the Hulk the advantage of having both brains and brawn. I saw her point but in the end we agreed to disagree.

Our food arrived. We started with a tasty plate of grits and shrimp. For the second course, Mama got barbecue ribs and I got fried chicken. For dessert, we shared strawberry shortcake and chocolate cake so decadently rich it made my eyes water.

Over the course of the meal I found myself scanning her face for her reaction to each bite and asking if she was enjoying herself. It pleased me to no end that she was. After our meal and on the ride home, the car was full of the pleasant aroma of the tangy sweetness of Mama's leftover ribs sitting in a doggy bag on her lap. Mama, who loves to cook, was thinking out loud as she tried to mentally reconstruct the ingredients in the sauce used in the shrimp and grits recipe, which she planned to re-create at home. I noticed that in addition to the doggy bag and the rose, she had also taken the brunch menu from the restaurant.

When she saw I had noticed, she said a bit shyly, "I want to show my friends what they was serving."

I was genuinely sad to drop her off in front of her house. We kissed and exchanged "I love you's!" and she was out of the car. I took a few moments to flick through my notebook in search of directions from her house back to my hotel. When I looked up, I see that her friends from across the street seemingly materialized out of nowhere and had joined her on her front porch. As I pulled away, I could see she was flashing a broad toothless grin with her friends and passing what looked like the menu to one of them. On the drive home, my mind's eye envisioned her also sharing the ribs and a detailed description of our day. Cute.

CHAPTER 20

I WENT TO TEXAS to visit my niece Latasha. Last time I saw her, she was a curious little girl just barely out of diapers who secretly marked the walls and furniture of our apartment with slashes of purple marker. Now she was thirty-four years old and the mother of seven. She had invited me to Houston to attend a large family reunion. It wasn't a Williams family reunion. Latasha was abandoned in Houston by my sister Donna when she was just fourteen years old and her little brother was ten. My sister left them with a great-aunt one morning, said she was going to work and never came back. It took just a few days for our great-aunt to catch on that Donna wasn't coming back. Latasha, after nearly twenty years, was still hopeful.

Tasha met me curbside outside of baggage claim at George Bush Airport on a hot and humid afternoon in Houston that threatened rain. As she approached, I could still see the tiny girl in the pretty woman with the solid frame typical of the women in my family. She was a no-frills type of gal. No makeup. No jewelry.

From her father's side she had inherited light brown skin with reddish undertones, which folks from the South called "redbone." She also had a healthy dusting of freckles sprinkled across her cheeks and nose, not unlike Uncle Landon. Her hair was thin (a trait from my mother's side of the family) with a loose curl pattern, which she wore in a slick ponytail. Otherwise, she said, the humidity would turn it into an untamed cotton ball. She was dressed in an oversized T-shirt, Capri pants and sandals. She approached me with a shy smile. When she got within touching distance, I reached out and embraced her, kissing her cheeks deeply and repeatedly the way I did when she was a little girl.

She led me to a black car that belonged to her best friend, Sista, a very large woman with a shaved head, flawless makeup and eyebrows so manicured they looked as if they were stenciled on. She wore a sleeveless top that highlighted the soft rolling contours of her arms. Sista had the figure of the ancient beauty woman artifacts of old—flesh upon flesh that does not repel but beckons you near. When she hugged me, she smelled of flowers and her skin was cool and soft despite the heat. Her nearly hairless head accentuated the flawless symmetry of her face and the impish gleam in her bright eyes. Also present was Latasha's eight-year-old son, Maurice, a beautiful redbone like his mother. After we got in the car, he sat quietly in his mother's lap, which Tasha said was completely uncharacteristic of the boy, who can be a terror. While she told me this, he looked back at me from the front passenger seat with a little face dominated by big brown eyes and a cherub mouth with an expression that seemed to say, *"Lies! All lies!"*

We left the airport and headed toward Tasha's home, where we would spend the night and get picked up the following afternoon for an hour drive into the country for the reunion. I learned that Sista is the daughter of the woman who eventually took Tasha in after Donna left.

Tasha and Sista met in high school. Sista, who has always been very overweight, was being teased by a group of students. Tasha witnessed the bullying and decided to step in and defend Sista. She told me she did it not because it was the right thing to do but because, since her mother left, she had been holding in a lot of anger and used every opportunity she could to vent. That day she unleashed her anger in defense of Sista. They became fast friends. When Tasha became pregnant with her first child at sixteen, it was Sista's parents, Mama and Pop, who gave her support and encouraged her to complete high school despite her pregnancy.

Because Sista is an only child and had no interest in having children, Tasha became a second daughter, and her subsequent children the grandchildren of Mama and Pop. Tasha's oldest son, eighteen-year-old Ladarian, who was about to graduate high school, lived with Mama and Pop.

During the drive to Tasha's house, I told her about my memories of her as a child. About the night Donna went into labor and denied she was pregnant all the way to the hospital. I told her what I thought when I went to the hospital to see her for the first time. I was ten years old and thought my two-months premature niece hooked up to wires in an incubator was the ugliest baby I'd ever seen. She looked like a wrinkled old white man.

I told her how much I loved her when she came home. How everyone loved her. How I mourned when Donna took her and moved away. Tasha listened to my recollections with a small smile on her face. When I was done, she told me that sadly she had no memories of me. I told her we would make new ones.

Tasha lived in low-income housing on a very rough side of town. As we pulled up to her place, the end unit of a series of townhomes surrounded by a high fence, Tasha joked that the fence was to keep the residents in, not the bad elements out. Sista dropped us off with the promise to pick us up the following afternoon and was gone.

Owing to the fact that Tasha is a single mother with six children living with her, ranging in ages from two to sixteen years old, I didn't know quite what to expect of the living conditions in her home. I knew the house I grew up in with five siblings was nearly always in disarray. Chores were often neglected, bickering between us was constant.

When we entered her five-bedroom duplex, I saw that it was clean and bright. Family photos lined the walls. I was relieved to exchange the sweltering embrace of a Houston summer afternoon for a spot on her sofa in the air-conditioned coolness of her living room.

Within minutes, my great-nieces and -nephews came down the stairs and indoors to greet me. The two oldest girls were in high school and seemed to be the closest of friends. Kieaira was sixteen and looked exactly like her mother in complexion and personality. Breannah, thirteen, was the spitting image of my sister Donna, with her dark, smooth skin and athletic build. The opposite of her big sister, she was smiley and bubbly. Elton was eleven and a bit on the shy side but was very polite and inquisitive. He also resembled my sister Donna. A'Mya, nine, was in my lap from the moment

I sat down and was full of questions. Maurice had shaken off his innocent angel routine and was solidly competing with his sister A'Mya for my attention. But the star of the house was two-year-old Hailey. She was an adorable little bundle of baby pudge and attitude in full-blown Terrible Twos mode. She had no interest in letting me touch or hold her and seemed to be just barely tolerant of my presence in her kingdom. Tasha told me the quickest way to her heart was through her stomach, a bottomless pit from which no food is excluded.

I attempted to bribe her with bland, wafer-thin rice crackers I had brought to eat on the plane. I wasn't confident she would find my offering appealing, but I gave it a go because I was desperate to get my hands on baby flesh. Surprisingly to me, but not her mother and siblings, she liked the cracker I gave her and begged for more. Within a few minutes she was munching happily in my lap.

I spent the afternoon chatting and playing with the three youngest children, the teen girls having more important things to do than spend the afternoon with a great-aunt. While Tasha prepared a dinner of fish and chips, she told me all she ever heard about me was that I was adopted by a rich movie star. She had expected me to be snooty and she thought I'd have reservations about staying at her place. I told her that her place is the Hilton compared to places I have slept during my travels. I shared with her stories of the Appalachian Trail, Africa and Antarctica. She listened and asked lots of questions.

Over the course of the evening I was touched by how close and loving her relationship was with all of her children. She was affectionate but when necessary chastised with love. There was no fear or anger in this house. The children freely shared sweets and toys with one another, something rarely seen when I was a kid. The youngest children were not allowed to wander the streets at will. Each and every one was accounted for with updates every half hour. There were thank you's and yes ma'am's.

After dinner and after the children had been put to bed or on the sofa to watch a video, Tasha and I sat in plastic chairs on her back porch in the lukewarm night under an inky sky. It was Friday and Tasha pointed out that per usual there was a fight in the parking lot of the convenience store across the street. Knuckleheads from the neighborhood. We watched the pushing and shoving from our seats behind an eight-foot wrought-iron fence. I was secretly worried about one of the combatants whipping out a gun but Tasha didn't seem concerned so I relaxed. After the fight broke up, I asked Tasha more questions about her life with Donna.

I remembered, as a young child, how close Deborah and Mama were. How they joked and gossiped like girlfriends. So when Deborah left, I knew that Mama had not just lost a daughter but her friend. I was happy to see Donna fill that role. She became the one who always rode shotgun and was the boss when Mama wasn't around.

This all changed not long after Tasha was born. The once close relationship Donna had with Mama quickly deteriorated. They began to fight about money, the state of the house and about Tasha. Donna was very possessive of her baby and was quick to brush off any attempts from Mama to give her advice regarding the infant. Mama's drinking was getting worse, too, and this did not help the situation.

Just before Tasha's first birthday, Mama and Donna had a big falling out. One night there was lots of cussing and threats coming from both sides. I lay in my bed in the dark not daring to leave the security of my room but unable to block out the yelling that easily penetrated the paper-thin walls. All seemed normal the next morning when I got up for school. Mama was asleep and Donna was changing Tasha's diaper. I kissed the baby and tickled her ribs, making her giggle so hard Donna shooed me away fearing I'd make her rewet her diaper.

When I came home from school at the end of the day, Mama was on the couch with her beer and a blues album was blaring from the record player. I went to play with the baby only to find the room she shared with her mother was empty. The crib was gone. The toys were gone. Their clothes were gone. All that was left was the sweet scent of baby powder lingering in the air.

I didn't know where they'd gone. I didn't ask. I accepted that the people I loved were not always going to stay around. I pouted for about a week and moved on. It would be a now grown-up Tasha who would fill me in on what her life was like after she left our home.

Donna took her baby and moved to Texas to stay with our great-aunt. Donna got a job and a boyfriend. Tasha tells me she had a happy childhood for a while, then a little brother came along. The boyfriends came and went. There was abuse. Abuse from the boyfriends and abuse from Donna.

Tasha told me of a time she heard a little girl on TV call her mother "Mommy" instead of the term "Mama," which is how she was taught. She said the word "Mommy" sounded much more loving and playful than "Mama." She decided she would stop using "Mama" and start using "Mommy" instead. One afternoon after school, she went home and called out to Donna using "Mommy" and Donna responded by slapping her in the mouth. She told Tasha never to call her Mommy again. "What you trying to do? Act white?"

I could see by the pained look on Tasha's face that the memory and the sting of that unwarranted slap still lingered. She rose from her seat on the back porch and opened her back door. I could feel the chill of the air-conditioning, which she liked cranked up to an arctic blast, on my bare arms. It made me shiver.

"I need a beer," she said. I could hear the television and the children talking inside. Then the door closed and I was alone again.

When Tasha returned, she told me how hollowed out she felt when Donna abandoned her. Despite the abuse, she still loved her mama. She still needed her. The great-great aunt who cared for her and her little brother believed in raising kids the old-fashioned way. Tasha's brother, being a boy, didn't have to do chores or stay in the house. It fell to Tasha to cook and clean, and playing out-doors with friends was strictly forbidden. On top of that, Tasha's brother had close family in Texas. His father and his father's family lived nearby and they'd often come over to take him on outings and made sure he had new clothes and toys to play with. Tasha had no one.

A few months after Donna left, Tasha got in the habit of keep-ing a telephone book in her bedroom. She'd scan the Williams section looking for Donnas or even D initials. There were a lot. She'd call these numbers and say, "Hello, my name is Tasha. I'm looking for my mama, Donna. Is this her house?"

Tasha stopped her story, shook her head and giggled to herself.

"What's so funny?" I asked.

Tasha told me that it wasn't funny then, but what she did made her think of an old joke told by the stand-up comic Katt Williams. It's a joke about how annoyed black people get when a wrong number calls but how friendly and helpful whites are in comparison. The joke goes like this:

Brrring!

White Lady: Hello? . . . No I'm sorry there's no Shaqueeta here. . . . Well, what number did you dial? . . . No, it's a nine not a seven. . . . Well, try it! . . . If it doesn't work, call me back! We'll figure this thing out!

We had a good chuckle. Tasha told me that story because she encountered a lot of annoyed black folks during her calling sessions. But this didn't stop her from making the calls. Then one evening a white lady answered. Instead of hanging up, the lady asked questions and when she heard that Tasha had been abandoned and had been calling all the Williamses in the phone book looking for her mama, the white woman burst into tears and asked Tasha if there was anything she could do to help. It was an awkward encounter for Tasha. She politely thanked the lady and hung up. She never made another one of those calls again.

When Tasha was fifteen, she got word that Donna was working in a store downtown. Tasha went to the store and sure enough there was her mama behind the counter. It had been more than a year since she'd left. She greeted Tasha warmly and told her curious coworkers that the girl was a friend. Then she sent Tasha on her way. When Tasha came back to the store a few days later, the manager told her Donna had quit. He didn't have contact information. Years would go by and Tasha, in an attempt to build her own family that would not leave her, would have four children. Though she was a grown woman with children and a valued member of a chosen family, Tasha still secretly longed for her mother. She got a tip that Donna was living in a residence in Houston and went by after work to follow up. She knocked on the door and Donna answered. Donna seemed resigned to the fact that yet again she had been tracked down. She let Tasha in. A young girl came out of the kitchen.

"Mommy, who is this?" she asked.

"A friend from work," Donna replied before ordering the girl from the room.

Tasha said the moment that young girl called Donna "Mommy" really stung. For the first time, she realized why Donna had left them. She wanted to forget about her old life and kids. She wanted to start over and she did. Tasha had never felt any anger toward her mother. She'd been angry but the anger was generalized. But after hearing the girl call her mama "Mommy" and hearing her mama deny her to her face yet again, she felt her anger build.

Donna offered her a seat and they made small talk. Donna told her she had two girls and was doing well. She asked Tasha if she had any children. Tasha told her she had four.

"Damn! Four? Why you have so many kids?" Donna asked in disgust.

"I have the same number as you. I just kept all mine," Tasha calmly responded.

The look on Donna's face went from disgust to shock to anger. Tasha took it as her cue to leave. Despite this last encounter, Tasha still hoped to reconcile with her mother. Her children have never met their grandmother. She had her mother's phone number and called from time to time. Donna blocked the number, so Tasha used her friends' phones. Her half-sisters have been told to hang up on her if she calls. They still didn't know that she was their sister. I offered to call from my phone and tell Donna who I am. Tasha looked hopeful then dismissed the thought.

"I'm OK with things as they are. At least I know where she is."

I was amazed at how much Tasha and I had in common. We were both abandoned (she literally, me emotionally), both taken in by another family and cared for, but we have handled our abandonment totally differently. I hated my mother. The further the distance between us the better. When my anger got too great, I stuffed it down, tucked it away. Like Donna, I wiped the slate clean and started over with a new family. When I felt the void, I traveled. I could blame that disconnect on being in a foreign land, foreign situations with foreign people. That's why I'm lonely, angry, scared. Not because my mama checked out. She was history. Irrelevant. Water under the bridge.

Tasha on the other hand never stopped loving her mother. To fill the void she created family. Her children. To erase the trauma of her past, she became the mother she always wanted. We sat on the back porch talking until just before dawn and we both had so much to say. Unable to keep sleep at bay, we turned in. In the moments before I drifted off to sleep, I admitted to myself that I didn't expect my visit to see Tasha to be pleasant. Women who have been dealt the cards she has rarely turn out to be pillars of the community. But I was happy to see that my niece was well and that she was raising intelligent, kind and interesting children. She was a wonderful example of how one need not look to the rich and famous for inspiration. I found it in refugees from Africa and now from a single mother of seven living in the projects. As sleep took me, my last thought was that it has been a long time since I'd had a more pleasant and enlightening evening in conversation with anyone as awesome as my niece, Ms. Latasha Williams.

As promised, Sista arrived the following afternoon to pick us up. Latasha and I had spent the morning and early afternoon trying to get the kids ready for an overnight stay while also getting the house in order for our departure. Sista's mama arrived a few minutes after Sista in a truck. We needed two vehicles to transport all of Tasha's children.

Mama was well-dressed in a light summer pants suit. Her hair was long with streaks of gray. Her skin was light brown and unwrinkled. Like her daughter, her face was lovely in its symmetry. She greeted me warmly and then immediately began herding the children into the two vehicles, along with their overnight bags. Though Tasha and I had been attempting to get the kids ready to leave since early afternoon with little success, Mama, like a veteran drill sergeant, was able to get the crew ready and strapped in the vehicles in no time.

The reunion was held in the backyard of a little farmhouse an hour outside of Houston. When we pulled into a dirt parking lot behind the little shotgun farmhouse, I saw three large smokers the size of short schoolbuses spewing smoke and permeating the air with the mouth-watering scent of roasting goat, pork and beef. A man in overalls was overseeing a large fryer filled with boiling grease in which he was dropping pieces of fish. There were tables with canopies and picnic tables enough to sit a small army. There was music blaring, a mix of pop, rap, R&B and old-time blues. Beer was flowing freely. There were at least three hundred people milling about, most wearing the family colors, red and black, represented by red T-shirts with black lettering.

The smaller kids were let loose to join the others in chasing after a large litter of puppies that were seeking refuge under the porch. The older kids propped themselves self-consciously on the benches and people-watched as the neighbor's cows in the pasture next door took in the scene with befuddled expressions.

After introducing myself to a few people, I took a seat in the shade next to Sista and Tasha. Tasha pointed out Pop to me, one of the men tending the large smokers. Tasha told me that despite all the alcohol that would be drunk that afternoon, there was never bickering or fighting at their family reunions. I spent most of the afternoon playing with the children, chatting with guests and watching Tasha revel in being a part of her big, welcoming family. I reveled in the fact that I had my girl back.

CHAPTER 21

JANE CAME to the Bay Area in June 2012 to meet Mama in person for the first time. Jane had spoken to Mama on the phone months earlier and offered to take her out to lunch the next time she was in the Bay Area. Mama told her she'd go if Jane didn't mind that she didn't have any teeth. Jane assured her this would not be a problem for her.

After their conversation, Jane called me to tell me my earlier assessment of Mama as cute and funny was spot on. When Mama called me to tell me of the invitation from Jane, she told me she was a bit self-conscious about her wardrobe. I told her not to worry and offered to take her shopping. She insisted on going to Wal-Mart. When we got there, she was suddenly shy about picking out the clothes.

"Pick out what you like," I encouraged her.

"I don't know. What do you like?"

"You're the one who's going to wear it, not me."

"I know but . . ." she trailed off, looking overwhelmed.

On and on we went as we made our way through the store. This interaction reminded me of the first time Jane took me clothes shopping. I knew I needed the clothes but I struggled with my pride. I didn't want to feel like a charity case. I think Mama was feeling the same way.

I decided to handle the situation the same way Jane did with me. As we walked through the store, I paid attention to the items my mother's hands or eyes lingered on and suggested she try those things on. This strategy worked, and eventually we were able to select several outfits, several pairs of shoes, scarves, a muumuu and a purse.

The afternoon before the meeting, Jane and I met in Berkeley to see a play called *Emotional Creature*, written by her friend, the playwright and activist Eve Ensler. The title aptly describes how I've been feeling the past few months. Since coming to the Bay Area to see my family, I've been an extremely emotional creature. I've cried nearly every night for the past few months and wanted to cry nearly every waking moment. When I see Jane waving happily at me from across the theater, I want to burst into tears at the sight of her. I've been rough on her the past few years. She has borne the brunt of my Terrible Forties like a saint and I want to thank her for keeping her promise to love me even if I'm not perfect. Even if at times I'm not lovable.

After hugs and kisses we settle into our seats clasping hands. For the next few hours we hear the stories of girls from around the world. Girls who have been silenced, raped, abandoned, excluded, forgotten and, by the end, awakened, made whole, validated and imbued with the power to shake the world. Jane cries through most of it but as she'll tell you herself, "A Fonda will cry at a good steak." I see myself, Tasha, Mama and even Jane in these stories. It's too much right now and I shut down so as not to blow a fuse in my emotional motherboard.

After the play we catch up on the family. My sister Vanessa had sent her kids to Chicago to visit with Troy and his wife, Simone, and Jane had joined them. I smile to see Jane so happy as she tells me how proud she is of her grandchildren. She asks how I'm doing and I tell her about being emotionally overwhelmed and conflicted. One moment I love my birth mother, the next I'm full of rage. We talk of the meeting tomorrow and I can see Jane is nervous. All I can do is pray for the best.

The night before the meeting, I call Mama to make sure she will be ready for the chauffeured car that will pick her up at 10:30 A.M. I also remind her that we will be taking photos, so she should wear a nice outfit. She assures me she will be ready. She asks me what she should wear and we discuss several of the outfits I bought for her. I tell her she should wear the fuchsia top with the black slacks and her ballerina flats. She dismisses that suggestion and asks if she should wear a print blouse instead. Exasperated, I tell her to wear whatever makes her comfortable. She is quiet for a while then says, "Lawanna, I don't know nothing about fashion. I think you should come over and help me pick an outfit." It's ten o'clock at night and I'm not about to get out of bed for this and I tell her so. By the end of the conversation, I've convinced her she will look beautiful no matter what she wears and she allows me to finally hang up.

The next morning the photographer and I meet Jane in her suite an hour before Mama is to arrive. She isn't quite ready, so we leave him to set up in the living room. Jane is busy getting dressed and packing; she will fly out after our lunch with Mama. I woke up late and neglected to eat breakfast. Somehow Jane senses this and encourages me to eat what's left of her breakfast: a bowl of fresh blackberries. There is also a bowl of fruit in the living room she won't be able to eat and she tells me to put it in a paper bag for Mama to take with her. She goes to the bathroom to put on her makeup and emerges with a pair of antique earrings. "I never wear these. Take them," she says, and folds them into my hand. Her nerves are showing and it makes me nervous too. Especially since I dreamed Mama wouldn't show.

Right on time the concierge calls to say that Mama has been dropped off and is waiting in the hotel lobby. The photographer wants to get a few shots of Jane and me alone and suggests I get Mama after we shoot. Jane insists I go down and bring her up immediately. I do as she says. When I get off the elevator, I see Mama calmly reading the morning paper. I greet her with a kiss and notice she has decided to wear the print top after all. I ask her how the ride was. She tells me she told all her friends that a chauffeured car was coming for her, and they were all outside waiting when it pulled up to get her. She chuckles at the thought. I wheel her onto the elevator while she tells me that she asked Teresa to come over to help her pick just the right outfit.

When we get to the suite, Jane greets her with a kiss on the cheek and beams down at her for a few seconds before bursting into tears. I knew she'd cry. She tells Mama what a great kid I am and how proud she should be of me. Mama asks her why she's crying and Jane says, "I thought you'd be mad at me for taking her away!" "Oh, no!" Mama says, "I think it was a good thing that you did." "Really?" Jane asks. "Yeah!" Mama says. They hug. With that out of the way, they move right along and quickly find something to talk about that they are both familiar with: ailments. Jane talks about a recent back surgery and Mama tries to trump her with her COPD, asthma and high blood pressure. Jane asks if she has diabetes and is relieved when Mama tells her she doesn't. Then they are discussing pain medication. Mama suggests Jane take Motrin, which she uses to dull the pain of arthritis. When Jane, who possesses a freakishly high tolerance for pain, tells her she tries to avoid using pain medications, Mama looks at her duly impressed.

When the photographer announces he is ready to take the photos, Jane quickly reaches for her makeup bag and returns to powder Mama's nose. "There! That ought to do it!" We are ready for our close-up.

After the photo shoot, we have lunch downstairs in the restaurant. Jane fusses over Mama, making sure the waiter finds a space nearby to park Mama's scooter, pulling out her chair for her, folding a napkin in her lap and suggesting menu items.

"Do you have any dietary restrictions?"

"Oh, no! I eat everything. Even without my teeth I eat it all!"

They chuckle and reminisce about the Party days. Mama is bashing former Party leaders Huey Newton and Elaine Brown. Regaling Jane with gossip about their corrupt activities and lifestyles. Jane listens attentively, offering commiserative "Umphs!" and "Tsk, tsks!" I can see Mama is getting righteously angry reliving those difficult years. Her voice is rising and I can see she's beginning to flail her arms a bit. I jump into the conversation before she starts dropping F bombs in this quaint little eatery in Berkeley.

"Doesn't Mama's hair look nice? She let me give her a haircut last week."

"Yes, she looks beautiful. I see where you get it from."

Then Jane reaches over and takes Mama's hand and says, "You should be so proud of Lulu. You are a big part of why she is such a wonderful woman."

"*We* did a good job," she retorts with a shy smile.

After lunch we climb into the chauffeured car to take Mama home before dropping Jane at the airport. When the car pulls up in front of Mama's house, I notice there is a little crowd of neighbors out across the street watching us. Jane asks Mama if she can come in for a short visit. "Of course!" We all get out and a man from across the street yells, "Hey, Jane!" Jane waves and proceeds to follow me as I push Mama up the ramp and onto her porch. We go inside and Mama invites Jane to take a peek at the family photos on the wall. Jane asks about Marsellus Wallace and Mama tells her to go to the back of the house and pull back the drapes on the sliding glass doors. Jane does so and is greeted with a quizzical bark from the Rottweiler. We chat for a while, and then Jane and I hug Mama good-bye. On our way back to the car, the little crowd is still there. They snap more pictures as we get into the car. As we drive away, I think Mama will have a lot to talk about next time she hangs out with her friends.

EPILOGUE

BRINGING MY MOTHERS together felt like catching sight of a Hobbit riding a unicorn down Main Street. Surreal. It wasn't long ago that I held little hope that I'd muster the courage to see Mama face to face, let alone coordinate a meeting with us all. Seeing them together emphasized just what polar opposites they are. One could not imagine two more different women.

I had no idea that the road I was on would lead to this meeting. There were many dead ends I had to maneuver around. I left everything and everyone I knew many times along the way. But the farther I traveled, the stronger I felt, despite the fact that there were times when the urge to divert down Easy Street was nearly overwhelming. The only thing that kept me going in the right direction was the fact that I knew not doing so meant losing myself forever.

So here I stand. My emotional Everest peaked. My flag planted. My reward? I've gained family in Oakland and Texas that love me and accept me. I've strengthened my bond with Jane. After our visit with Mama, Jane tells me how adorable Mama is. She'd anticipated anger but instead got a sweet, funny, curious woman—the woman I remember so vividly from my early childhood. Jane and I are nestled in the cool dark interior of a chauffeured car headed to the airport. East Oakland slides by in the bright afternoon and, to the unknowing eye, looks like a not too bad place to raise a family. Still looking out the window I tell Jane, "Mama wants me to come spend Thanksgiving and Christmas with her." There is a brief pause before Jane asks, "Will you?" And I tell her, "No. I'm going to be where I belong. With you."

There hasn't been a fairytale ending with my biological mother, but our story isn't over yet. What I did not expect was to find some things hadn't changed and never will. We will continue struggling to connect, she will battle her demons and I mine. Now, though, I can honestly say that I love her and respect her, and that I need her presence in my life. Our differences, our fears, our fights won't run me off like last time. And so where one road ends, another begins. This time I've unburdened myself of my savior complex. I can't save my mama from her life, any more than she could have saved me from mine. For this leg of the journey I'm traveling light.

No matter under what circumstances you leave it,
home does not cease to be home. No matter
how you lived there—well or poorly.

—JOSEPH BRODSKY

ACKNOWLEDGMENTS

Before writing my own book I scoffed at writers who equated writing theirs to giving birth. After the fact, I can't think of a more fitting analogy. I could not have conceived of and delivered this book without the help and support of many people. I must thank my book's "baby daddy," Dave Eggers. Thanks, friend, for "planting the seed" and encouraging me to write when I didn't believe I could. And thanks to my literary OB/GYN (aka, the world's greatest agent), Edward Orloff. You rock! Not only did you open your home to me, you did a fantastic job monitoring my growth as a writer. Of course I had to have a doula. I found her in my wonderful editor, Sarah Hochman. Sarah, thank you for making a potentially painful and difficult process one of the most rewarding experiences of my life. I'm thrilled that together we have delivered a book we can both be extremely proud of. Thanks to Blue Rider Press—David Rosenthal, Vanessa Kehren, Aileen Boyle, and Brian Ulicky—and to Penguin USA.

I'd also like to acknowledge the love and support of my friends and family: Jane Fonda, Mary Nell Kennedy, Deborah Williams, Uncle Landon, Neome Banks, Aunt Jan, Aunt Ora, Aunt Nell, Grandma, Ayaan Gates Williams, Thembi Williams, Indigo Williams, Aunt Virginia, Petik Williams, Kim Williams, Kijana Liu, Yupo Liu, John Williams, The Awesome Latasha Williams, Teresa Williams, Louise Williams, Donna Williams, Randy Williams, Clara Jean Williams, Vanessa Vadim, Troy Garity, Simone Bent, Nathalie Vadim, Ted Turner, Jimmy Brown, Debbie Masterson, Joe Masterson, Eileen Masterson, Laura Turner Seydel, Rutherford Seydel, Teddy Turner, Rhett Turner, Jenny Garlington, Beau Turner, Rosina Seydel, Scott Seydel, Pat Mitchel, Thouraya Raiss, Juan Jose Alonzo, Yasmine Alonzo. My Phonzis: Andrea Carter (S) and Terese Smallwood Whitehead (M), Laila Benchekroun, Rachida Benchekroun, Omar Chaabi, Vendela Vida, Valentino Deng, Patrice Gaines, Peter Frick Wright, Tom Hayden, Barbara Williams, Steven Bennett, Karen Averitt, Jim Averitt, Marin Marcus, Kristy Davis, Susan Johnson, Pat Durett, Robin Laughlin, Carol Mitchell, Tommy Mitchell, Shawn Barton, and David and Laurel Hodges. If I have left anyone out, I'm sorry and I'll make it up to you later.

Last, I'd like to thank the amazing folks at the Student Conservation Association (SCA) for providing me with beautiful places to live, work, and contribute to the preservation of our country's wild spaces. It was while working with the SCA, from the moonscaped deserts of Southern California to the grizzly-bear-infested forests of Alaska, that my mind was quieted enough to allow me to work on this book.

ABOUT THE AUTHOR

Mary Williams's work has appeared in *The Believer, McSweeney's,* and O*: The Oprah Magazine.* She is the author of the children's book, *Brothers in Hope: The Story of the Lost Boys of Sudan.* She lives in the Southwest.